W9-BPO-601

Embedded Systems: Desktop Integration

Oliver H. Bailey

Wordware Publishing, Inc.

Library of Congress Cataloging-in-Publication Data

Bailey, Oliver H.
    Embedded systems: desktop integration / by Oliver H. Bailey.
      p. cm.
    Includes index.
    ISBN-13: 987-1-55622-994-1
    ISBN-10: 1-55622-994-1 (pbk.)
    1. Embedded computer systems   I. Title.
    TK7895.E42B3267 2005
    004.163--dc22   2005006854
                                     CIP

© 2005, Wordware Publishing, Inc.

All Rights Reserved

2320 Los Rios Boulevard
Plano, Texas 75074

No part of this book may be reproduced in any form or by
any means without permission in writing from
Wordware Publishing, Inc.

Printed in the United States of America

ISBN-13: 987-1-55622-994-1
ISBN-10: 1-55622-994-1
10 9 8 7 6 5 4 3 2 1
0503

Windows, Windows XP, and .NET are trademarks of the Microsoft Corporation. NetBurner is a trademark of NetBurner, Inc. EAGLE Layout Editor is a trademark of CadSoft Computer GmbH. Kylix and C++Builder are registered trademarks and Delphi and C++BuilderX are registered trademarks of Borland Software Corporation. Qt is a registered trademark of Trolltech. PIC, dsPIC, MPLAB, and PICMicro are registered trademarks of Microchip Technology, Inc. 1-Wire is a registered trademark and DS is a trademark of Dallas Semiconductor Corporation. PSoC is a trademark of Cypress Semiconductor Corporation. BASIC Stamp is a registered trademark of Parallax, Inc. FreeBSD is a registered trademark of the FreeBSD Foundation. Linux is a registered trademark of Linus Torvalds. UNIX and Motif are registered trademarks and GNU is a trademark of The Open Group. Cygwin is a trademark of Red Hat, Inc. I²C and I²C-bus are trademarks of Phillips Corporation.

    Other brand names and product names mentioned in this book are trademarks or service marks of their respective companies. Any omission or misuse (of any kind) of service marks or trademarks should not be regarded as intent to infringe on the property of others. The publisher recognizes and respects all marks used by companies, manufacturers, and developers as a means to distinguish their products.

    This book is sold as is, without warranty of any kind, either express or implied, respecting the contents of this book and any disks or programs that may accompany it, including but not limited to implied warranties for the book's quality, performance, merchantability, or fitness for any particular purpose. Neither Wordware Publishing, Inc. nor its dealers or distributors shall be liable to the purchaser or any other person or entity with respect to any liability, loss, or damage caused or alleged to have been caused directly or indirectly by this book.

All inquiries for volume purchases of this book should be addressed to Wordware Publishing, Inc., at the above address. Telephone inquiries may be made by calling:

(972) 423-0090

Dedication

To those who have gone before me:

My father,
Hurshel J. Bailey
1919–1988

My sister,
Cozette M. Bailey
1960–1997

Our beloved greyhound,
Jelly Bean
1990–2004

Contents

Part II — Implementation

Foreword

Oliver Bailey has taken a unique approach in this book by using a real product design process, complete with imaginative requests from a marketing department and managers. Early in the book, I identified with many circumstances that regularly occur in our office when we're considering a new product. It reminded me that there's so much more to product design than a schematic, some microcontroller code, and a printed circuit board. It's a reminder that designing the prototype is 90 percent of the fun and 10 percent of the work, and that you can swap these two numbers to bring a product to market. With his business-minded approach, Oliver challenges us to put thought into the software integration, operating systems, hardware design, and marketing department requests up front. The result is that the prototype will be more complete, and completing the project will involve less feature creep. This is what it will take, because embedded developers are always looking at desktop integration alternatives.

Many books dealing with microcontrollers are very firmware (microcontroller code) and hardware (circuit design) oriented. They provide code examples, a schematic, and a description of how the design should work. They rarely cover the hardware connection solutions (USB, serial, Ethernet), not to mention the variety of operating systems and drivers for the hardware. Knowing more about microcontrollers than operating systems, I spent all of my time reviewing the sections on designing cross-platform user applications and their programming environments. From reading microcontroller discussion forums it is clear that most users need support with the subject. Now they have it in one place. These considerations are far more important to embedded developers than they used to be.

We have lots of confidence in Oliver's ability to research and recommend the right technical solution for the project. For example, Oliver spent many days using the USB to serial chips with different operating systems. The result is that he chose a common implementation with FTDI and off-the-shelf drivers. In our office we had gone through the same process a few months earlier and spent at least 40 hours before we came to the same design conclusions. Use this book to help you choose and develop the interface, because you can have confidence the research was done correctly before any conclusions were drawn.

This book is also very timely. Oliver provides overviews of the most popular new USB solutions and several microcontrollers. And with the GNU tools maturing and developers looking at alternative operating systems more each year, I'd say this book was just in time.

Oliver's triple-decade experience is now yours. *Embedded Systems: Desktop Integration* fills a void in the industry by presenting the communication solutions between microcontrollers and PCs, by developing cross-platform executables from a single source code base, and putting it all together in one place. Writing this book was clearly no easy task considering the scope, but it all came together in a way that we can understand. His research will save us a lot of time on our next project.

Finally, Oliver's writing style is really easy to follow. You'll be part of the project and appreciate the conversational approach he uses along the way. There's no stuffy desktop-reference book approach anywhere in this book.

Ken Gracey
Parallax, Inc.

Preface

If you ever want to realize how much you don't know about something, write a book about the subject. This has been a humbling experience but a fun adventure as well. For me it all started when I was doing machine tool design in LaPorte in the late '70s. I needed a tube for a black and white TV so I went to the local Radio Shack store. While I was there I noticed this ugly gray monitor and keyboard just sitting in a corner playing Pong. I asked the manager what it was, and he explained it was a computer that was fully programmable. That Radio Shack became a regular hangout for me both before and after I bought that old TRS-80 (which I still have).

What happened next was nothing short of a miracle. LaPorte, Indiana, in those days was a small town of about 10,000 that sits on the Indiana-Michigan line. Rich in heritage but nestled in the corn fields away from the big city and big business. Not long after I bought the TRS-80, a blind ad ran for a programmer who had TRS-80 experience. I applied for the job and as it turned out the employer was none other than Howard W. Sams Publishing, a company moving into the software industry. Never would I have thought that a software opportunity would present itself in a small, sleepy town like LaPorte, Indiana. But it did and the rest is history. From 1979 to 1986 I developed operating systems, accounting software, programmer tools, and numerous other products. In 1986 I began developing embedded machine control systems and have either been on my own or owned companies since that time. Over the years I have written hundreds of articles, spoken at conferences, and even appeared on video for a variety of topics.

Over the years, the software industry and America has changed. In recent years I've decided to leave the software and hardware industry to move into something else. So I decided to share my experience and insight with the software and hardware community before moving on. This is the first in a series of books that cover topics such as embedded systems, communications, host application development, Java, Internet communications, and wireless embedded systems. I hope you enjoy reading this book as much as I have writing it.

Acknowledgments

While I may have written the content, there are a lot of people who supported this effort. Wes Beckwith and Beth Kohler at Wordware Publishing deserve a lot of thanks for their efforts. Karen Giles, Troy Kitch, and John Ray Thomas at Borland; Ken Gracey and Erik Wood at Parallax; Tom Kenney at NetBurner; Jeff Schmoyer at microEngineering Labs; Eric Sells, Brian Schneider, and Dan Butler at MicroChip; Corey Wilner and Louis Bolma at Cypress Semiconductor; Pavel at PicAnt.com; Dr. Robert Miller at Trace Systems; Sara and the support staff at HI-TECH Software; Susie Penner at Trolltech; my old friends at Custom Computer Services (CCS); the folks at MotherBoards Direct (thanks for your help, Dave); Jack Schoof at NetMedia; Alan Towne at Saelig; the fine people at Sysvestor; Matthew Daughtrey at Embedded Ethernet; Frank Miller at Pulsar; Jan Axelson; the folks at Linx Technologies; Keith Dingwall of FTDI; Adam Lintott of Matrix Orbital; Dave Smiczek of Dallas Semiconductor; and my reviewers, John Wilczynski and Keith Kehl.

Introduction

In this book, we design a thermostat that interfaces to a host system through RS-232, USB, and Ethernet. To make things fun, the device layer and user applications have to run on Windows, Linux, and FreeBSD. We build three prototype thermostats using the BASIC Stamp, PIC Microcontroller, and PSOC Microcontroller. We implement RS-232 using the old-fashioned line drivers, and then implement USB using three different USB components. We also implement Ethernet using two different components. In the end, you'll have experience with three different microcontrollers, two different Ethernet controllers, and three different USB interfaces, three different compilers and user interface builders, and five different embedded compilers and languages.

The book is divided into two parts. Part I includes Chapters 1–6 and focuses on project design. Part II includes Chapters 7–11 and discusses the implementation of the project.

Intended Audiences

There is something for everyone in this book. If you're new to electronics, then go through all of Chapters 1–8. If you have some experience, I would suggest reading Chapters 1–6, 7, and 9, as building the PIC-based prototype is more challenging than the BASIC Stamp for someone with prior electronics expereince. If you're a master of electronics, then I suggest sinking your teeth into the PSOC prototype. The PSOC is a fun little device that has endless possibilities for configurations.

Writing Style

I write in a conversational style. In other words, I talk to you, not at you. Even though we aren't face to face, you are actively involved in the conversation. I have tried very hard to present this in a real-world scene as much as possible. You will notice that occasionally I will even change direction or implementation methods or parts because that's how it is done in the real world. If I take out important information simply because we don't use it, then I haven't given you, the reader, the full experience.

What Is Not Covered

I don't cover programming languages as there are thousands of books devoted to those topics. This is not a book on structured program design methodology. It also doesn't include a large amount of program listings in the text. Program listings and other information that may change during the life cycle of the book can be downloaded from www.wordware.com/files/embsys or www.time-lines.com.

Part I

Design

Design Requirements

Overview

Our programmers and hardware engineers have been given the task of implementing a new intelligent heating and air-conditioning control system. The marketing group has determined that a niche market exists for a product that can work either stand-alone or integrated into a single PC or PC-LAN. To take full advantage of this market opportunity, the marketing department has defined three separate products.

The first is a stand-alone intelligent thermostat that has an LCD display output, three control buttons, four direction buttons, power LED, alarm LED, and internal temperature management and monitoring capabilities. This is a stand-alone device with full environmental management capabilities. External heating and cooling can be controlled through the use of two relay-controlled outputs.

To program the device and monitor it from a desktop computer, an RS-232 port has been built in. This is the least expensive device and can only be connected to a single computer. The device is powered by a 5-volt supply with an internal battery backup.

Following is an artist's drawing of the unit.

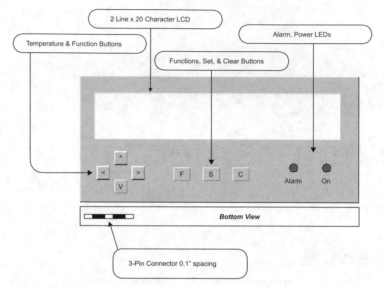

Figure 1-1: RS-232 port thermostat

Product number two replaces the RS-232 port with a Universal Serial Bus (USB). This allows a single host system to control multiple units and also allows the device to function as a data-acquisition system to be used for the monitoring and control of multiple rooms or floors within a building from a single PC. As it ended up, the prototype was powered from an external source with USB power being an option.

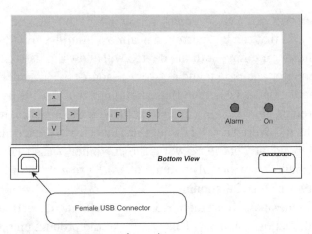

Figure 1-2: USB interface thermostat

The third product has an Ethernet interface that replaces the RS-232 or USB interfaces. Ethernet allows this device to be connected to a local area network (LAN). This product serves the small- to mid-sized business owner who needs flexibility in expansion and may require greater distances between units.

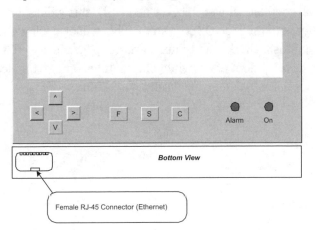

Figure 1-3: Ethernet interface thermostat

This provides a one-to-many relationship, and the number of devices that can be controlled is almost limitless. Building the Ethernet interface into the device will allow the use of existing computer equipment and network resources. This will make the installation less costly in those buildings that already have a LAN wired in, allowing for a quicker return on the investment and reducing overall cost of ownership. Since each device also works independently of the network, the customer is assured that environmental control will continue to work properly in the event the network stops functioning.

One final requirement from the marketing department is multiplatform support. This will make the product unique in two ways. First, no other competitor has offered a unit that can be integrated into a network this inexpensively. Second, to attract the widest audience the units must be accessible from Windows, UNIX, and Linux. This requirement will make the device compatible with IBM mainframes, Microsoft Windows, Linux, and the Macintosh. After researching the various versions of UNIX, a decision has been made to support FreeBSD. As over 70 percent of all commercial web servers use BSD, this will assure compatibility with the Mac OS X system. This will also allow the Macintosh, UNIX, and Linux markets to be addressed with a single development effort while eliminating some of the licensing concerns associated specifically with Linux.

The Development Teams

Management realizes that a project of this scope has never been undertaken within the organization before. While it is believed that a cost savings can be realized by initial multiplatform support, they also are aware that the project can go over budget and be improperly implemented without solid design and management from the start. They have chosen to select a management team that provides a dedicated design architect and project manager. These two individuals will manage the design, implementation, and deployment from start to finish. They have also chosen to have three team leaders, one each for the hardware, device interface, and user application groups. Each team leader will report directly to the project manager and architect. Each team will be responsible for a very focused part of the project.

Hardware Group (Embedded Device Design/Implementation)

The hardware group has been developing stand-alone electronic controls of this type for many years. But this will be the first time that an external interface has been added for the purpose of monitoring and controlling via a personal computer. This will require some change in thinking from prior products in how to handle control logic. In the past, all control has been internal to the device. Now the hardware group will have to consider what changes need to be made to allow the device to be monitored and controlled from an outside source or from the keypad of the device.

Device Interface Group (Device Interface and Device Drivers)

There is a systems department within the main IT group that routinely writes applications that extend or interface to the operating system core. But their experience is limited to the systems on which they run their business applications. Taking this into account, management has decided to use existing device drivers wherever possible. This will reduce the amount of custom work needed but will still require support for multiple platforms. So, through a collaborative effort with the hardware engineers, the focus will be to develop device interface software that provides a consistent application interface across all platforms.

User Application Group (User Applications for UNIX and Windows)

The applications group of the IT department feels very comfortable with this task. But they have never before supported multiple operating systems for the same application. They are concerned about making the best use of cross-platform tools to maximize their development efforts while minimizing the amount of redundant work needed. They also have never been involved in developing a device protocol or hardware device interface. They are concerned about the learning curve needed to make this happen.

Concerns and Issues

Since the hardware group has never built a product with RS-232, USB, or Ethernet interfaces, there will be a definite learning curve in implementing these interfaces in both hardware and software. There are also concerns about understanding what changes in logic and components will need to be made to get a working system. To aid in the prototyping stage it has been decided that off-the-shelf solutions should be used to design the products and gain an understanding of the logic and component changes that will be required for the finished products.

The software group will need to research the cross-platform solutions that are available to make a single-source solution a reality. Since the tools they have been using are exclusive to Windows, they will also have to learn UNIX and Linux development. Most important of all, however, they will need to learn how UNIX and Windows differ. The systems group has been given the job of defining the device drivers to make the thermostat and PC talk. They must gain the knowledge needed to properly define working protocols that can bridge not only Windows, UNIX, and Linux, but the embedded system side as well. All three groups will work together to define a standard message protocol so the device can communicate through software with the systems group taking the lead in protocol development.

Platform-Independent Software Requirements

Making a user application platform independent is not only a high priority but also of great concern. To gain the best experience and choose the best implementation strategy, two development approaches will be pursued. The first approach develops a cross-platform solution by using commercial products for the development efforts exclusively. To expedite the development effort, the selected commercial products must work identically on each platform. Each separately hosted tool must compile the source code identically with a resulting program that looks and behaves identically on every platform supported.

Management is aware the device drivers will have to be supported separately for Windows and UNIX/Linux. Even so, the preferred approach is to use existing drivers if possible that are already supported by each system. This would limit the development effort to writing a shared library that would give each driver the same look, feel, and function calls on all platforms. This would assure that no platform-dependent code would need to reside in the user application and place all platform-dependent code closer to the device driver layer.

All of the chosen platforms support text mode and at least one graphic user mode. After investigating development options it has been determined that a graphic user interface will be used. The reason is twofold. First, more development will need to be done if a text mode is used. There are also concerns about using text mode interfaces when almost all currently developed products use a graphic mode interface. More important, however, is the fact that more tools and a wider selection of commercial cross-platform tools are available to the developer who uses a graphic interface.

The second approach is to develop the product using the free GNU compilers. Unlike commercial tools, this compiler suite allows full cross-platform development on either target to be fully compiled and executable programs delivered. Rather than depending on a vendor, this integrates products from several sources. Since cross-platform development will be required on all future projects, developing under these conditions will allow the best development path for future projects yet to be selected.

Embedded Device Requirements

The embedded device takes input from one or more temperature sensors to increase or decrease temperature and control air flow. The device works stand-alone or managed by a desktop computer. Even if the device is not managed remotely, it has the ability to send data to a remote PC for environmental monitoring. An LCD display is used to display current unit status and settings. Two to four pushbuttons are on the front of the unit to change settings and display current environmental status. The temperature sensors use the Dallas 1-Wire network. Using the 1-Wire device allows us to expand the number of temperature sensors by simply adding the device to the existing wire and resetting the unit. Each temperature sensor has a unique device ID that associates it with a fan and environmental control unit. We program each temperature sensor with a high and low comfort temperature. Once programmed, we poll the devices periodically; any device that indicates the temperature has risen or dropped beyond the comfort temperature will generate an alarm, telling us it needs to be serviced. Once the alarm is cleared, the environmental controls and fans are turned off. This simple approach eliminates the need for a complex multitasking system. User input and display information is handled in between checking comfort ranges. Communications to the desktop computer are also handled in between comfort checks, which eliminates the need for a high-end processor. Two paths of device development will be pursued. The first makes use of off-the-shelf products for the prototype. Concurrent with prototype building will be a second development effort building components of the unit from scratch. The end result will be a combination of off-the-shelf products and scratch-built pieces.

Device Interface Requirements

It has already been established that all platform-specific code will reside in the device interface layer. It has also been established that RS-232, USB, and Ethernet will be supported as external device interfaces. To meet the objectives of these requirements, a shared library will be developed to be distributed and installed according to platform. If done correctly, this approach will allow new platforms to be supported with the addition of a single file: the interface library.

One additional component will be a part of this project: a developers kit. By allowing developers access to the device interface layer new software products can be developed for the aftermarket. The RS-232 unit will also be included in the developers kit. This kit will be sold to developers who wish to add additional intelligence like X-10 support. This will allow consumer-installed fans and heaters to be integrated into the system, allowing it to be easily expanded. The marketing department believes this product has a very bright future. USB support is being provided to offer a mid-range product that is both expandable and reasonably priced. With the USB product, a desktop computer can monitor and control several devices (or zones). USB cable length is limited to 16 feet, but even with this limitation marketing believes a demand in smaller homes and offices exists. Care is being taken to support only those host systems where USB support is a native part of the OS. The USB standard allows for a human interface device (HID) to be integrated in a fairly simple fashion and with minimal programming. Care has been taken to limit USB input to a few buttons, a single LCD display, and two LEDs.

Developing an Ethernet interface is not such a trivial task. Much thought was given to this feature before including it in the specifications. While this interface is the most expensive to implement — both in terms of hardware and software — it offers the greatest opportunity for medium to large facility sales. The

Ethernet-based device will be sold for a much higher price; however, it will offer the ability to build very smart environmental control systems. There is also another benefit: While the temperature sensor cannot replace a smoke detector, it can measure how rapidly temperatures increase and decrease. This allows a computer to not only monitor temperature changes but also notify the user when rapid temperature changes occur. This additional feature makes the device suitable as an early warning detection system for a potential fire or industrial refrigeration failure before much damage is done. Finally, the Ethernet unit allows a network of temperature sensing and control devices to be built, paving the way for additional add-on products in the future.

Desktop Software Requirements

While it may seem that the applications group has the least amount of work to do, no one has a bigger research project ahead. There are industry standards to which both hardware design and device interfacing must adhere. There are no industry-specific standards on how operating systems should work or on implementing cross-platform tools. The only standard that can be applied here is the ANSI standard for the C and C++ languages. Using a commercial tool approach, the vendor list will be narrowed to those companies offering either development tools for all the required platforms or language tools that support the same. Development tools include editors, cross-platform libraries that support application development, and complete design systems. Non-commercial alternatives include editors, development libraries, and compilers. There is also the possibility that a good solution will include a mixture of both free and commercial products. Any free product used must include source code. This will allow the continued use of the product even if the product developer stops supporting it. A second requirement is that either the library for each required platform be included or the makefiles to

build the libraries are included. Management expects a considerable amount of time to be spent researching the right solution
and even building simple test programs to validate actual cross-
platform compatibility.

Operating Systems Support

Microsoft Windows has several versions in use. To make the
widest use of the Windows development effort it has been
decided to only support Windows 2000 and later versions. This
allows development to concentrate on a consistent device driver
model. It also allows support for Windows kernels that support
pre-emptive multitasking. It has also been decided to support
Linux kernel versions 2.4 and later. This decision is based on
USB support being complete in these kernel versions. FreeBSD
is based on the Berkeley system that was modeled after the original UNIX source code. The Intel versions of all BSD operating
systems provide support for Linux executables by configuring
the system at startup. This is one approach. However, another
approach would be to cross-compile for the BSD version during
the development cycle. While both approaches will be tested,
support is leaning toward native FreeBSD support. It has not
been determined yet if non-Intel platforms will be supported. If
native FreeBSD is supported, then cross-compiling for
Macintosh OS X should be straightforward. If Linux compatibility
mode is selected instead, the initial release will be limited to
Intel platforms. If this is the case, management has decided to
see how much additional effort would be required to support
non-Intel platforms. This approach could lead to compatibility
with a much wider base of computers, including not only
Macintosh, but also DEC and IBM mainframes as well.

Requirements Summary

At first glance this project seems daunting, but after some careful thought it is very clear that it is not only feasible but also can serve as a model for all future projects that require host integration and cross-platform support.

This is the requirements list:

■ Embedded environmental control that can be used stand-alone or integrated to a Windows, UNIX, or Linux host for monitoring and controlling purposes using RS-232, USB, or Ethernet interfaces

■ A temperature sensor network that can dynamically add or remove sensors via a simple device reset

■ A host interface that can run on Windows, UNIX, and Linux with identical functionality and a consistent look and feel

■ Consistent device interfaces that keep platform-specific issues at the device interface layer, thus allowing for a single-source solution for the user applications and distribution of a single platform-specific library

■ Embedded device development using off-the-shelf components for the prototype and a mixture of custom-built and off-the-shelf products for the final product

■ Single-source desktop application development using commercial tools, a combination of commercial tools and free tools, or the complete use of free tools under the GPL or GNU licenses

Data and Control Flow Management

Embedded systems development has some unique challenges that don't exist in normal end-user application development. Let's take a look at these differences:

- The application starts when power is applied to the processor.

- User input is not limited to a mouse or standard keyboard.

- User output is not limited to a color monitor.

- Events are triggered by external events in addition to user events.

- Application errors must be handled without human intervention.

- Power requirements must be minimal and battery backup is required.

Unlike a desktop application, the embedded application initializes when power is applied or a reset condition exists. A reset condition can be a drop in power or other external event such as bad sensor detection. Since we cannot assume that a person will be around when these conditions are triggered, error handling is different than in a user application. Upon an error condition we must write the error to a memory area that will remain constant even if power is removed and reapplied. In this case, when the power is applied an initialization process will check memory, keys, and outputs, then initialize the sensors and begin the task of monitoring temperature, comparing it to the limits and reporting temperatures when they exceed or fall below those limits. Relays are also turned on and off to control heating, cooling, and/or air circulation.

In embedded systems, input is rarely done using a keyboard or mouse. Keyboards are not used for generating alphanumeric characters but rather to identify a function specific to the system. In this case we have a total of seven keys. Three control keys select the function, set the changes made to a permanent state, and clear the changes to start over. There are also four direction keys. These keys raise and lower temperature settings and move to the next or last setting for adjustment. When a key is pressed, a character is not returned but rather a key identifier showing which function to process. When control codes come in from a remote host, those codes will be processed as if they were pressed on the local keypad.

Next we have user output. Unlike a PC we don't have a color monitor to output graphics and text. In its place we have an LCD display that has one or two lines of 10 to 20 characters to display user messages, functions, help screens, and temperature. There are no graphics capabilities but we do have the ability to create custom display characters. To get the user's attention we will use a small low-power buzzer. This will be used to flag error conditions and emphasize important information.

When you develop an embedded system you have the operating system, user input, output, data handling, and everything else rolled into a single program that can range in size from 1 K to 64 K or so. Considering that Windows and Linux can take several gigabytes of disk space, an embedded system is only a tiny portion of this. When we consider that an embedded system is developed for a specific purpose rather than general computing, these constraints are not of concern. Having said that, how we process events will vary depending on which microcontrollers we use. When using the BASIC Stamp, the main program will be constantly polling to detect events. When using the PIC or PSOC processors, we will handle the event directly as an interrupt to the main program. This will conserve power by allowing the processors to go into a sleep or low power mode.

Application errors will be written to an area of memory that will retain the last several errors, the date and time of errors, and any other important information. This log will be circular, which means that when the last entry is written the first entry will be overwritten on the next error. This log can be displayed on the LCD or PC.

Finally, we need to address power supply and consumption. The temperature sensors require a minimum of 5 volts to be set and read. The LCD display also requires 5 volts and the processors require from 5 to 7 volts to operate. To be consistent, the units will have an external power connector and battery backup inside. This will be either a rechargeable lithium battery or four standard AA batteries. The USB unit will allow power to be used from the host PC when connected. RS-232 and Ethernet units will require external power. For those of you who have intelligent thermostats in your home or office, you are probably asking why those units don't require external power rather than battery backups. Those units get power from the wires attached to the furnace or air conditioner.

Note:

In this project, temperature management triggers an increase or decrease in temperature depending on settings and season. When it's time to turn on or off a heater or air conditioner, an event is sent or detected by the main controller. This would be the same as having a person stand in front of the thermostat and watch the change in temperature every minute to simply turn a switch on or off.

Project Management and Data Modeling Tools

To make sure everyone communicates design information in a clear and consistent fashion the project manager has decided code diagrams will use the Unified Modeling Language. UML is designed to provide object diagrams that illustrate how objects or functions interact with each other and what types of properties (variables) have been defined in the interface. This will be especially useful when defining the device interface layer, as it will provide the necessary documentation to implement function calls to the device layer from all chosen platforms.

Data Flow Diagrams

Embedded Device Functional Layout

This device can be used stand-alone or integrated to a desktop computer. There are two or four pushbuttons that allow temperature settings to be increased or decreased. For the sake of simplicity, no clock is required for the initial trial, so there will no time of day or date display. The device communicates to the user through an LCD display that shows user settings and current temperature. Inputs are received from up to 64 temperature sensors. Each sensor has a unique 48-bit serial number that associates it with a zone. Each zone is associated with a fan output so temperature can be controlled for individual comfort. The temperature inputs are handled 1-Wire. The following flow diagram depicts temperature input, fan or environmental control output, user input, and user output. Three keys are defined to select the control menu, save the current settings to memory, and cancel the control mode restoring the prior settings.

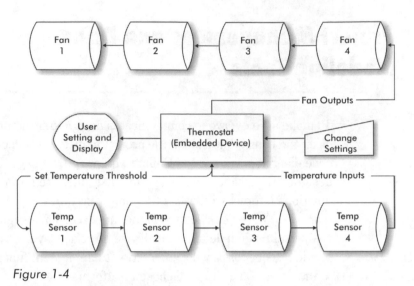

Figure 1-4

RS-232 Interface

The embedded device provides the desktop system with temperature logging data and control information via a serial cable. From this information the desktop system can send control commands to reprogram the device or override control commands. This control information consists of high and low temperature thresholds that start and stop fans and air-conditioning or heating equipment. When the system is being controlled from a Windows or UNIX host, the monitor replaces the display as the output device and the keyboard replaces the device buttons. The mouse can also replace the up and down buttons as well. The thermostat has limited logging capabilities due to a small amount of memory. As a result the computer will also act as an unlimited storage device for log records. These records can also be formatted and printed by the user using the time and date functions on the computer. This eliminates the need for a real-time clock and additional memory in the embedded device. A serial interface limits us to a single computer connection. It should be noted, however, that the device could manage 64 temperature sensors and 64 fans. Even with a simple serial interface a large building can be easily monitored and controlled. The following diagram shows how the computer can be used as an alternate control device.

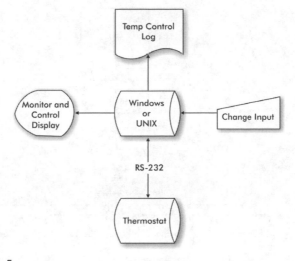

Figure 1-5

USB Interface

While USB allows a single computer to manage many devices, the probability of doing that is actually pretty small. Normal USB cables are 6 to 8 feet in length. Why support USB when a serial cable allows for greater distances? Simple — some computers may not have an RS-232 interface. Newer systems being built are no longer offering the old serial connection.

Note:

Since USB is now included with every IBM-compatible PC there is no longer a need for serial ports. As a result, manufacturers are warning consumers that the old serial port will be removed from new systems delivered within 12 months.

The following diagram shows how the USB interface offers a many-to-one control solution.

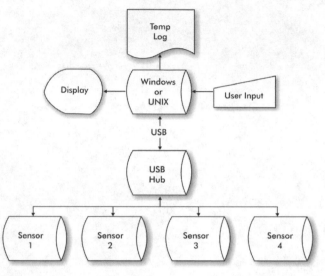

Figure 1-6

Ethernet Interface

Ethernet provides capabilities that RS-232 and USB lack. That's not to say RS-232 and USB interfaces should not be used; in fact, quite the contrary is true. In reality, an Ethernet interface provides the following benefits:

- Peer-to-peer support for the embedded devices
- A many-to-many relationship to a desktop computer system
- Internet accessibility
- X-10 monitoring and control
- Unlimited expansion

Peer-to-Peer Device Networking

This architecture has many benefits. These devices can communicate with each other independently from the desktop systems. Using this technique we can build extremely energy-efficient systems by using surrounding zone devices as supplemental control when large temperature swings occur. We can even reroute heating and air conditioning from those zones when necessary. Following is a diagram that shows how device-to-device, device-to-host, and host-to-host communications work.

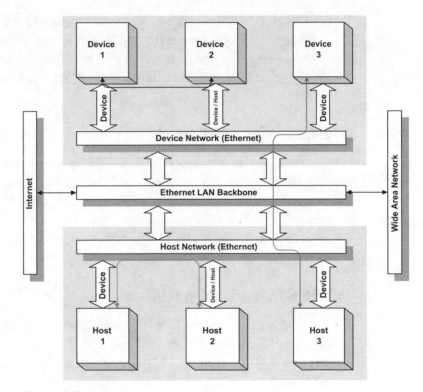

Figure 1-7

Many-to-Many Peer Networking

Using Figure 1-7 it becomes clear how easy it is to manage multiple systems from a single host. But many hosts can monitor a device at the same time even though only one can actively manage the device. Using the above model you can see that local, regional, and long-distance monitoring and control of the heating and air-conditioning devices is easy.

Internet Accessibility

While WAN and Internet accessibility aren't covered in this book, extending the protocol to support a wide area or international network is easy. The design requirements take this into account, as WAN and Internet control will be a part of future product specifications.

X-10 Monitoring and Control

By using Ethernet, additional devices can be monitored and controlled using the X-10 protocol. Additional fans, heaters, dehumidifiers, and other appliances that assist in controlling the environment can use this same technique by adding adapters or communicating through a host system. Future products will allow expanded intelligence through the use of this network.

Unlimited Expansion Capabilities

Providing an Ethernet interface allows for almost limitless expansion. We can expand devices by adding them directly to the Ethernet backbone or by attaching them through host systems already on the network. The following diagram shows how our devices are monitored and controlled via the Ethernet interface.

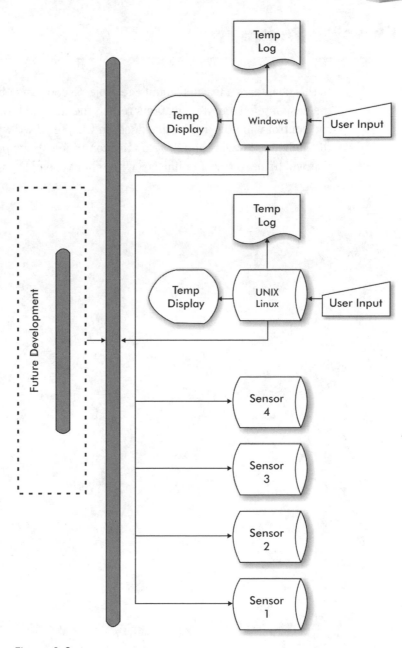

Figure 1-8

Chapter Summary

In this chapter we learned about the project scope and objectives, the design team, communications requirements, and how data and control will flow and be managed. In Chapter 2 we will design the embedded device and develop the communications protocol that will be used to communicate with other types of systems.

Embedded System Design

Overview

In Chapter 1 we defined the project scope and addressed issues with each development component. In this chapter we begin the task of designing the embedded system. When we design a network of devices, there are always many design choices to be made. Each of us tends to use technologies we are comfortable with. When we most need to take time to explore technological alternatives is when we have the least amount of time to spend exploring those alternate methods. The old saying "There's never time to do it right but always time to do it over" is very true in developing complicated embedded systems. In this chapter we break down the function of the embedded system until we have a functional task list. That task list will be used as the foundation for the functional specification and design of the embedded system.

Special Skills

There is normally a clear line separating the responsibilities of software and hardware people. Some of the typical "gray areas" are protocol development and device driver development. Both of these areas are involved with how the hardware and software systems communicate. These areas of development typically overlap both hardware and software groups as shown in Figure 2-1.

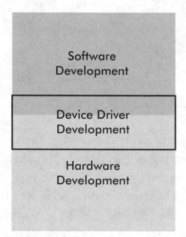

Figure 2-1

Device driver development requires a thorough understanding of how the hardware works. But the device driver developer has to also be highly skilled not only at software but also at writing software at the core of the host system's kernel. Just as important is the design and implementation of communication protocols. Unlike the device driver developer, the protocol developer is writing software to allow systems of different architectures to communicate. Developing protocols again requires a variety of skills as shown in Figure 2-2.

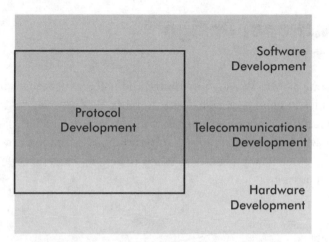

Figure 2-2

As you can see, knowledge of telecommunications is very helpful when developing a communications protocol. Having knowledge of different processors and how they handle character data is very important. Byte ordering is one example of this. The Intel and Motorola processors handle byte ordering in different fashions. Understanding this and other processor-dependent items, like variable size, can mean the difference between a well-developed protocol and meaningless data. When it comes to interfacing different types of devices, a good working knowledge of each device, hardware, and software is a must to properly implement a good working protocol.

The Functional Design

Compared to Windows or Linux, the embedded processor is much simpler in design. Less memory, no operating system, and a finite number of peripherals and external device interfaces make the development task easier. Figure 2-3 shows how simple the embedded processor is when developing an embedded application.

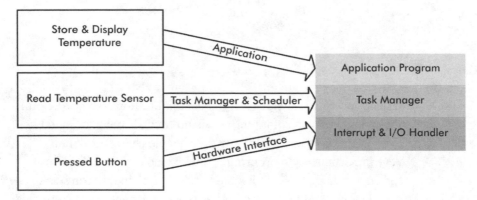

Figure 2-3

As you can see, when a button is pressed it will interrupt the program to take action. Temperature readings will occur at a preset time interval and a clock in the thermostat will measure the frequency of the readings. The result will be stored and displayed on the local LCD or transmitted to the host for logging and display. This sums up the defined purpose of this device, but there are two functions that need to be placed in the diagram before we have a completed definition. The first is our power monitor, which will simply increment a counter each time the unit is initialized. The second and final task is the communications handler to the host system. The power monitor will be part of the program initialization, so it will be at the application layer. The communications handler, however, isn't quite as simple. Data is only sent if the host is connected. In addition, host control can occur at any time. Because of this, data received from the host will be considered a priority and, if possible, treated as an interrupt. Data going to the host is either the result of an inquiry or a routine temperature update. To handle this properly, inbound host communications will be handled at the I/O level and outbound communications will be handled at the application level. Figure 2-4 shows these additional functions.

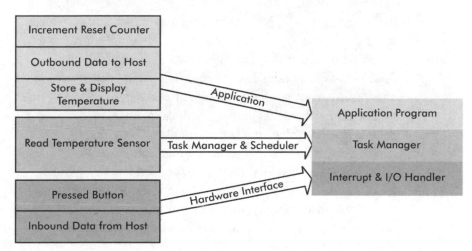

Figure 2-4

We've just developed our functional definition of the embedded system. It has to:

- Process pressed buttons on the thermostat.

- Process incoming data from a host system.

- Read temperature sensors at periodic intervals.

- Store temperature readings.

- Display temperature on LCD.

- Send temperature readings to host (if host is connected).

- Maintain a count of reset conditions.

The Embedded View of the World

An embedded system sees everything as input or output. A keypress or incoming data is input, whereas data to the host system or LCD display is output. Some embedded processors handle only analog or digital data, while others handle both. This means that events can be either analog or digital, depending on which processor is used.

What makes analog and digital data differ is continuity! Analog data is a continuous voltage while digital data comes in streams. Most embedded processors made today can handle analog and digital input and output. Keyboards, mice, modems, and data displays can all be defined as simple I/O devices.

There are three methods of communications that can be used to interface an embedded system to the world: serial, parallel, and TTL. All of the devices we will use to implement this system are capable of all three types of input and output. Table 2-1 describes each type of I/O including variations on each method as it applies to this project.

Table 2-1: Communications methods

Input/Output Type	Description	Analog/Digital
TTL	Transistor-to-transistor logic. Uses varying voltage levels.	Analog
Parallel	Sends single bits on multiple wires at the same time. Uses a clock line to synchronize data.	Digital
Serial	Sends all data in a single wire one bit at a time. May use separate clock line or baud rate generator, which requires a clock at both send and receive ends.	Digital

All of the communications methods we will implement utilize one or more of these methods or a variation of these methods. How the device communicates to the outside world is very important. Many factors have to be considered when designing an embedded system of this type. In contrast, when a software product for the desktop is developed, processor speed, memory, and storage requirements are simply defined and conveyed to the end user, and the end user is responsible for meeting these system requirements. Embedded systems are a much different story. If your desktop or notebook computer runs low on memory, you can go to the store and buy more. This isn't the case with an embedded system. If an embedded system runs out of memory while it is running, the results can be disastrous. At a minimum the system will crash, but depending on the use and purpose of the system, damage to property or life can result.

In the United States, government agencies regulate the requirements of such systems when used in life support or industry. In some cases days, weeks, or even months of documented tests and results have to be done before the device can be put into everyday use. For many years I designed machine control systems for special use in machine and print shops. While these machines were software driven, they were required by OSHA (Occupational Safety and Health Administration) regulations to have hardware disconnects, and if the system crashed it still had to shut down safely. This assured that no matter how confused the software ever got, pressing the big red Stop button would physically disconnect the power, preventing the loss of limb or life, and always guarantee a quick and reliable stop.

These factors should always be considered when designing any embedded system (they actually should be considered in *all* software and hardware projects as good engineering practices). Power requirements play a vital role in embedded systems. Our system will run in a house or business so we will use power from an electrical outlet. Since this is a new product we will keep it simple. In future generation products we could add a backup battery for time stamping temperature changes or allowing the user to change the comfort level based on time of day or season. A backup battery could assure these settings are saved even if the main power is lost. These considerations together help us determine the type of embedded system to choose for the application. There are almost an unlimited number of devices available and most can handle almost any of these tasks. For our purpose our primary requirement is communications based, as the embedded controller needs to communicate with each of the following individually: the host computer, LCD display, input buttons, and temperature sensors.

For this project we will use asynchronous serial communications. This will allow the embedded system to communicate with anything that supports the RS-232 standard. The RS-232 standard was the original serial communication method of choice for desktop computers. In addition to RS-232, we will also configure an additional processor pin to support a clock for communicating with synchronous serial devices. Using a transmit, receive, and clock pin, varying analog voltage levels can be used to send synchronized data. This technique will be used to expand our communications support to USB and Ethernet interfaces.

Serial Communications

Earlier we discussed the methods of communications available to the embedded system developer. It should be noted that these methods are built in and require no additional devices for support. Of course, external components can make the job easier, but these methods can be implemented without external hardware components. Now let's examine serial communications a little more in depth.

While the term "serial communications" is used in a generic sense, the different methods of serial communications are not. There are many different ways of communicating serially between different devices but they all fall into the categories explained earlier: synchronous and asynchronous. All serial communications techniques send data one bit at a time over the same wire. There are numerous variables associated with the stream of data. How the data is sent — LSB (least significant byte) or MSB (most significant byte) — is selectable; this is known as the byte order and was mentioned earlier. Other variables include baud rate, character length, number of stop bits and start bits, flow control options, and parity variables.

Asynchronous Serial Communications

Asynchronous serial communications uses only a single data pin but requires the data be clocked at the source and target. RS-232 requires setting baud rate, stop bits, and parity alike at both the send and receive sides. If the settings are not the same, the data will not be properly deciphered or will be seen as complete garbage by the receiver. Following is a flow diagram of how asynchronous data communications work.

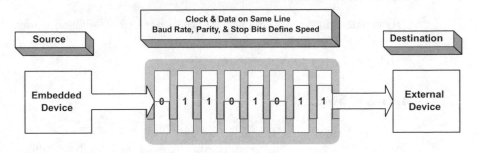

Figure 2-5

Byte Ordering

Most processors in use today are at least 16-bit processors. This means that if an instruction is 1 byte long, two instructions are processed per clock cycle. When an application is executing between processor memory this is handled automatically, but when we send data between systems of different processor types, confusion can quickly arise. Some processors handle data from the low-order bit to the high-order bit. This means the byte stream is handled as executed. But some processors handle the data high order to low order and then process the data after performing a swap. If you are sending data between processors that handle byte ordering differently, be certain to swap the bytes correctly or the data could get mangled.

Baud Rate

The baud rate is the speed at which the bits are sent over the serial line. Timing is arranged by calculating the delay between characters at a given clock rate. This time factor is then used to transmit the data. At the receiving end, the same delay is used to reassemble the data bits to form characters. Baud is represented in kilobits per second (K). You can calculate the actual number of characters sent and received by adding the start, stop, character length, and parity bits together and dividing the baud rate by the result. This will give a pretty close estimate.

Character Length

This is the number of bits in the actual character. Usually 6, 7, or 8 are the choices. In the early days only 6 bits were used, but today 8 bits is a typical character length.

Start and Stop Bits

A start bit is actually a synchronization bit that indicates the start of a character is being transmitted. The start bit is represented in a transition from a negative voltage (also known as a *mark*) to a positive voltage (also known as a *space*). Stop bits are always represented as a negative voltage (*mark*). Depending on the character frame size (which is determined by baud rate, data bits, and parity), the number of stop bits can be 1, 1.5, or 2.

Flow Control

There are several types of flow control that use both hardware and software. Hardware handshaking uses control lines to signal transmit and receive conditions. Data Set Ready (DSR), Data Terminal Ready (DTR), Clear To Send (CTS), and Request To Send (RTS) are the standard hardware handshake signals for RS-232. This translates to two additional control lines being used for hardware flow control. There are also software flow control signals — XON and XOFF, which stand for Transmit On and

Transmit Off, respectively. Both techniques are used in RS-232 communications. If you don't want to use two additional processor pins, then use software flow control if you aren't transmitting high volumes of data.

Parity

This is the number of 1's at the end of each character. Even, Odd, or None are serial communication selections. These represent 1 (Odd), 2 (Even), or Don't care (None). Just as start and stop bits are used to identify the beginning and end of a character frame, the parity value is used to provide a consistent number of bits for the actual character.

Synchronous Serial Communications

Synchronous communication requires two lines between the devices. One line carries the clock pulse while the other line carries the data. This method allows data transfer speeds that are governed by the processor speed without setting baud rates, parity, and other settings. Data transfers occur at the clock rate of the sender. Most embedded processors today support data rates as high as 150 MHz. A slower embedded processor would send the data at the clock rate. The embedded processors we will be using range in speed from 4 MHz to 50 MHz. Figure 2-6 shows a synchronous communications diagram.

Synchronous communications define a separate data and clock line. The sender always provides the clock so the receiver can synchronize data transitions. Since the clock is provided by the sender, data transitions are guaranteed to be correct and there is no need for setting baud rates, parity, or stop bits. Faster clock rates allow faster data transfers without any additional software.

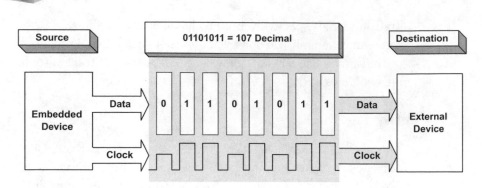

Figure 2-6

Comparing Asynchronous and Synchronous Communications

You may be asking why asynchronous data transfers would be used since they require more effort. RS-232 is an EIA (Electronics Industry Association) standard and was one of the first asynchronous standards defined by the EIA. RS-232 baud rates are supported by almost all devices and use a separate baud rate generator rather than the system clock. While synchronous data transfers are much faster by comparison, the higher speeds are only good for short distances unless high-quality cable is used. This makes synchronous data transfers more cost effective for short distances, while asynchronous methods are more cost effective for longer distances because less expensive cable can be used. RS-232 is also a standard at the signal level so the interface will always work between different devices when it comes to data handling. RS-232 defines handshaking between devices. In each RS-232 session one device is defined as Data Communications Equipment (DCE) and the other as Data Terminal Equipment (DTE). Over time there have been some misunderstandings on how to define DTE vs. DCE, which have led to communications problems. If you use RS-232, always be certain to make one side DCE and the other DTE or you may have difficulty sending and receiving data.

Synchronous Transfer Types

Synchronous data transfers have been around for many years. This method of communication was originally used by IBM as a means for remote terminals to access mainframe equipment. This technique allows high-speed data transfers even in large networks with high data traffic volume. Synchronous data transfers differ in software implementation. I²C, SPI, and Dallas 1-Wire are all variations of synchronous communications. We can also define our own protocol or just shift data in and out by simply defining the clock and data lines and sending the data.

This project will use synchronous data transfers for data exchange with the RS-232, USB, and Ethernet controllers, which will be on the same board as the embedded controller. This makes internal data exchange easy and fast and requires minimal software so we won't be using all of the embedded system resources to send and receive characters. This technique also simplifies software development because we will always be only one layer away from the actual hardware communicating with external systems.

Parallel Data Communications

Parallel communications are not used in this project but have been considered. To round out your knowledge of communications techniques a short description of how parallel communications work is presented here. Parallel communications are common for moving large amounts of data very quickly on slower processors. Printer manufacturers use parallel communications to allow the printer to keep pace with constant data delivery. Parallel communications allows printer makers to move the data to the print head pins a full character at a time. This also increases printing speed by a factor of 8 since all 8-character bits are transmitted at the same time. The following diagram illustrates how parallel data communications work.

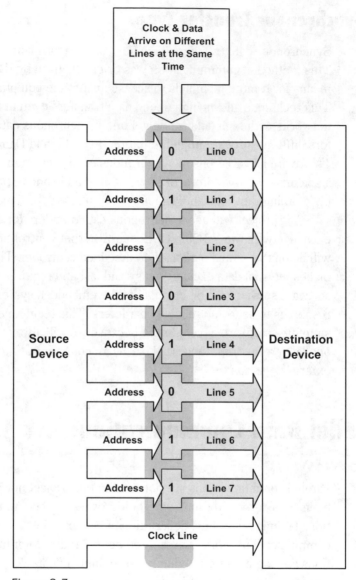

Figure 2-7

The Communications World of Windows and UNIX

Because embedded processors are used in out-of-the-way places and because they usually manage some type of mechanical or electrical control or appliance, the developer must be familiar with the actual hardware. Windows and UNIX systems were designed to be used by humans. Because of this there are many more layers of software between the hardware layer and the user. Device interfaces are handled at a much lower level, keeping human interaction minimal when using the system to address external devices. To make a system intuitive and easy for a person to use, much effort must go into the design and implementation under the hood. Unlike the embedded system where a single layer acts as the handler of all data, I/O, and user interaction, Windows and UNIX have a presentation layer that communicates with the user, a file handler that reads and writes file I/O, and a device layer that moves data between devices, files, and user interfaces. Rather than looking at the actual electrical signals in a device, the device is opened and the driver acts as the interpreter between the actual hardware and desktop application. This means the programmer doesn't have to be an electronics engineer to address the hardware. In fact most applications programmers have little or no knowledge of the hardware. They simply open, read, write, and close files or device names.

The Protocol, a Bridge between Different Worlds

The protocol is the software that bridges the embedded system and Windows, UNIX, and potentially any other system. Once the embedded hardware is defined, the protocol message categories are defined. Defining the message types and data definitions allows us to build a software bridge.

On the embedded system the protocol is implemented in software but becomes functional in hardware once the code is burned into the processor. On Windows and UNIX the protocol is developed as a shared library, or DLL. This allows the protocol to be seen by the application as a black box and prevents tampering with the protocol, thus keeping its integrity intact. The application programmer will open this black box by name or as a file and through a series of defined record or structure layouts will simply send these records off and await a response. Figure 2-8 graphically illustrates the differences between the embedded system and the Windows and UNIX hosts. The first block shows the embedded device model. There is no device driver layer because the embedded system deals with events and device interfaces directly. The second block is the physical interface layer. This would be the RS-232, USB, or Ethernet cable that connects the physical interface to the device. The third block contains two sections. The first is the device interface and protocol layer. This is functionally the same as the embedded system, interfacing directly to electrical signals. The second portion of this is the application layer. The application layer formats the messages and sends them through a device driver layer and eventually to the embedded system.

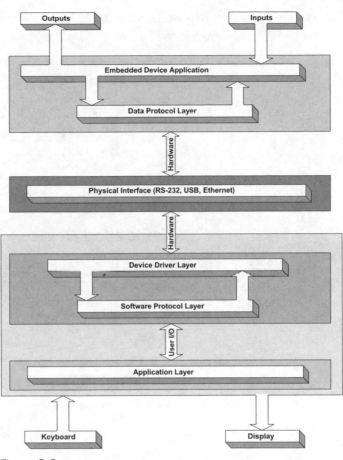

Figure 2-8

Embedded System Protocol Functions

In specifying a protocol we must define a formal set of rules that allow the embedded system designer and application software engineers to communicate. We then eliminate the possibility of miscommunications between these devices by specifying a procedure that allows all the devices to communicate only when it is their turn. Using this strategy we can convert data so it is always properly interpreted by the host and embedded system. This formal type of communication is called a protocol. As the embedded system design process evolves it is broken down into a logical flow of data as shown in the following diagram.

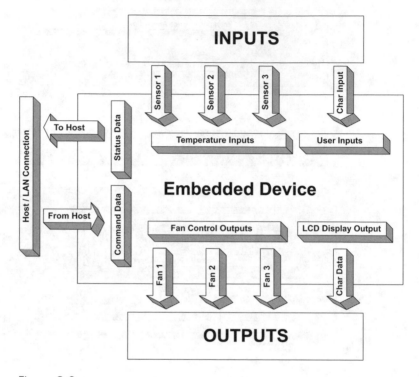

Figure 2-9

In Figure 2-9 you can see the embedded system does little more than read inputs from temperature sensors, adjust outputs to control fans and other environmental equipment, process host commands for logging and control messages for climate over-rides, and provide data to the host and end user for monitor and display purposes. As our design progresses the arrows will eventually turn into processor pins on the embedded system that monitor or control environmental functions. The data flow arrows identify a serial, USB, or Ethernet connection to the host. Since we now have a defined flow of data and control within the embedded system, we will establish the foundation for a communications protocol between the embedded system and the desktop computers. A message sent that doesn't conform to protocol definitions will be ignored. Expanding the system in the future simply requires additional message types, categories, and message fields. To maintain backward compatibility the protocol will contain a protocol version. Adding new message types in the future will increment the version number. This assures a path to expansion while being able to process legacy messages without modifying the hardware in the field.

Communications Protocol History

Protocols have existed in the communications industry for many years. Datapoint developed the ARCNET protocol as the first broadband network protocol many years ago. ARCNET was the basis of what eventually became the Ethernet protocol. Today, Ethernet is the most widely used network protocol for LANs and WANs. Ward Christenson developed the X-Modem protocol in Chicago over 20 years ago as a way to transmit files from one computer to another and assure no data was lost or garbled in the process. These are two excellent examples of why protocols are developed and the functions they serve.

For our purpose a simple protocol will suffice as a simple means of establishing communications between the desktop computers and the embedded systems. We are simply establishing a format by which the two systems can talk and a priority handshake by which each party can take their turn speaking to prevent data collisions. Protocols are implemented every day for many different types of communications. In their simplest form they establish a set of commands or words each party or computer understands. In their most complex form they introduce error checking to make sure every word is spelled properly and used in proper context. Every protocol is different and is based on a specific need or requirement.

Building a good protocol is done in small steps. By illustrating each step we go from concept to working model by checking our query and response tables against our real-world requirements. It is very easy to write down the requirements and develop a working protocol; this is done all the time. There are several reasons why I am taking smaller steps. They are:

- Proper data size definitions need to be established across all platforms
- Thorough query definitions
- Thorough response definitions
- Functional completeness

Protocol Definition Considerations

By breaking down the requirements from Chapter 1 into smaller pieces we can determine how large a data message will be and how many commands our protocol will require. The following diagram shows detailed information on the data flow of the embedded system.

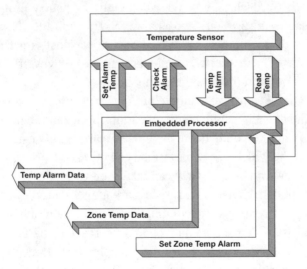

Figure 2-10

From Figure 2-10 it is clear the data flow for the temperature sensors, temperature alarms, and zone temperature information is sent to the host but only if the host is connected and requests the information. The host can send zone alarm limits back to the embedded processor. This allows the host to monitor temperature and temperature alarms and set the temperature alarm triggers, which in this case is setting a high and low temperature for each sensor to act upon. If the temperature range is between the high and low settings, no action is taken. If the range goes above or below those range settings, an alarm condition will cause the embedded system to start the heating or air conditioning and the associated fans for air movement. Addressing each sensor through its unique ID sets temperature ranges. The temperature can be read or a query can be generated to see if an alarm condition exists.

For the purpose of this book we will be controlling a small fan that turns on or off depending on temperature and/or alarm conditions as shown in Figure 2-11. The fans are managed completely by the embedded system through the use of an electronic switch. Since we are working on a small scale, a single byte is output to the switch to turn the fan on or off. Each bit that is turned on will turn a fan motor on. Each bit that is turned off will turn the fan motor off. The single byte used to manage the switch is stored in non-volatile memory, which allows the status

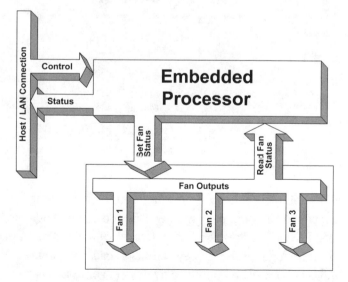

Figure 2-11

to be retained even if power is lost. Upon request the host can
have the embedded processor retrieve the data and send it to the
host for display, logging, or control purposes. The host can also
tell the device to change the fan status by simply sending a new
message to replace the old one. So, in addition to our temperature data, we can add a simple fan monitor and control message.

After temperature measurement, user input and display messages need to be included in the protocol. A single byte gives the
ability to read eight switches. While there are currently two buttons, using a byte gives us expansion capability. In Figure 2-12
we see how user interface information flows.

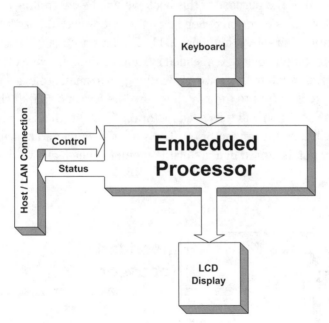

Figure 2-12

This completes the data flow picture for each function the
embedded system performs. Our protocol will handle keyboard
and LCD messages in addition to controlling and monitoring the
system in general. The keyboard is a read-only device. While an
LCD is typically an output-only device, some LCDs have the ability to store special character sets and read them back. LCDs may

also allow their display contents to read by location, line, or all character positions at once. Since LCD designs are constantly changing, our protocol will be flexible enough to handle varying device types without making code changes. We have now mapped all the functions of the embedded system. Next we will take this information and implement the protocol.

Designing the Device Protocol

We start by listing the functions of the embedded system and placing those functions in categories. The following table illustrates the functions of the embedded system and the categories we have assigned them.

Table 2-2: Embedded system functions

Function	Category
Collect and monitor temperature changes	CLIMATE
Respond to temperature changes and alarms	CLIMATE
Monitor, control, and override fan controls	CLIMATE
Monitor remote user input	SYSTEM
Output remote display data	SYSTEM
Change remote message text	SYSTEM

Next we list the functions monitored by the host systems and assign each to a category. Table 2-3 illustrates these functions and categories.

Table 2-3: Desktop system functions

Function	Category
Collect temperature data	CLIMATE
Set temperature alarm	CLIMATE
Temperature alarm response	CLIMATE
Manual climate override	SYSTEM
Monitor remote user inputs	SYSTEM

Function	Category
Manage remote message output	SYSTEM
Edit remote display messages	SYSTEM

We have now completed the function and category tables for both the embedded system and desktop systems. Using the categories we have just created we will build our message tables. Since we have accounted for both the embedded system and host system functions, we can now consolidate the rest of the protocol definitions into a single table. In Table 2-4 we have taken each function in the previous two tables and assigned each to a message type. Once our categories and message types are defined, we can determine the parameters that will be associated with each function. Here I have assigned a message type and parameter type to the function categories.

Table 2-4: Message definitions

Category	Type	Message Definition	Parameters
CLIMATE	MONITOR	Request temperature	Sensor ID
CLIMATE	CONTROL	Set temperature alarm level	Sensor ID, Hi/Lo Level Alarms
CLIMATE	MONITOR	Check temperature alarm	Sensor ID
CLIMATE	MONITOR	Check all temperature alarms	None
CLIMATE	MONITOR	Get fan status	Sensor ID
CLIMATE	CONTROL	Set fan status	Sensor ID
SYSTEM	MONITOR	Check keyboard	None
SYSTEM	MONITOR	Get current display message	None
SYSTEM	CONTROL	Display user message	Message ID
SYSTEM	CONTROL	Change display message text	Message ID
SYSTEM	MONITOR	Request status	Status ID
SYSTEM	CONTROL	Set status	Status ID, Message Length

Protocol Message and Variable Size Considerations

We are now ready to assign a variable size to each message. We are doing this so we can make certain we always use a variable of the same size for each system that uses the protocol. Using the data from the above tables, the variable definitions are as follows:

Table 2-5: Message variable size

Variable Name	Size
Sensor ID	I byte
Alarm Type	I byte (0 = Low, I = High)
Alarm Temperature Setting	2 bytes
Message ID	I byte
Message Size	2 bytes

We have now completed the protocol definition from the host (or desktop) query side. We have two message categories: climate and system. We also have two message types: monitor and control. In our final step we allocate a size to each variable we have defined. In Table 2-6 I have completed the definition structure.

Table 2-6: Completed message definition structure

Name	Variable Size	Accepted Values
Message Category	I byte	0-255
Message Type	I byte	0-255
Sensor ID	I byte	0-255
Alarm Type	I byte	0 = Low, I = High
Temperature	2 bytes	0-65535
Message ID	I byte	0-255
Message Size	2 bytes	0-65535

To provide the flexibility of being able to add new messages without modifying the hardware I have added a variable called Message ID. Each message type will have an associated ID. Since a single byte can hold a value of 0 to 255, we have plenty of room for additional messages without changing the protocol. This means we can design several generations of this product or use this same protocol for several product lines without making further changes to the embedded or host system software. We've also declared a Message Size variable that holds the complete message length. This allows us to have messages of varying length (such as display text messages) and also allows us to change the size of existing messages without any changes needed to the protocol itself.

Embedded System Protocol Responses

Message categories, types, variables, and sizes have all been defined. During the implementation phase we will build a device response for each query from the host. Since our protocol is now completed, adding the responses during implementation will simply give us a list of possible responses. In order to visualize our protocol, following is a query and response table.

In Figures 2-13 and 2-14 the Control column is the host system making the control request. The Status column is the embedded system's response. The Message Type column is the message class as viewed from the host side. Figure 2-13 shows the monitor class messages while Figure 2-14 shows the control class messages.

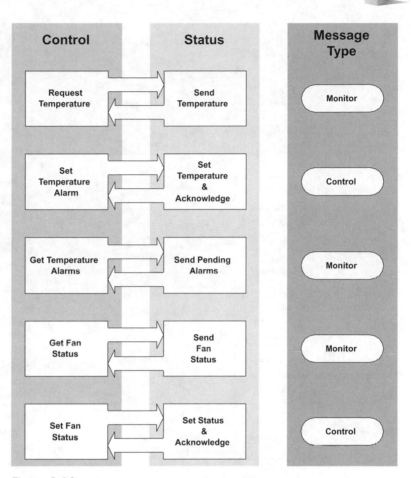

Figure 2-13

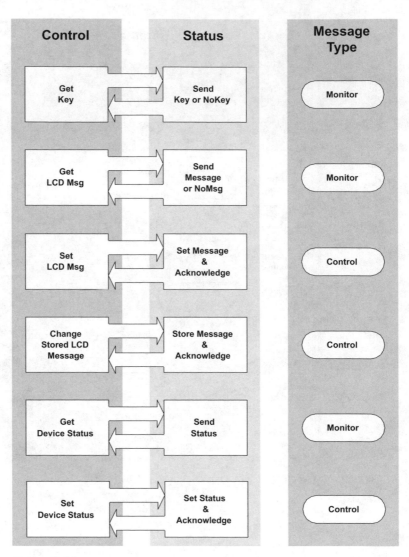

Figure 2-14

Embedded System Summary

By defining each duty the embedded system is responsible for we have created a functional description for all device inputs and outputs. Using I/O definitions allowed us to define a protocol that a host computer can use to communicate with the device. Defining this information allows us to develop a complete protocol that can be used by the device and other systems to communicate.

Protocol Summary

We have now thoroughly defined a communications protocol by which our embedded system, Windows, and UNIX systems can all communicate. Message categories, types, variable names, and sizes have all been defined. We have made our protocol expandable by having room for new message types and varying message sizes.

When the need arises for a communications protocol to be developed there are always many details to consider. Walking through the protocol development process one step at a time assures that all the little details have been thought of and dealt with properly. Using this technique you are assured of building a solid protocol that will meet current and future needs without constant changes.

Chapter Summary

The embedded system now has a formal language that allows it to talk to the world. While this is a simple example, it covers handling device input, device output, display output, user input, and the remote monitoring and control of the environment. In the process of establishing a protocol we have narrowed the differences between desktop systems and the embedded system to the interface or device driver layer on the host systems. Our device input and output seamlessly interface to a protocol that the device driver layer uses to send and receive messages to a remote system. On the host side this protocol interfaces to the device driver, which will in turn interface to the desktop application layer. In the next chapter we will design the device interface layer to handle the differences in the hardware layer and the differences between UNIX and Windows. This approach will lead us to design a user application that will interface to the device driver layer the same way across platforms.

Chapter 3

Designing Portable Device Interfaces for Windows and UNIX

Overview

This is by far the most difficult chapter of this book and the largest chapter so far. If you have never written a device driver I recommend reading this chapter twice — the first time to learn the architecture and the second time to understand the design.

While there are many similarities between the current Intel-based UNIX and Windows 32-bit architectures, there are just as many differences. There are many factors that contribute to how portable a device driver can and will be. Some of these factors are:

- **Language portability** — C, C++, etc.

- **Existing OS support** — Whether some level of driver support is already present

- **Legacy driver support** — Whether a similar device driver has already been developed in prior OS versions

- **Device type** — Whether past versions of the OS supported this device type
- **Driver structure** — Whether a complete driver needs to be written or a mini-driver or "wrapper layer" will suffice

Designing a portable device driver isn't a decision that will be made at a given point in the development cycle. It is a decision that will be made from the project start and will influence decisions throughout the development cycle. This single decision can have the largest impact on the overall cost of a project. In an ideal world the implementation phase of this project would be the easiest since it would merely be implementing the work already defined. But as we all know, this is not an ideal world. Technology industries are constantly forging ahead with new ideas, products, and enhancements to existing products. It is not uncommon for one or more operating system updates to be released between the design of a product and its implementation. For that reason, any experienced software architect knows a certain amount of flexibility needs to be incorporated into the design. If this isn't done, you can expect what I call the infinite design cycle implementation. Each time the implementation team gets the design, some changes need to be made to support the latest OS changes, so the design is sent back. Well, guess what happens by the time the design changes are made, reviewed, approved, and sent back. You guessed it — the whole cycle starts again.

Let's examine each of the above considerations and the effect they have on the portability of the device layer. Unlike the hardware implementation, this side of the development is dependent on many outside forces. OS vendors and third-party suppliers to those vendors have a major influence, as do security updates due to virus threats and other market conditions. So how does one design a device driver under these conditions? Following a few simple rules not only allows your design to be current, but also develops the highest quality driver with the longest life cycle.

The Basic Driver Design

There is a world of difference between designing hardware and designing software. I've been involved with hardware and mechanical design for almost 25 years, and it is nothing like software design. Here's why: Software is only one dimension, so when it works you cannot visibly see how the pieces fit together. That is one reason people tend to think software works by magic. There are no naming conventions defined in software, so learning a new operating system or user interface can take months or even years depending on how complex it is and the number of functions that exist. Can you imagine not having nut and bolt thread standards? You could spend weeks trying to find a nut or bolt exactly like the old one. Fortunately we were smart enough to realize that having standard thread dimensions was not only in the best interest of the consumer but the manufacturer as well. This approach has never been taken in software because everyone has a better idea than the next guy (or so they believe).

As a hardware and software designer you cannot control what others do or don't do, so to design device drivers that can be implemented and maintained without a lot of ongoing design changes, try the following:

- Keep your design document to the important points without defining implementation. This means making sure the developers know what is up to their discretion in implementation and what rules must be adhered to strictly. While a protocol must be coded as defined, the details of how the vendor and product ID are implemented can be left to the developers.

- Point out items that will impact system performance by documenting these issues, but again leave implementation details to the developers. This will assure they account for these considerations while having the flexibility of developing to their breadth of knowledge.

- Use senior people with proven development skills as lead developers. This is one of the most important points to consider. The more development experience people have, the more comfortable they are in their realm and the higher the quality of work. This can easily translate to shorter development cycles and longer product life cycles.

- Partner your junior developers with experienced developers. This has several benefits during the development process. It builds team spirit among the development team and allows the experienced developers to share their experiences and tutor junior people. If done constructively, this is a very good way of mentoring new development people.

- Never be so inflexible as to not listen to the developers. I've seen too many times when the architect refuses to listen to ideas from the developers. If a developer sees something he is concerned about, listen. Give developers the flexibility to show how they would do something while reserving the right to make a call. This builds rapport with the developers and also sets forth an environment of true team spirit.

- At the end of the project, update the design document to reflect the actual implementation. This will provide a clear starting point for the next-generation product and a detailed accounting of design vs. real-world development.

As you can see, many of these items are more people related than technology related, but they are just as important to the project's success. This allows a good design to be turned into a terrific product. Documentation is one of the most important yet most neglected areas of most projects. While we were once a nation of people who could only communicate in writing, we now seem to neglect writing altogether.

When you put your design on paper and look at it a day or so later, you will always find a way to improve what may already be a good or even a great design. You also are leaving a trail you or someone else can always follow and start from again without worrying about forgotten details. Any product worth developing is worth documenting; at the same time your documentation may prove your idea was first in case of an intellectual property dispute.

These are just some of the things to consider when designing device drivers. All of these items are important because you are designing the software that will determine how well the system performs and may be the difference between a good error log or a system crash. There is no greater responsibility than designing or implementing device drivers for an operating system that supports many concurrent tasks and users.

Language Portability

Choosing the right development language for device driver portability is different from choosing a language for application portability. We will be using the GNU C and C++ tools for one application development platform and the Borland compilers for Linux and Windows as another option. For device driver development, C is generally the language of choice. C is ANSI supported and provides a good balance of syntax while allowing easy access to system resources such as memory and ports. Some people consider C a high-level language, but it is actually a mid-level language that is one step above assembler in features and syntax. In fact, C was developed as an alternative language for writing operating systems by the original authors at Bell Labs. For device driver development on UNIX and Linux, we will use the GNU C compiler. This compiler is supported across all UNIX and Linux platforms in addition to being supported on Windows. In addition to the C language, the compiler also supports Fortran, C++, and Java as other mainline languages. Less popular languages are also supported such as Objective C (which is an object-oriented version of the C language) and Pascal. The GNU compiler suite also supports several Java-related features. The GNU compiler suite allows Java code to be compiled into the normal byte code for the Java virtual machine or as a native executable on the target machine. While there are versions of the GNU compiler suite for Windows, the Microsoft Device Driver Kit (DDK) only supports drivers written using Microsoft languages. Microsoft compilers, like most others, support ANSI standards as well as their own. Since device driver architectures are somewhat different between Windows and UNIX/Linux, it is very unlikely that low-level Windows drivers can be cross-compiled for any other platforms.

Existing Operating System Support

Careful selection of interface techniques can greatly reduce the amount of effort needed to integrate new devices. There are several considerations to keep in mind during the decision-making process regarding this issue. One of these considerations is speed. We have chosen three types of hardware interfaces to accommodate a one-to-one, many-to-one, and many-to-many relationship, but each of these techniques also handles data at different speeds. Generally speaking, the longer an interface has been around, the more likely it is to have built-in operating system support, but it is also likely to be much slower than current interface technology. Let's examine each interface method we have chosen to see how well each is supported in the operating systems we will be using.

The RS-232 Interface

Commonly known as the serial interface, this was one of the first methods of computer networking used to connect terminals, printers, and other types of external equipment to mainframes, and mini- and microcomputers. This interface is defined at both the hardware and software levels. The hardware is generally defined as DTE, which is short for Data Terminal Equipment, or DCE, which is short for Data Communications Equipment.

UNIX, Linux, and all Windows versions from Windows 95 and later support RS-232 internally and in a similar way. All three systems treat RS-232 much as a file that has the ability to open, close, read, write, and manage through the use of I/O hardware control functions. There are also many third-party serial toolkits available that use RS-232, although few if any support cross-platform development.

The Ethernet Interface

Unlike RS-232, Ethernet devices were not integrated on computer motherboards until recent years. In addition, Ethernet connects the computer to a network rather than a terminal, printer, or modem. Because of these differences, Ethernet has multiple tiers, or layers, of support by the operating system. Of course there is the hardware layer that is the physical interface and the device driver that allows the system to communicate with the hardware. But there is a second layer known as the socket layer. The socket layer is where the TCP/IP implementation resides. Each host platform has this layer, which is software only. The following illustration shows where it fits in the scheme of our design.

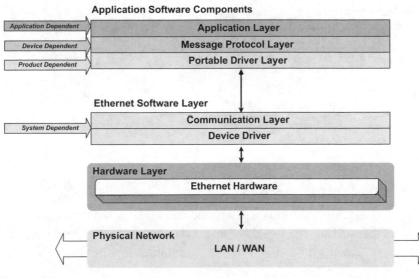

Figure 3-1

The TCP/IP or socket layer is addressed through the use of the Socket API on UNIX/Linux and WinSock on the Windows platform. If we were designing a network application for a standard PC or even a mainframe computer, using the socket layer would allow the program to communicate across the building or across the planet to any type of computer that also supports the Socket interface. Since we are interfacing to an embedded system instead, adding the TCP/IP interface will come at the expense of memory and speed. If we don't want the device to be accessible from a WAN or the Internet, then bypassing the socket layer will not only conserve memory and increase speed but it will also provide an additional layer of security. This layer of security is minimal since it is not encrypted. If we bypass the TCP/IP layer, the developers will need to address the hardware layer directly for sending and receiving data to the device as shown in the following illustration.

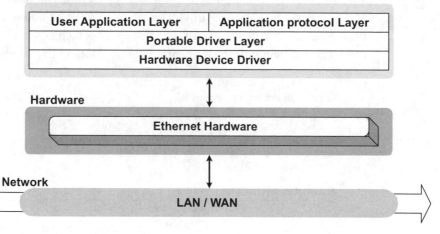

Figure 3-2

Eliminating the TCP/IP layer may cause additional development effort; however, this will be handled in the portable "wrapper" that will be developed for device communications. Since we have designed a protocol for device communications, some of the additional work will be minimal. For the purpose of this project we will examine both methods of implementation from a hardware and software perspective.

The USB Interface

I left this method until last because USB is not like either of the hardware interfaces already described. USB supports up to 127 devices. These devices can be from the same vendor but more than likely are many different types of devices from many different vendors. This device interface has been slated to replace both the existing RS-232 and parallel printer interfaces. As I write this book many of the new systems being delivered no longer have serial or parallel interfaces, opting instead to have multiple USB ports instead. Currently there are hardware products for parallel to USB, serial to USB, and Ethernet to USB; all work very well. Keyboards, mice, game paddles, and a wide variety of devices are currently available for USB.

USB has two specifications: 1.1 and 2.0. The USB 1.1 specification is a low-speed data interface with a maximum data throughput of about 10 MPS (megabits per second). USB 2.0 increases that speed to 480 MPS, or by a factor of 48. Both versions support cables that can be a maximum of 16 feet in length. USB is fully self-contained and self-powered, providing 5 volts to peripheral equipment. Even though USB is powered by the host, care should be taken to keep current requirements low or provide an external power supply.

USB is multiplexed through the use of hubs, which take a single USB connection and multiply it by four or eight additional devices. Both USB 1 and 2 specifications support a maximum of 127 devices. Hubs can be powered by an external source or can be parasitic by using the 5 volts already available from the host. Once again, current requirements must be kept low. As a rule, when you add more USB devices you should use powered hubs to provide enough power to drive the external bus and eliminate the potential of current overdraw.

Chapter 3

Microsoft began supporting USB devices in Windows 95 OSR 2 but Windows 2000 and Windows XP provide much greater support for USB 1.1 and 2.0 protocols. UNIX and Linux provide thorough support for USB in kernel 2.4 and much better plug-and-play support in the current kernel, 2.6. FreeBSD began supporting USB in the 4.7 release, and the 5.1 release has full USB support that is impressive. Both UNIX and Linux have excellent USB support for the 1.1 protocol.

Like Ethernet, USB has tiered support at the OS level. Unlike Ethernet, this support is not used to standardize communications with the world. Every device attached to a computer via USB has a device classification type, vendor code, product code, and optional revision code associated with the device. Since USB is known as "hot-pluggable," which means a device can be connected and disconnected while the system is running, the second-tier drivers are loaded and unloaded dynamically as devices are attached, removed, and reattached, all while the computer is running.

USB communications are referred to as "endpoint to endpoint" communications, which means that while 127 different devices may be attached on the same bus, each device communicates directly with its associated driver on a one-to-one basis. The device ID, vendor, product, and revision codes tell the system which driver to load. The device type ID tells the kernel which branch of the kernel driver should be used as the data pathway to and from the device. This is the simple explanation that omits much of the complexity of the USB architecture. We will examine that complexity in Part II as we build, test, and integrate our embedded system.

The Windows Driver Architecture

Windows has a long history of development. It started as little more than a task manager that ran over DOS (Windows 1.1), then evolved to a subsystem over DOS (Windows 3.1), and on to a GUI that hosted DOS as a subsystem (Windows 95 and 98). In the early 1990s Microsoft borrowed Dave Cutler and his team from DEC to build a new operating system that would have a real multitasking, multiuser core and support the Windows GUI. Dave Cutler was the architect of the VMS operating system that DEC had used for its mini-computers for years. That effort resulted in the core architecture of Windows NT, 2000, and XP. While Windows 98 is still in use and supported, that architecture is at the end of its life cycle and no further development on that kernel is being done. For our purposes we will go with current technology and address only the Windows 32-bit architecture found in Windows 2000 and Windows XP.

The Windows Boot Process

Windows starts the boot process by starting the hardware abstraction layer, or HAL. This program checks for attached devices, timers, and motherboard features and sets up basic hardware initialization and communications. Next the Windows kernel mode driver is started and a process manager, kernel mode memory manager, and kernel logging is started. Once the kernel is started, the Windows executive is brought online. The executive is responsible for loading higher-level device drivers, system-level security, and networking. Once the executive is fully operational the user layer is initialized and the logon prompt is displayed. At this point the system is fully functional and ready to start servicing user program needs. One of the interesting liaisons between the kernel and user modes is the service manager. The service manager handles starting and monitoring of all background tasks. After a user logs in, any applications that start automatically for that user will be invoked and running. This includes taskbar managers, special user interface components, user I/O programs for telecommuting, etc. Services are the bridge between kernel mode drivers and user mode applications. Applications that run as services do not need to have any user interface at all. But if the developer needs user input or display capabilities, what is known as an interactive service can be written to allow user mode display and input from, essentially, a kernel mode program. Windows services are a major difference in how Windows and UNIX are designed.

When the Boot Process Fails (The Recovery Console)

At the very beginning of the boot process, the console mode can be entered through the recovery screens or by entering a special startup mode that allows a single user to do maintenance, cleanup, and repair tasks. Windows is a true graphics mode operating system and while Windows, UNIX, and Linux can be made to look similar, the fact that Windows is a native GUI adds complexity to writing device drivers.

As you can see, the services layer of Windows has access to both user mode and kernel mode drivers, and resources. This is important since all of the communications methods we have chosen have some internal support in Windows. Our goal is to develop a "wrapper" around the device driver layer that hides the platform-dependent calls.

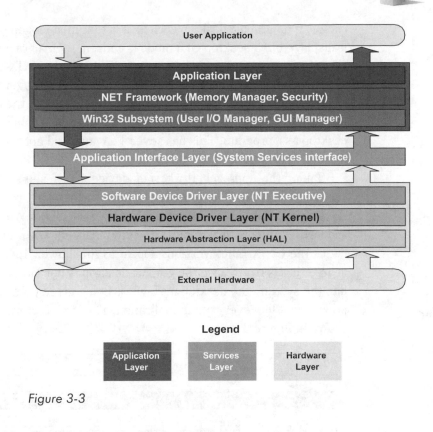

Figure 3-3

The UNIX System Architecture

UNIX/Linux take a simpler approach to system architecture. Before Windows, operating systems used keyboards for user input and simple monochrome text displays for output. Fancy graphics were unheard of in those days. UNIX/Linux have their roots in text mode as opposed to graphics mode. The UNIX/Linux systems begin by reading configuration files that start different kernel components with the startup parameters. Once the kernel is running, the task manager is started along with any background tasks that are designated to run automatically. If graphics mode is the defined user startup mode, the X server is started, followed by the chosen graphic desktop of choice. If no graphic desktop is chosen, a text mode logon prompt is displayed. If a desktop GUI mode is chosen, then a graphic version of a user ID and logon prompt are displayed. In UNIX-style operating systems, the X server is the screen I/O manager and mouse handler at the lowest level. The X server shifts the display into graphics mode and then loads the chosen graphic desktop as a program. This has several obvious and not-so-obvious advantages.

Taking this approach, the kernel, device driver, and system services layers are all text mode applications that don't require any graphic desktop to load or use. If you've used both Windows and UNIX/Linux with a graphical desktop manager you will notice the UNIX/Linux versions appear to run slower. To some degree that is true. Since the graphic desktop is not integrated into the system, the desktop manager is being given processor priority just like every other application. This architecture is shown in Figure 3-4.

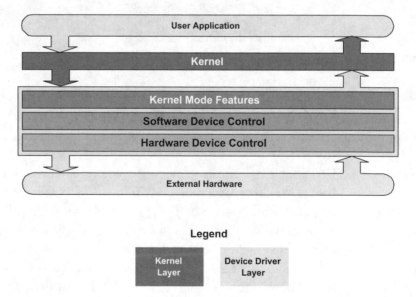

Figure 3-4

Unlike Windows 2000 and XP, the UNIX device driver layer is simpler in design. Since the graphic desktop is another program, access to the kernel and device layers is much closer to the application layer and easier to develop for. This doesn't mean writing UNIX/Linux drivers is a cakewalk, but rather that fewer considerations need to be given to graphic desktop integration. This architecture by design gives higher priority to tasks that run closer to the core of the operating system, again reducing some of the considerations that an integrated graphic desktop may pose.

Device Driver Types

Though the architecture of Windows and UNIX are different, they share common ground when it comes to the device types supported. These types of devices are discussed in this section.

Character Devices

Keyboard, terminal, and serial devices are known as character-based devices. These are devices that send, receive, and process data one character at a time.

Block Devices

Block devices process data in blocks, that is, more than one character at a time. Disk files, disk drive interfaces, SCSI controllers, scanners, and cameras are all examples of block devices.

Network Devices

Originally network devices were block devices, but in the last few years they have been broken out into their own device category. The most recent UNIX and Linux kernel updates (2.4 and 2.6) provide fairly extensive network card support. Windows also has extensive network card support. FreeBSD (UNIX) and Windows have thorough wireless network card support also. New Linux kernels have excellent support, while the older 2.2 kernels have limited wireless support. Both architectures support a tiered or mini-port driver layer. This allows developers to add multiple levels of driver support for different application needs while sharing the same physical device driver.

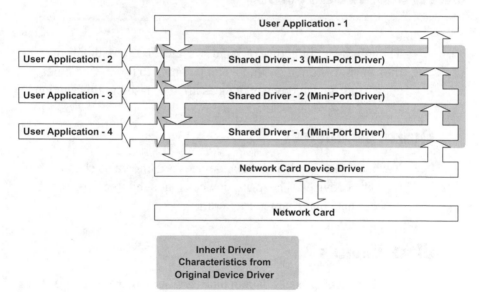

Figure 3-5

Each driver layer inherits from the original device driver, and changes are implemented to meet application specifications. These are known as "mini-port drivers," or "tiered drivers." These drivers allow specific functionality to be implemented without writing a complete device driver. The base device driver may be inherited. Each driver has a unique name that differentiates itself from the other drivers in the chain.

USB Devices

USB (or universal serial bus) allows for layered device drivers to be added and removed while the system is running. Because USB is defined as a "hot-pluggable" architecture, this layered (or tiered) device driver structure is unique when compared to other device drivers. Unlike other devices, USB has a core driver manager designed to detect the attachment and removal of a device while the system is running. This means that drivers for each device are loaded and unloaded dynamically. If an application is started that addresses a USB device, it must be able to handle the device being removed and take an orderly shutdown action accordingly. This may sound complicated, but USB is well defined and well thought out to handle this type of implementation. Because of its architecture, USB has a device handler that is part of the operating system. When a new device is attached, the device announces itself to the system. The core driver then performs handshaking and interrogates the device header, which provides vendor- and product-specific information. This information is used to look up the driver name and location for this specific device. That's the abbreviated description; more detail will be covered as we implement the interface in Part II of this book. Developing a USB driver requires the developer to write the specific functions for handling device-specific I/O, startup, and shutdown. USB allows the driver developer to focus on features specific to that device and not spend as much time interfacing to the operating system

Even though a core driver is available at the system level, each device must provide a second-level driver to support specific device I/O. USB hubs and the core driver handle device detection, initialization, and shutdown while also providing a pathway for the data to travel.

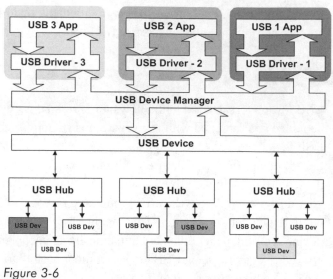

Figure 3-6

Portable Device Driver Requirements

Now that we have provided some background on the target platforms and how they handle devices we can start defining our portable device layer. The goal of having a portable device layer for our application is to simply hide the platform-specific details of the device interface, while providing the functions required to send, receive, and process data.

Since we have already defined the protocol between the user application and the embedded system, we only need to concentrate on host-specific device communications as they pertain to:

- The specific device driver for a given device type (RS-232, USB, Ethernet)

- A mini-port driver to handle high-level communications between the device and the application (USB initialization, shutdown, etc.)

- Providing platform-independent device driver management

For the purpose of this chapter, the definition of "processing" data is simply seeing that it is properly sent and received between the embedded system and the user application. You may be asking yourself why we aren't concerned with embedded system control at this point and potential error conditions in this layer. The answer is very simple: We want to be certain that communications control and data control are handled in their proper layers and are independent of each other. If we mix data and communications control, or worse intermix that control in multiple layers, we will defeat the purpose of portability and complicate the debugging process (debugging will be covered in Part II as we implement our system). This approach allows us the benefit of breaking the entire system down into smaller pieces

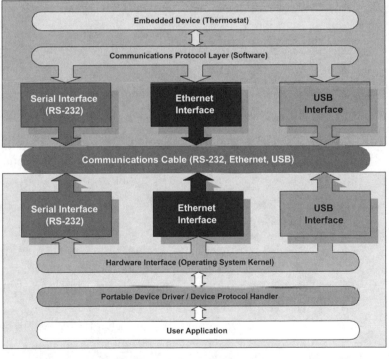

Embedded Device (Thermostat)

Communications Protocol Layer (Software)

Serial Interface (RS-232)

Ethernet Interface

USB Interface

Communications Cable (RS-232, Ethernet, USB)

Serial Interface (RS-232)

Ethernet Interface

USB Interface

Hardware Interface (Operating System Kernel)

Portable Device Driver / Device Protocol Handler

User Application

Legend

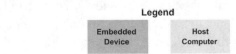

Embedded Device

Host Computer

Figure 3-7

and addressing only those design concerns for the piece we are currently working on. Now, you may be thinking that by taking this approach we will miss something important. There are several remaining pieces in the design of this system, and the final chapter in this section will be a complete design review. In design review we will look at each piece of the system and see how well the puzzle fits together in detail.

Our portable device driver is sandwiched between the user application and the hardware interface layer of the operating system. Since we defined the objective, now let's outline the functions our driver is responsible for:

- Providing uniform function calls to the embedded system from UNIX, Linux, and Windows

- Formatting outgoing data into device protocol format before sending

- Formatting incoming data into device protocol format before passing it to the user application

- Verifying data buffers have been sent properly

- Acknowledging data has been received properly

- Formatting data to be sent and received by the proper hardware interface while maintaining transparency and platform independence to the user application

- Porting the protocol handler to Windows, UNIX, and Linux for use

While this is a short list of requirements, it will take some effort both in the design and implementation stages to meet the goal of portability. Figure 3-8 illustrates the requirements of the portable device layer in more detail.

Now that we can visually see what tasks need to be implemented by our driver layer and we have a short list of requirements, the next step is to define each of the required tasks in detail to be certain we haven't left out any features that are needed. We will do this starting with the task closest to the hardware transport and then moving up to the user application interface.

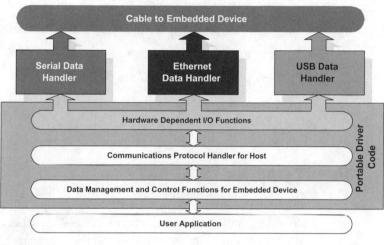

Figure 3-8

Hardware Function Calls

This is the software that communicates directly with the hardware. There are two categories of functions: generic and device specific. Generic functions are those that are required no matter which hardware interface is used. Device specific are those required only for a specific type of hardware.

Generic Device Functions

Let's begin by examining the generic function list. These are functions that will be used across all hardware interfaces. The first of this group would be to open and close the device for transmitting and receiving data. We will name these functions g_device_open and g_device_close. Next we need to send and receive data from all devices so we will define g_device_write and g_device_read. Finally, we need to be able to get and set the status for all the devices so we will define the g_device_get_ status and g_device_set_status functions. This gives us a list of the following six functions:

- g_device_open — Opens a device for reading and writing
- g_device_close — Closes a device that is currently open
- g_device_read — Reads data from an open device
- g_device_write — Writes data to an open device
- g_device_get_status — Gets current device status
- g_device_set_status — Sets device status

Device-Specific Functions

Device-specific functions are a little more complicated since we have to be familiar with the features of RS-232, Ethernet, and USB. This feature list is dependent on the hardware interface and parameters that each device can accept. Let's examine each hardware interface and build our function list for each.

RS-232-Specific Functions

The RS-232 interface is managed by the system in Windows, UNIX, and Linux environments. The interface has both software and hardware controls associated with it that control baud rate, data flow, and physical port number. Since we aren't sending large amounts of data we will use a simple handshake that controls the hardware handshake CTS and RTS signals. To handle the RS-232-specific functionality we will add the following function calls:

- serial_set_baud — Sets baud rate on current port
- serial_get_baud — Gets baud rate on current port
- serial_flow_off — Toggles hardware control line to stop sender
- serial_flow_on — Toggles hardware control line to start sender
- serial_set_port — Sets port number

- serial_get_port — Gets current port number
- serial_write_data — Sends data buffer
- serial_read_data — Processes incoming data buffer
- serial_port_open — Opens port for use
- serial_port_close — Closes serial port

Ethernet-Specific Functions

Since Ethernet can be addressed in several different ways we want to keep our dependent functions generic enough to accommodate the needs specific to our application. With this in mind we will first outline the functions common to all access methods. All Ethernet transmissions require a source and destination IP address. If we use TCP/IP, the network interface will send and receive data via Sockets or WinSock. If we don't use TCP/IP, then we will send and receive raw data directly to the network card. Since we have defined the communications protocol to the device separately, we can use either Sockets or Direct Access. Figure 3-9 shows how the Ethernet software layer handles these two different types of communications.

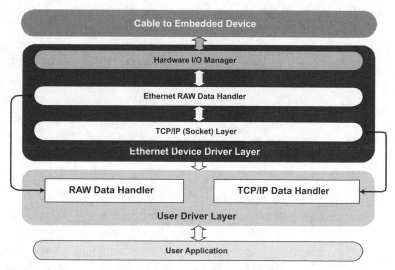

Figure 3-9

While it appears we could use both methods simultaneously, only one layer can be open at a time. This prevents two applications from writing at once and turning the data into garbage. To keep application access simple we will define which method to use when the device is opened. This will be a parameter passed with the open command that is a value of RAW or TCP. Now we have a manageable set of Ethernet-specific related methods. They are:

- ethernet_open — Opens the device for communications
- ethernet_close — Closes an existing Ethernet session
- ethernet_set_src_ip — Sets source IP address
- ethernet_set_dest_ip — Sets destination IP address
- ethernet_write_data — Writes data to output buffer
- ethernet_read_data — Moves received data to buffer for processing

To complete the open process at least one parameter will need to be passed to tell which method of communications will be used. Since we have documented the parameter we will leave final definitions until the implementation phase.

USB-Specific Functions

As discussed earlier, USB differs from any other communications method in several ways. Since USB allows devices to be added and removed while the system is running, a unique scenario is created. In simple terms, USB allows devices to be booted and shut down anytime while the host system remains running. To handle this situation, Windows, UNIX, and Linux have a USB core driver that detects the addition and removal of USB devices. When a device is connected, it forces the USB core driver to run through an enumeration process for the newly attached device. This process will eventually determine the USB device class and the vendor, product, and optional revision codes contained in the device. The class type determines which part of the USB core driver will handle the device I/O. This information is then used to load device-specific drivers that handle the device, vendor, and version-specific data.

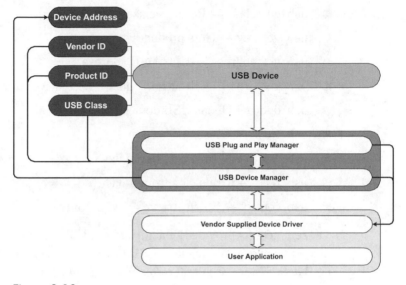

Figure 3 10

When a new device is attached, it starts as device 0. Device 0 is reserved for newly attached devices. The host interrogates the device to get the vendor ID, product ID, USB class ID, and optional product revision ID. This information is used to find the best match of a vendor-supplied device driver. Some types of USB classes are supported by the operating system if a vendor driver is not available. Keyboards and mice are two examples of devices that have internal support for certain USB classes. Keyboards and mice are known as human interface devices (HID) and can have built-in support at the system level if no device-specific driver can be found. Until the device is identified, the USB initialization driver (device ID 0) is used to communicate with the USB device. When a USB device is removed, the event triggers a query of connected devices. A comparison is done against the current device list and the device not responding to the inquiry is removed. Given all this information we can determine that the following functions are needed:

- usb_get_vendor — Returns vendor ID
- usb_get_product — Returns product ID
- usb_get_class — Returns class ID
- usb_get_rev — Gets product revision info
- usb_get_address — Gets USB address
- usb_get_driver — Returns vendor device driver info
- usb_open — Opens USB device
- usb_close — Closes USB device
- usb_write — Writes data to device
- usb_read — Reads data from device
- usb_control — Sets/retrieves device control

These functions provide the ability to get USB device information; open, close, and manage USB devices; and send/receive USB data. Even if we don't implement all the code for each function, the function stubs will remain available for future releases as needed.

Note:

USB has many other parameters that can be accessed from the host system. These parameters will be covered in detail in Part II, the implementation section. The information provided here is to facilitate the high-level design.

Putting It All Together

Since we have covered all three methods of communications between the host and the embedded system, let's examine our specific functions to see how everything fits together. Figure 3-11 shows how our generic function calls have been translated to device-specific calls.

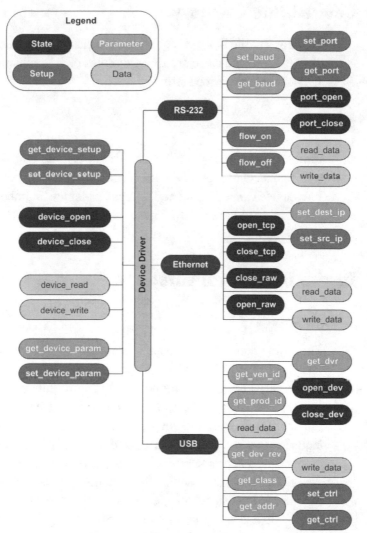

Figure 3-11

Now that we have all the functions defined for our design, we can break them down into four categories. They are:

- State — On, off, open, close
- Setup — Port number, source IP address, driver control
- Data — Read data, write data
- Parameter — Flow control, data bits, baud rate

Device State Category

Functions in the State category make a change in the state of the device. Open and close are two examples of functions that cause a change in the device state.

Device Setup Category

These functions or parameters are required before device state can change. One example of this type is the RS-232 port number. The device cannot be opened unless a valid port number is defined first, whereas flow control can be changed without affecting the current device state of opened or closed.

Device I/O Control Category

Data Category

These functions control features associated with sending and receiving data to the device. Baud rate, flow, control, and IP address are just some examples of I/O control functions. These parameters differ from setup parameters because they aren't required for opening the device or in some cases are simple inquiries to get information from the device such as vendor ID, product ID, and product revision. In some cases, these settings are required for setup while changing their values would be considered I/O control. One example of this scenario is set_src_ip and set_dest_ip. In Figure 3-11 set_src_ip is a setup function and set_dest_ip is considered I/O control. Setting the source IP address is required before a valid socket can be opened. Under certain conditions, however, a socket may have multiple sessions going at the same time. The IP address of the destination may not always be required to open a socket but is always required before sending data. These functions manage sending and receiving data to and from the device. Sending data requires having the device open to send/receive data and having a data buffer available to pass data to and receive data from the device.

Function Parameters

Any experienced software or hardware engineer is likely asking why we haven't filled in the function parameters and return parameters list. The reason is because we are defining what type of control and data functions are required. While we could define the parameter lists and return parameters, they would more than likely change if an experienced engineer were to develop the project. If the engineer working on this project is inexperienced, he or she may not realize the written definitions are simply suggestions or to be used as a starting point. By providing the high-level design and omitting the details, we are merely setting boundaries or guidelines for the implementation engineers to use. During the implementation phase these values will be provided as implementation and testing progress.

This philosophy differs from traditional software design methods. There are a couple of reasons for this difference. First, the system we are implementing is not just an IT system. IT consists of both hardware and software. Setting too many rules before the prototype has been built can lead to infinite hardware and software changes. The electronics need to be well defined before any software is written. But the firmware that brings the electronics to life will actually be subject to changes as the software for the host systems is developed. This is unique to the hardware/software design process, as traditional engineering disciplines allow for mechanical and electrical definitions to all be set before the prototype is built. Blueprint changes are generally made during the prototype phase. Hardware/software systems are more fluid during the prototype stage, unlike their mechanical counterparts. For this reason we need to leave a little more flexibility in how the hardware/software systems integrate than we would with mechanical systems.

Designing for True Portability

True portability between all systems exists only in an ideal world. In our case achieving this is accomplished by designing portable functions during the high-level design. During implementation the developer will make several decisions that will affect how much and how easily portability will be achieved. From the designer's perspective, using devices that have some built-in support in all the systems that are targets will be a good start to true portability. The more built-in support that exists at the OS level, the less work the developers will have and the higher the degree of true portability. In our design RS-232 and Ethernet are portable across all the platforms we are targeting. USB is supported but there will be some code required that is specific to our product(s).

Because of this we most likely have two separate pieces to our driver layer. The first piece will take our generic function calls and wrap them into system-level calls for RS-232 and Ethernet. We will provide wrappers for USB calls as well, but we need to develop the data handler for our USB device and use it to handle the actual device I/O. At this stage of the design process we've defined the functional interface to the device.

The wrapper layer will be portable across all platforms and any platform-specific code that handles device I/O will reside at the driver layer. We are dealing with USB, so even though some code will be needed at the driver level it will be minimal on all the supported platforms. Windows calls this a mini-driver and it has several uses, such as for USB and developing printer drivers.

Similar to USB, the printer port has generic functions that handle data. Formatting commands for positioning characters, changing fonts, and other data that is printer specific is handled by developing a mini-driver.

Chapter Summary

While developing 100 percent portable device drivers isn't possible, a large degree of portability can be attained. Careful planning and design, and using devices that have some degree of built-in operating system support can go a long way toward creating portable device drivers. When developing software that will control external hardware devices, there are always control, state, and data management categories. Device parameters may fall into any or all of the mentioned categories. Keep design simple. By focusing on the requirements and leaving development issues to the developers, a solid design compiled with a maximum driver life cycle will be the benefit. A complete review of our design will be given at the end of Part I. In the next chapter we examine the issues that need to be considered when developing cross-platform user applications.

Chapter 3

Chapter 4

Designing Cross-Platform User Applications

Overview

Designing user applications that run on multiple platforms can be both rewarding and challenging. Each operating system has its own set of rules for application development, hardware interfacing, and task scheduling. There are an abundance of program editors, programming languages, third-party developer libraries, and desktop managers (GUIs) that all play key roles in the design and implementation process. There are no national or international standards defining how user interfaces are built or components work, so finding the best method of cross-platform development takes research. Nonetheless, once these challenges have been overcome, developing single-source user applications can become a fun and rewarding experience and can be done with a minimum of additional time. In this chapter we explore the options available to the developer and the impact on development time and project cost.

The Windows Application Programming Interface (API)

We covered the architectural differences between Microsoft Windows and UNIX in the previous chapter. Windows is difficult for developers coming from other environments to understand. The reason for this long learning curve is due to the fact that a Windows application can have many windows within it and each window is an independent object that processes messages, events, and data.

Traditionally, programs were written with a main loop that handled data, messages, and events, so becoming accustomed to this fundamental difference takes time. To implement this object-oriented approach, Microsoft makes use of callback routines. Callback routines are functions that reside within the application that are called from outside the application by the OS or another program. This feature makes a Windows application completely event driven. This in and of itself is not a difficult concept to understand, but when you have several windows in an application the method of gluing each of these objects together is not terribly obvious or intuitive.

There are many tools on the market to assist in developing Windows applications. You can write all of your code the old-fashioned way with any text editor, or you can use a visual development product like Visual Studio, Delphi, or C++Builder. Manually writing Windows API code is not on my top ten list of things I want to do. It can take hundreds or even thousands of lines of code to accomplish even simple tasks in Windows. With that in mind let's look at how Windows, UNIX, and Linux user applications compare functionally, and then explore cross-platform development options to make the most of time and tools.

Windows Application Programming Layers

The Dynamic-Link Library (DLL)

Microsoft has taken a unique approach to distributed computing. First, they introduced the dynamic-link library (DLL). This is a shared code library that allows a single instance of code to support many applications at the same time. This conserves the use of memory in exchange for the overheard of switching between different application stacks that may be using the library simultaneously. In short, you save memory at the expense of speed. Since time-critical portions of code normally run at the driver or OS level, this usually has little effect on overall program performance. A counter keeps track of how many applications are using the library, and when the count reaches 0 the library is closed and eventually released from memory.

The Visual Basic Control (VBX)

Because of the amount of labor it took to build good Windows code, Microsoft responded with the VBX control architecture. This allowed developers to write controls that could be used in any language that supported the VBX package architecture. While it didn't reduce the amount of labor it took to build program components, it did allow the components to be included in other programs while not permitting the original code to be tampered with. The architecture was slow to be accepted by the development community due to its complexity.

The ActiveX Controls

VBX was eventually repackaged and expanded to support 32-bit Windows platforms and to be more easily imported into other programming languages and environments through the use of a visual interface.

The Component Object Model (COM)

Next, Microsoft added interprocess communications through the use of remote procedure calls (RPCs). This allowed a nonvisual means of communicating with a control or other component such as a function or method. It also provided a means to use or control a component, function, method, or complete application. Since RPC is a network protocol, it became the foundation for allowing network users access to COM objects.

Network COM (COM+)

The COM (or COM+) mode added the ability to control and access objects across a network or the Internet. A separate technology known as Microsoft Message Queuing (MSMQ) was integrated into the COM+ layer, allowing remote transaction handling to be queued or managed even in an offline situation.

The .NET Specification

In 2001 Microsoft introduced the .NET (pronounced "dot-net") specification. The .NET framework was the result of that specification and the first step in accomplishing several goals. First, it introduced developers to the "managed code" architecture. Managed code allows the operating system to chaperone the execution of programs and shared libraries by managing the memory space they reside in. This eliminates the need for a programmer to manually allocate and free memory, thus eliminating memory management problems that have plagued Windows development over the years. .NET compiles code at run time rather than at compile time. Until .NET, most development languages for Windows generated machine-executable code. With .NET, however, an intermediate file is generated. This intermediate file is then translated into machine-executable code when the program is executed. One obvious advantage of this is the ability to create a single intermediate program file that can be run on any system with a .NET framework installed. This means that you can distribute your program to any system that supports .NET and it will run. Linux, Solaris, UNIX, and even mainframe systems will eventually support the .NET framework. While this is an advantage, there are also a couple of disadvantages. First, the intermediate code can be easily reverse-engineered so anyone can see your program and intellectual property. There are, however, tools available to encrypt the intermediate file so the code cannot be seen. It also takes longer to load the program since it has to be compiled at run time. Not all systems have .NET integrated yet, so your program may also run slower after it has been compiled to machine language.

Using .NET means the compiler vendor will parse their language file and send the resulting code to the Microsoft intermediate compiler. This will all but eliminate some of the advantages that other compiler vendors have gained over the years in speed and performance. When an update is made to the current .NET framework, programs will be able to take advantage of the features immediately and without a new distribution of the program from the vendor. All in all, the .NET strategy does make sense if implemented properly. There are two development projects currently going on to implement .NET on UNIX and Linux. When completed, you should be able to take your Windows program and execute it on UNIX and Windows (if all works as expected). Currently the .NET framework is available for Windows 98, ME, NT, 2000, and XP as a download. Windows Server 2003 and later operating system releases will have .NET integrated into the core OS. The following diagram illustrates how .NET integrates into existing systems.

Chapter 4

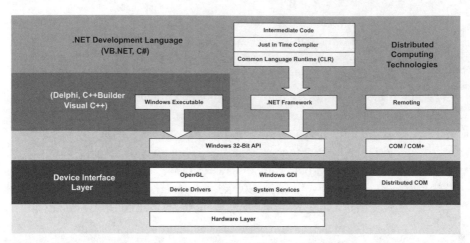

Figure 4-1

As you can see, Windows has several layers associated with user application development, depending on the development language or platform (native language vs. .NET), and whether local or distributed computing is being used.

The UNIX Application Programming Model

The UNIX application model is somewhat different from Windows. UNIX was written years before color monitors were available, and graphical user interfaces have only been widely used for the last 15 or so years. Prior to that, suitable hardware was either not available or was simply too expensive for the mass market. This made providing backward compatibility while supporting current input and display technology a unique challenge. How users interacted with the computer was changing. Research at the Xerox Palo Alto labs had introduced a pointing device (mouse), and display technology was becoming both cheaper and more functional in high-resolution color displays.

In the early 1980s, MIT introduced the UNIX world to X Windows. Since UNIX was not originally designed as a graphics-based system, its graphic desktop implemention was developed in layers. The lowest level layer was the display manager or server. The display manager was combined with a graphic server with the task of collecting input from users (keystrokes and mouse data) and responding with the data for those requests. To display the data in a display-independent graphic format, the client was written as a separate program that could be run either on the local machine or on a remote desktop. Separating the display manager and display client allowed a single display manager the ability to handle multiple displays of different height, width, and color depth. The client in this case was responsible for the display parameters and the server was responsible for seeing that input and output requests were handled in an orderly fashion.

A layered approach also provides more of a building block type approach to user application development. Each layer can build upon the previous layers, which allow high-level user interfaces and developer libraries to be implemented. This architecture also allows cross-platform tools and libraries to be more easily developed as shown in Figure 4-2.

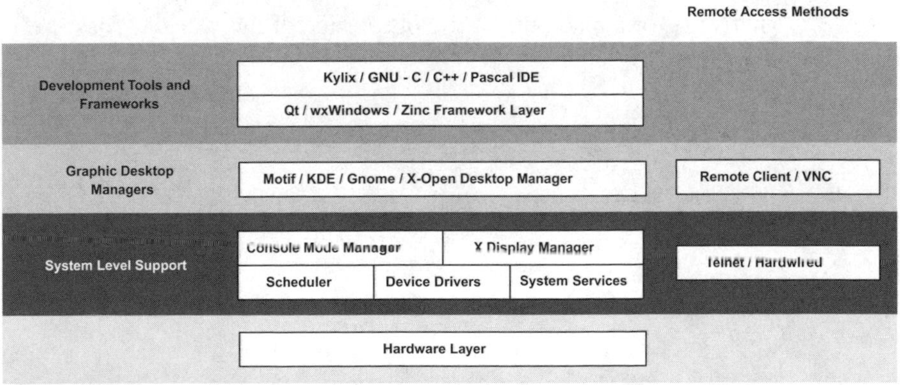

Remote Access Methods

Development Tools and Frameworks	Kylix / GNU - C / C++ / Pascal IDE	
	Qt / wxWindows / Zinc Framework Layer	
Graphic Desktop Managers	Motif / KDE / Gnome / X-Open Desktop Manager	Remote Client / VNC
System Level Support	Console Mode Manager	X Display Manager	Telnet / Hardwired
	Scheduler	Device Drivers	System Services	
	Hardware Layer	

Figure 4-2

This figure breaks down the different layers of the UNIX display management system. There are many desktop managers available to the UNIX and Linux user including X Windows, Motif, KDE, and GNOME, to name a few. These desktop managers combined with either a framework or X Windows are the equivalent of the Windows API layer. Qt, wxWindows, and Zinc are just a few examples of portable application frameworks. These frameworks are also available on the Windows platforms, and toolkits are available for Windows developers.

X Windows in Depth — A True Client/Server GUI

The X Windows server is also known as the X Display Manager (XDM for short) and is used as a functional model for other popular desktop managers like KDE (KDM) and GNOME (GDM). XDM routes graphic I/O to and from the client desktop. A single display manager handles all graphic desktop sessions on that or any remote machine attached to XDM. The client program manages the graphic desktop, mouse, and keyboard input from the user. The client may be run on the local machine, a network machine, or a machine on the other side of the world across the Internet.

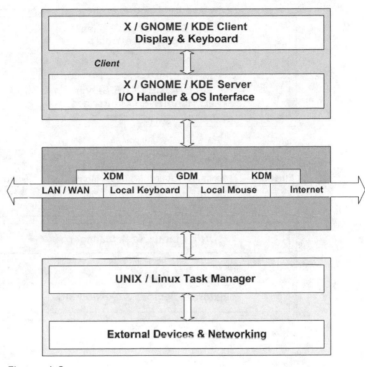

Figure 4-3

As you can see, a display manager can serve clients on remote machines as easily as it can on the server machine. The UNIX or Linux server task manager communicates with the X Server layer, which is located in the same layer as the physical transport layer. The physical transport layer handles both local and remote clients in addition to keyboard, mouse, and network communications.

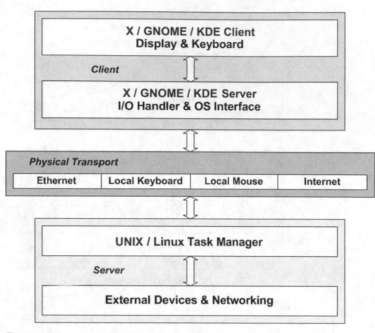

Figure 4-4

A remote X Client application appears as just another application when it is running. The only indication the application is actually hosted on a remote machine appears in the upper-left corner of the main application window. The host machine name and display number indicate the application is running remotely. This means that while it appears you have several programs running on your computer, programs connected to remote X Servers are simply using your system for user input and display output. The actual programs are running on the machine in which the X Server is running. It is possible to run as many remote sessions or programs as desired using this method. Display output is configured to the display parameters on the client machine (where the output is displayed). It is also possible to run a client on Windows machines using any X Client/Server designed for Windows. Red Hat's Cygwin has a free XFree86-based server that I use on Windows 2000 and XP, which works very well. Products that allow an X Windows client on Windows may have the X Server built into the same application as the client. The available X Window client/server products have a wide variety of price ranges and features.

Alternatives to the X Windows Approach

There are alternatives to using the X Client/Server approach. Now you may be asking why a developer would want to use an alternative if this approach is truly efficient on resource usage. The answer lies in how much time you can afford to spend setting up the X environment for remote access and how familiar you are with X Windows setup and administration.

Setting up a suitable X Windows client/server environment can be a very time-consuming task. It requires the altering of setup files on the client and server machines and additional network setup as well. If you are going to use this feature across the Internet, a secure socket layer is strongly recommended, which adds even more complexity to the setup process.

One alternative to X Windows is the Virtual Network Computing product (VNC). VNC was originally developed by Bell Labs of the UK (the former Olivetti development center). VNC also requires some setup on the client and server but is easier to learn and does not require an understanding of how X Windows works. VNC displays an entire desktop rather than a single application window. If you use Secure Sockets, the difference is running a single application versus displaying and accessing an entire desktop session as a client. If user security is an important issue, providing access on an application basis is worth the additional effort and learning curve of X Windows.

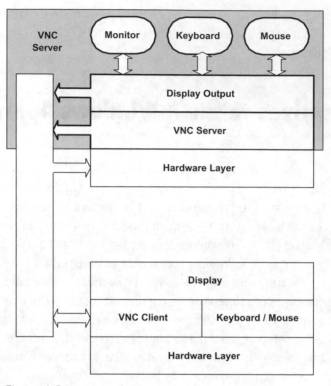

Figure 4-5

VNC intercepts display and keyboard data and echoes the complete display to the client machine. All applications running on the desktop are available to the client in a view-only or full-access mode. X Windows provides more security since only the application running remotely is displayed, not the complete desktop.

Alternatives to Cross-Platform Development

Before leaving this topic we need to explore other alternatives to developing cross-platform applications. We've explored the native graphic interfaces for both Windows and UNIX, but there is one more approach yet to be mentioned. Several years ago Red Hat developed an interface layer for Windows that allowed many of the native UNIX desktops to run on Windows. This was accomplished by building a UNIX interface layer as illustrated in the following figure.

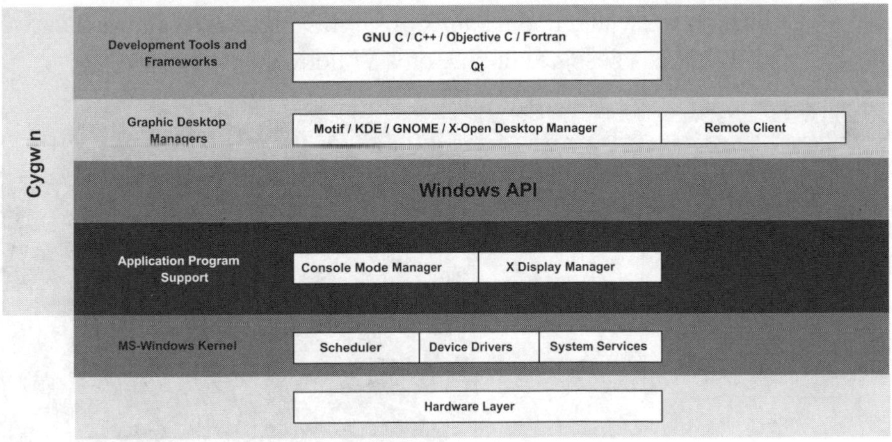

Development Tools and Frameworks	GNU C / C++ / Objective C / Fortran		
	Qt		
Graphic Desktop Managers	Motif / KDE / GNOME / X-Open Desktop Manager		Remote Client
Windows API			
Application Program Support	Console Mode Manager	X Display Manager	
MS-Windows Kernel	Scheduler	Device Drivers	System Services
	Hardware Layer		

Cygwin

Figure 4-6

Named Cygwin, this product is designed to provide UNIX shell emulation on Windows. A custom version of the GNU compiler collection was developed to support the Cygwin architecture. When invoked under Windows, the Cygwin product opens a Windows console window that provides a UNIX shell as shown in Figure 4-7.

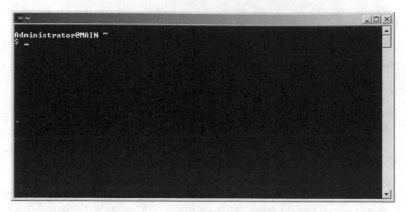

Figure 4-7

Once this shell is running we can start an X Windows session just as we would under Linux or UNIX. Figure 4-8 shows a native X Windows session running on a Windows XP machine.

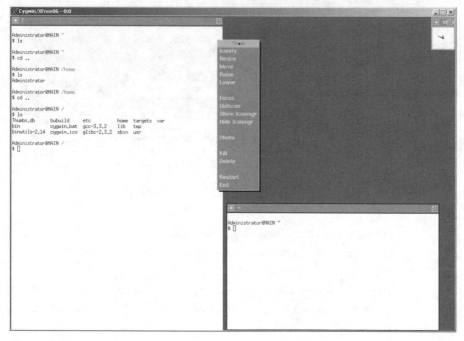

Figure 4-8

The familiar Windows title bar at the top is the only indicator that X Windows is running on a Windows XP machine. Now this in and of itself isn't anything other than a couple of applications running on Windows XP and emulating a UNIX command shell and X Windows server and client. However, as shown in Figure 4-6, desktop managers also run in this environment. KDE, GNOME, and several other desktop managers work well within this context.

Emulation vs. Native Execution

What makes this a unique approach is where the emulation is handled. The Cygwin emulator sits between the application layer and the Windows API. It translates Windows API calls to native calls for the chosen desktop manager. This allows developers to compile their existing UNIX/Linux applications by using the Cygwin libraries to generate a cross-platform target. In short, only two rules apply. First, a desktop manager must be chosen that is supported under Cygwin. Second, the platform in which the application is compiled must support the Cygwin target. Both of these subjects will be covered in detail in Part II.

Programming Languages

Next in our list of cross-platform considerations is the choice of programming languages. A suitable programming language can have a dramatic effect on project length and required resources. There are many factors to consider when choosing a programming language for multiplatform development. Not all languages and compilers are available on multiple platforms, which makes choosing a language and compiler less daunting, but the choice is very important nonetheless.

Employee Skill Sets

Above all else, employee or contractor skill sets must play a role in choosing the right languages. If you select a language without considering the skills of the developers, you may lose much more than you gain. Choose a programming language level that matches the skill level of the team. Before we delve into the specifics of programming language selection, consider the following factors before making a final decision.

- Are my developers experienced in the languages being considered?

- If they are not, have they had experience with a similar type of language?

- Are there languages available that the developers have experience in and that are available on all required platforms?

- If not, can the developers become fluent in using the selected languages quickly and still bring the project in on time?

Taking these factors into account early in the language selection process can save not only time but frustration as well. If necessary, ask the developers for their input and encourage them to be honest. There is nothing wrong if an individual is uncomfortable with or inexperienced in a given language or programming discipline.

Visual Application Development or Hand Coding

It wasn't so long ago that we hand-coded everything. Reusable code was defined as collections of functions that were added to libraries and the libraries were distributed with the products. Designing a graphical user interface in the old days meant adding color to the text and using crude ASCII characters that gave us block text graphics. Today it's an entirely different world. Almost all new user applications are graphic based. Today, input is managed by events instead of a program loop. This gives much better control over program flow, and the graphical user interfaces provide bells and whistles never even thought of 10 years ago. Event-driven software is designed much differently than the old DOS or text mode programs.

Hand coding event-driven software is a tedious and time-consuming job. It can easily be necessary to define thousands of variables that manage the user interface or capture mouse events. To streamline this process (and spend less than a lifetime writing a single application), we have visual designers and visual development systems that allow the developer to focus on the application rather than the mechanics. Visual development tools come in many forms and price ranges. There are complete development systems that include language compiler, visual controls, linkers, and even program installers. These products range from free to several thousand dollars depending on features, number of supported platforms, and other factors. Borland, Microsoft, and Metrowerks are just a few of the companies that offer these programming tools.

Visual Development vs. Development Framework

Development frameworks, mentioned earlier, provide a visual designer and libraries that work with several languages and/or platforms rather than a complete development platform. Instead of providing a complete development environment, a visual designer and libraries are provided that work with several languages and/or platforms. Again, these tools vary widely in price and features. In the UNIX/Linux environment many of these tools are open source, which means you can get the source code in addition to the object code. Many products may be available that perform a certain task. One example of this is visual designers. There are a wide variety of vendors that provide visual designers for these application frameworks. In some cases purchasing the add-on components to make the framework useful can be very expensive. You may also be dealing with many vendors instead of just one. In short, you need to examine these tools to see if they really provide a cost advantage or are more trouble than they are worth. Qt, GTK+, wxWindows, and the Zinc interface library are some examples of application frameworks.

Free vs. Commercial Products

Some of these tools and compilers have both free and commercially sold versions. This can be confusing! When can I use a free version and when do I have to purchase a commercial version? In most cases, if you are developing an open-source product that will be given away, then you qualify to use the free version and you can also distribute any required libraries for free. If, however, you are developing products for sale or you do not want to give away the source code, then you may be required to purchase a commercial license. If you develop an open-source product and later decide to sell it or no longer distribute the source code, you may need to purchase a commercial license at that time. You need to check each product you intend to use to see what the license states. Some products are bundled with commercial products and are freely redistributable only when using the compiler or language it was originally included with, so again check the license to see what your rights are.

GNU vs. GPL Licensing

There are also several types of open-source licensing. The two most common are GPL and GNU licensing. One license encourages free distribution of products both open source and commercially, while the other is much more restrictive when it comes to commercial distribution. Again, check the license and ask the advice of a lawyer. A few dollars spent on legal fees now may help you avoid buying your lawyer a nice house in the future.

Programming Language Selection

The most popular language used in the Microsoft Windows environment is Visual Basic. Visual Basic has English-like syntax and a coding style that most people find easy to learn and use, and are comfortable with. Visual Basic is very popular among people who are not professional programmers but have a need to write an application. For developers who like Visual Basic-like syntax but need more access to the operating system, there is Delphi. Delphi provides a visual environment much like Visual Basic, but is more object oriented and is based on the Pascal language, which has more robust type-checking and very strict programming rules.

More experienced developers who need more control over a device or the operating system and are less concerned with syntax and more concerned with language features may also choose C or C++. The C language has been around longer than Pascal and some programmers prefer it or are simply more comfortable with the language.

For those who want the ultimate in portability at the application level, don't need to interface with device drivers or operating system services, and are not concerned about execution speed, Java is an option. Java is object oriented, similar in syntax to C++, and is compiled to machine code at run time, much like the .NET programs. Java has been around longer than .NET and is written and supported by Sun Microsystems. Java is free to use and distribute and can be run on almost any computer from embedded systems to mainframes.

It's important to note that not all languages are cross-platform compatible. As with libraries, prices range from free to thousands of dollars depending on many factors. The following table lists by platform which languages are supported.

Table 4-1: Platform language support

Vendor/Compiler	Windows Support	UNIX/Linux Support
Microsoft C++	Yes	No
Borland C++	Yes*	Yes*
Borland Delphi	Yes*	Yes*
Borland Kylix	No	Yes
CodeWarrior C/C++	Yes	No
Intel C++ Suite	Yes	Yes**
GNU C/C++	Yes	Yes

*Cross-platform support uses CLX library.   ** Intel architecture only

As you can see, Microsoft compilers only support Windows platforms in native code form. Borland provides several suites of
tools that offer two different mechanisms of cross-platform development. With the exception of Visual Studio .NET, Microsoft
compilers only support Windows executables and native Windows API and generate machine code. They support
cross-platform development for Windows and Linux using their
CLX visual controls (CLX is based on the Qt graphic library).
When you purchase a Windows version of Borland C++Builder
or Delphi (Pascal) you also receive the Linux version of that language. Borland compilers that run on Linux are named Kylix
(although they are the Linux version of Delphi). If you purchase
Kylix as a separate product, you receive both the C++ and
Delphi versions of the compilers. Borland has begun shipping
Delphi 2005, which is Delphi for .NET and C#Builder for .NET.
Using Delphi you can write a cross-platform program using CLX,
which will generate a native executable for each platform or a
.NET program that can be run using the .NET framework.
Borland also supports cross-platform development for the C#
language, which is exclusive to .NET. The Borland product is
C#Builder and is a visual development environment for develop-
ers who are familiar with Delphi or C++Builder development
environments and the C# language.

CodeWarrior from Metrowerks supports Windows and Macintosh native compilers. Intel provides C, C++, and Fortran compilers for the Windows and Linux platforms, although I have not used them.

And now we have reached the GNU compiler suite. GNU compilers have been around for many years and support more platforms and processors than the other compilers mentioned here combined. The GNU compilers support all Windows/UNIX/Linux platforms on all supported processors for these operating systems, and are mature and full featured. Now the bad news: The compilers do not come with a standard IDE like the other products do. This means that no visual development environment exists that allows a user application interface to be visually created and integrated into the finished program, which means you may need to use several tools or even construct the user interface by hand. Using a trial-and-error method can take many hours to construct even the most simple user interface.

Programmer Editors

This is a final category of cross-platform tools. Again, there are products that range from free to several thousand dollars. Emacs is a free product developed originally for the UNIX and Linux environments. There are versions for UNIX, Linux, Windows, and several other systems as well.

Borland has introduced C++BuilderX, which is a development environment that supports multiple platforms and compilers. It includes Borland's own compiler in the Windows version and also supports Visual C++ 6 and GNU for Windows. The product is also available for Linux and Solaris. While I have not worked with C++BuilderX very much, it provides UML diagramming in the commercial versions and allows multiple targets to be generated with the GNU compiler suite. The product does not offer a visual GUI designer so other products would need to be acquired for the interface development. Metrowerks also offers a Linux editor for developing programs with the GNU compilers. I have not worked with the product so I cannot compare it to the Emacs and Borland products.

A Final Word about Free Software

During the course of writing this chapter I had some issues regarding cross-platform development using the GCC compiler suite. I wound up contacting the Free Software Foundation office because my emails were being bounced back undeliverable to the addresses on their web page. There was no acknowledgment of the problem, only a statement that the addresses should work. I was also informed that all of the developers donate their time and it is common for two to three weeks to elapse between a question being asked and a response being sent.

This is a very serious consideration when choosing a commercial product versus a free product. This caused me to go back a second time and take a closer look at the email address problems. When I took a closer look at some of the web pages, I noticed that some had not been updated in several years. I also noticed that some of the links from those pages were no longer active.

The Cost of Free

Taking the above experience into consideration, anyone using free software has to determine the real cost. While the software may be obtained free of charge, a three-week delay in a commercial project does not go without cost. Anytime a problem is encountered time is at stake. The time to research the problem has costs, the time to attempt a fix has costs, and even the time spent searching for the right person to contact has a cost. When you acquire a commercial product, the company that sells that product promises its support. While support may not be free, at least there is a single point of contact. It is very important to understand these hidden costs.

Shareware — The Middle Ground

While on the subject of commercial versus free software I want to mention the middle ground — shareware. With shareware you can acquire a free demo or trial product to use. If you like the product, you can purchase it; this also includes developer support. Over the last 10 or so years I have purchased several shareware developer tools (mostly libraries) for use in commercial products. I might add that the products I have purchased have come from all over the world including Russia and Japan.

My experiences have never been negative. I have found that support for these products rivals, and in many cases exceeds, the support of commercial software vendors. I would not hesitate to use or purchase a shareware product for commercial use.

Chapter Summary

In this chapter we have explored the options and concerns with developing cross-platform compatible applications. As we've seen, there are several approaches that can be taken for developing applications from a single-source code base that can run on Windows, UNIX, Linux, and other operating systems as well. In the end a developer will probably choose one of the following techniques:

- Cross-platform languages that support developing consistent user interfaces and code base for multiple platforms (Kylix/Delphi, Kylix/C++BuilderX, GNU tools, etc.)

- Developer libraries that provide consistent functions, methods, and user interface components on multiple platforms (Qt, wxWindows, etc.)

- A combination of developer libraries and visual designers (Zinc interface library)

There are options available even in cross-platform development compilers, tools, and libraries.

Chapter 5

Developing the Desktop User Application

Overview

In the previous chapter we explored the concerns and design considerations of designing cross-platform user applications. In this chapter, we will design the end user application. When we have completed this chapter, we will have a completed design specification. Remember that we are still in the design phase, so the implementation details have not yet been introduced.

Functional Requirements

Now that we've reached the traditional information technology layer, we need to stick to the rules of the road for a user application. That means we need to have functional requirements that are well documented. There are two reasons for this. First, there may be distributors who wish to either develop their own user applications or assist the end users in developing those applications. As a result, the documentation will serve not only for operating the system but also as a road map to developing a user application from scratch.

The function calls needed to communicate with, monitor, and control the thermostat are already defined, so our task now is to take that information and put it into a functional visual package that can be easily operated by the end user. We still have a few choices to make regarding the user interface.

Multi-Language Support

No, I don't mean C and C++. English, Spanish, and other languages are routinely used in software development these days. If the interface will be available only in English, the text for the user interface components can be hard-coded during the visual design phase. If other languages will be supported, then we need to use a separate file that can be easily translated.

Chinese, Japanese, and Korean Language Support

The Chinese, Japanese, and Korean languages differ from English in more than just phonetics and visual design. For instance, the Japanese language can have up to 13,000 different characters. There are several special considerations to support these various languages. First, the U.S. character set is relatively small when compared to the Far Eastern sets. To allow for the display of all foreign characters, a two-byte or Unicode character set is used. This allows up to 65,536 different text characters to be displayed, which is more than will be needed. To support the entry of these characters from an English-type keyboard, a software component known as an input method editor (or IME) is invoked. The function of the IME is to display character options and allow the user to select the proper character based on the context of the sentence.

Far Eastern languages require twice as much memory for storing messages that are displayed, and the screen metrics change because the number of characters in the message increase. To deal with this challenge, smaller characters should be used to display user messages. Help files also need to be translated, again keeping in mind the changes in message size and required storage.

Graphic or Text Mode Based Application

As we've already learned, all of the supported platforms provide both text- and graphical-based interfaces. Since that is the case, what are the deciding factors? Let's compare the text and graphical interfaces.

Text Mode Interfaces

It may appear that implementing a text mode interface is easier than using a graphic interface. After all, using block graphics has to be easier than graphic text fields, right? In the past that may have been true, but with today's high-resolution monitors and fast processors, implementing a graphic user interface is just as easy. Text mode displays were used for years because graphic displays were expensive and processor speeds were not able to handle the processing load. Text mode interfaces were also popular because they limited the amount of data needed to draw a screen of data on a remote terminal.

Several things have changed since those days. First, try to purchase a text mode (or monochrome) monitor for less than a color display. Today, even if you could find a green, amber, or white text mode monitor, they are considerably more expensive than high-resolution color. Second, compare the average speed of

Chapter 5

a computer today to one 10 years ago. 66 MHz Pentiums were common 10 years ago; today, 2+ GHz are standard. In short, today's computers are roughly 40 times faster than systems of just 10 years ago. Finally, operating systems today have the necessary developer tools that make writing graphic-based event-driven applications much easier. In fact, the developer tools available today in most cases have no text mode counterpart.

The Modern Graphic Desktop

Okay, so using a desktop manager or graphical user interface is the method of choice. What products are available to developers that support cross-platform development and work on multiple platforms?

There are many ways of developing graphic user applications on one or more platforms. In the previous chapter we examined cross-platform-specific options and considerations. The following sections look in detail at choices applicable to our specific project.

The Microsoft Windows Operating Systems

By limiting our development support to Windows NT kernel-based systems, we have the ability to retain a high degree of control over not only the application but the operating system as well. Windows NT, 2000, XP, and Server 2003 all allow the developer access to the pre-emptive task scheduler. This was not available in Windows 95, 98, and ME. Because of this, task scheduler applications are much less likely to crash the operating system should an error occur. Even if we use a desktop manager that is available on Windows- and UNIX-based systems, all API calls on Windows will eventually be processed by the Win32 API. With that in mind, the remaining considerations are the amount of memory consumed and how much processor overhead will be incurred.

Memory Usage

Microsoft Windows loves eating memory. If memory were junk food, Microsoft would win the award for the world's most obese operating system. It seems that every time I add another 512 MB of RAM, Windows consumes it on power-up, burps, and asks for another helping. The fact is pretty graphics come at a hefty cost in memory usage. With this in mind, let's compare the levels of application code using a graphic framework, a desktop manager, and native executable program.

Developer Libraries and Tools

As we've already learned, a graphic framework allows a developer to provide a consistent user interface on multiple platforms by translating native API calls into a uniform set of calls accessible on all supported platforms. Some of the more popular graphic frameworks available on Windows are the following:

- Qt library
- wxWindows library
- Zinc interface library
- GTK+

Qt Library

The Qt library from Trolltech has been around for several years. In fact, the Qt library is what provides the cross-platform visual components their foundation in Borland Delphi, C++, and Kylix products. The Qt libraries provide consistent interface components on Windows, UNIX, and Linux platforms, offering one solution to single-source cross-platform application development. The application is linked to these libraries statically when compiled. When the application is executed, the Qt library calls are translated into native calls for the operating system on which the application is being run. A separate binary image of the application and libraries is required for each platform the application is distributed on.

The following illustration shows how the Qt libraries fit into the memory management of Windows.

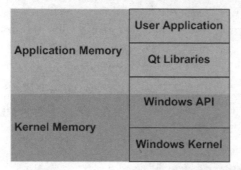

Application Memory	User Application
	Qt Libraries
Kernel Memory	Windows API
	Windows Kernel

Figure 5-1

By looking at how the Qt libraries use Windows memory, we can see they reside in user memory, which is shared with the application and interface directly to the Windows API. You will also notice that the Windows API resides partially in user memory and partially in kernel memory.

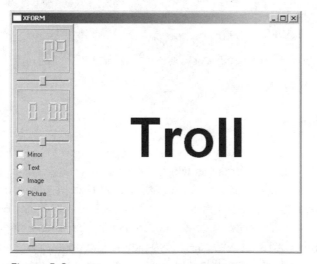

Figure 5-2

This image is a screen shot of a program developed using the Qt library that is running on Windows XP.

wxWindows

Like Qt, wxWindows is a library that provides a consistent "look and feel" wrapper for the end user and also provides a consistent API that translates native API calls for the developer.

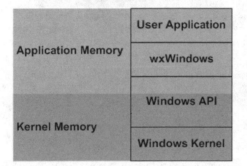

Figure 5-3

The memory model of wxWindows is identical to the Qt library. The main difference in these products is how they are licensed. The Qt libraries support both the GPL and commercial licensing schemes. This can be complicated for developers and can lead to a license violation by simply selling a single product. The Qt libraries also include a graphic designer, where wxWindows is supported by several third-party products, both commercial and free. wxWindows is a free product, so selling your first copy will not put you in license violation. There is also one more big difference: wxWindows supports the C++ language exclusively, while Qt can be used with a variety of languages including C, C++, and Pascal.

So how do applications developed using wxWindows look? Figures 5-4 and 5-5 are screen shots of Windows and UNIX versions of an application developed using wxWindows.

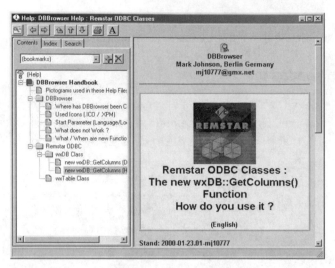

Figure 5-4: Windows version

The above application is a simple web page viewer and list display running on Windows. It looks like a standard Windows application. While it doesn't have a menu bar, it does have a standard Windows toolbar and tool buttons.

The following figure is the Linux version of this same program.

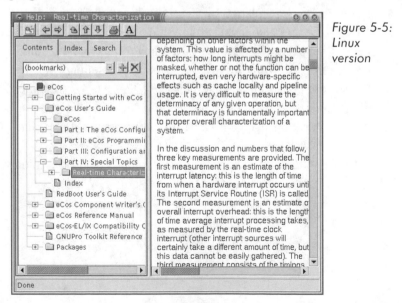

Figure 5-5: Linux version

Figure 5-5 shows a different web page being displayed than the one shown in Figure 5-4, but the same toolbar, tool buttons, list box, and page display are evident. The Linux display is running under the GNOME desktop manager.

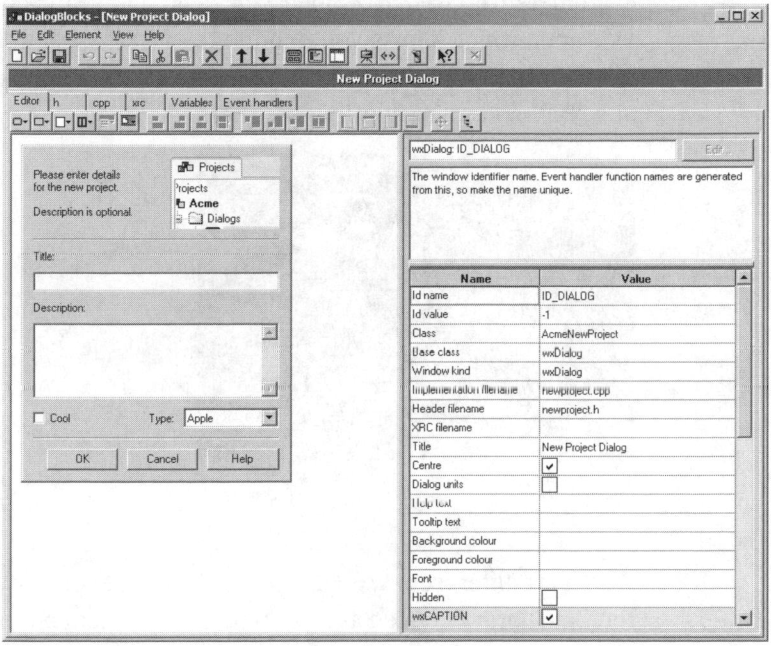

Figure 5-6

Figure 5-6 shows a screen shot of DialogBlocks, a design program for the wxWindows framework. It is very similar to other design tools, offering a visual designer and code access to include files, code files, variables, and event handlers for the current object being designed.

Zinc Interface Library

The Zinc library has been around for almost 15 years. Originally developed by Zinc Software, the product supports UNIX, DOS, and Windows. In the early days you could select a text or graphic mode DOS interface. Over the years Zinc has changed hands several times. Today the Zinc product is owned by Wind River and is available in an embedded version or the legacy Windows and UNIX versions. The UNIX and Windows versions are available under the GPL license scheme. Two versions are currently supported — version 5.3 and version 6. Version 6 is for Wind River customers who wish to embed Zinc. The library includes the Zinc Designer, which allows you to build the interface and then compile it for one or more targets. The Zinc interface toolkit, like Qt and wxWindows, resides in user memory.

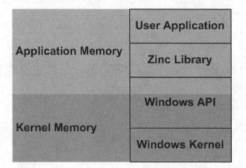

Application Memory	User Application
	Zinc Library
Kernel Memory	Windows API
	Windows Kernel

Figure 5-7

Zinc does differ from wxWindows and Qt in several ways. First, the Zinc library started as a commercial product and went through several generations before becoming open source. As a result, Zinc matured before being released to the open-source community and has thorough documentation. Next, Zinc has been ported to several embedded platforms and supports several embedded operating systems. Both Qt and wxWindows can be embedded, but Zinc has supported embedded systems longer. And last, Zinc is owned by Wind River, a company that specializes in embedded tools.

Following is a screen shot of the Zinc Designer running on Windows XP.

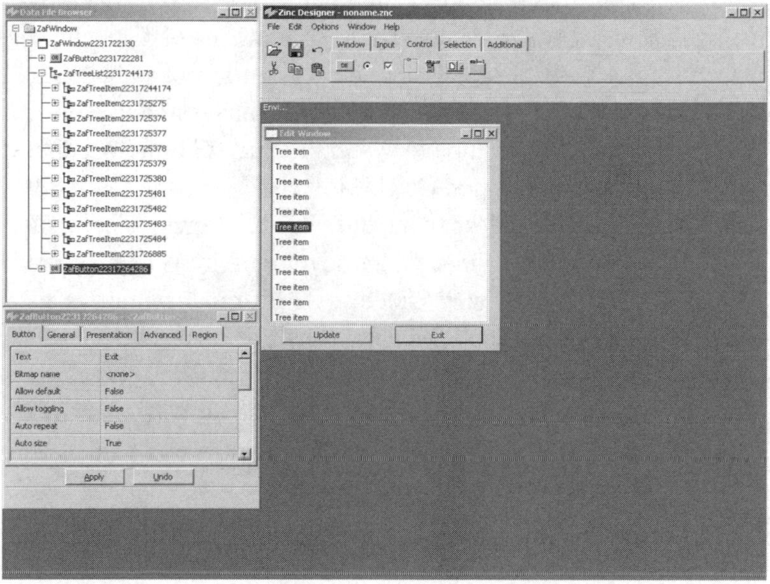

Figure 5-8

For those of you who may have used Delphi, Visual C++, or another visual development tool, the Zinc Designer will look somewhat familiar. The window in the center is what the end product will look like. The visual designer is the tabbed bar at the top right. The top window on the left is a list of components that have been inserted into the main window. The lower window on the left contains the properties of the currently highlighted object, which in this case is the Exit button.

GTK+

The GTK+ library is tightly coupled to the GNOME desktop manager. Originally started as a means of distributing networkable application objects on Linux and UNIX, GTK+ is the foundation of the graphics manager and user interface components. The complete system includes libraries, applications, and a visual designer. GNU C++ and Microsoft C++ are supported as the compilers to build the GTK+ environment, but many languages are supported for development. GTK+ is available for Linux, UNIX, and Windows 32-bit mode. There is also a Cygwin version available, which means there are two choices of implementation for the Windows platform. GTK+ is a part of the GNU software project, so it is free to use and distribute. GTK+ is a complete product, which is demonstrated by the following screen shot of AbiWord, a word processor written using GTK+.

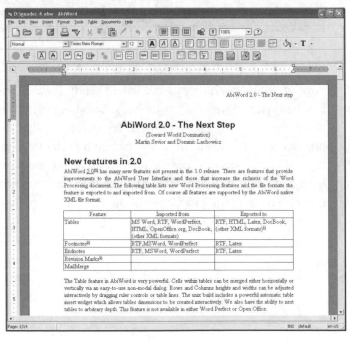

Figure 5-9

As you can see from the word processor application, GTK+ is a very complete toolkit. All of the standard edit controls are available to the developer including menus, toolbars, and document interfaces. The following screen shot shows the same program running on Linux.

Figure 5-10

Aside from the distinctive GNOME look, both applications look and function the same.

Comparing GTK+, Qt, wxWindows, and Zinc

On the surface, these four products seem to be almost identical. They all support the platforms required in our project. Each library either includes a visual designer or has third-party support that provides visual design tools, and all of these libraries have open-source versions. But if we look a little closer we find some important differences.

While it is true all of these libraries have open-source versions, three of these products have no commercial version available. wxWindows is a completely free product that is open source. The Zinc framework is also completely open source for version 5.3. Zinc does offer a commercial product for embedded developers. The Zinc framework includes everything necessary to install, compile, and visually design an application from start to finish on Windows and several UNIX and Linux platforms. The Zinc framework also includes PDF versions of the installation, quick start, and reference manuals. These are updated versions of manuals that shipped to customers who purchased this product. Zinc supports Linux, Windows, Sun Solaris, Hewlett Packard, SCO UNIX, and XENIX. GTK+ is also open source and has no commercial equivalent. Used as a core portion of the GNOME desktop and supported by the GNU Free Software Foundation, GTK+ is both widely used and well supported.

wxWindows is a very popular and refined product. Like the Zinc framework, wxWindows is covered by open-source licensing only, which means there are never any royalties for use. Unlike Zinc, however, wxWindows has no visual designer included. While that is technically true, the preferred designer shown in Figure 5-11 (DialogBlocks) was written by one of the committee members of the wxWindows team.

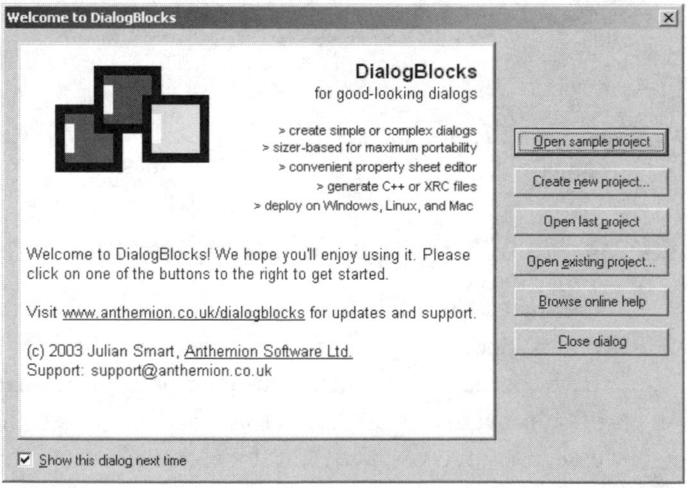

Figure 5-11

wxWindows is a mature product with plenty of support from third parties. The Borland C++BuilderX product provides a technology preview of a visual designer that uses the wxWindows framework. In addition, wxWindows is available on the Apple Macintosh. The Zinc interface library was never ported to the Mac, instead going in the direction of embedded systems. If Apple support is required, then you are faced with either wxWindows or the Qt library.

Now we come to Qt from Trolltech. Qt is unique in that a free noncommercial version is available for Linux but not for Windows. This means that Qt is only available as a cross-platform solution as a commercial product. The Qt library is not cheap — the Professional version starts at more than $1,500 per developer and the Enterprise version starts at over $2,500 per developer for a single platform. A multiplatform product is even more expensive. (Check with Trolltech for current pricing.) The reason for the Linux-only noncommercial version is due at least in part to the KDE desktop using Qt as its delivery framework. Qt is also included in Delphi 7, Kylix 1, 2, and 3, and C++Builder 6 and later as the foundation of the CLX visual component library provided by Borland.

Another concern with using Qt is the conditions under which you move from a noncommercial to commercial license arrangement. In short, once you begin selling your product you no longer qualify for a noncommercial license. If you sell your first program for $59, you could end up spending almost 50 times that amount immediately to legally use the Qt product. Finally, if you want support for Linux, Windows, and the Apple Macintosh, prepare for a big dent in your wallet. Pricing for multiplatform support starts at more than $3,000 per developer for the Professional version.

GTK+, Qt, wxWindows, and Zinc Interface Library Summary

The following table summarizes these products so we can determine how viable they are for our needs.

Table 5-1: Comparing libraries

Product	Windows	Linux/UNIX	Macintosh	License	Visual Designer	Source Code	Price
GTK+	X	X	1	GNU	Yes	Yes	$0
Qt	X	X	X	2	Yes; included	3	<$5 K[4]
wxWindows	X	X	X	GPL	Third parties	Yes; included	$0
Zinc	X	X	No	5	Yes; included	Yes; included	$0

Notes:

1. I have not found a Macintosh version of GTK+ but there may be support directly or through a version of GNOME for the Mac.
2. Noncommercial and commercial licensing
3. Noncommercial Linux only; commercial all
4. Price per developer
5. The license enclosed with Zinc is from the commercial product days. It is undetermined if Zinc follows GPL or GNU licensing. As of this writing, Zinc has not returned my inquiries to clarify this issue.

From the information obtained it would appear that Qt is aimed at the corporate developer. For commercial product development, either wxWindows or Zinc would prove to be a more cost-effective choice. In the end, however, I would choose wxWindows over Zinc. The reason is support. While both products include source code, there are two issues with the Zinc library: The first is licensing. Wind River has not updated the license to reflect that it is now an open-source product. While this is probably not to the disadvantage of the user, it could still present problems. More important, however, is the fact that development on desktop versions of Zinc seems to have stopped. This leaves it to the user of this product to maintain it and enhance it. That could easily erase any cost savings that using the library would bring. If we choose to use a library, we have several good options available to us.

The .NET Framework

The .NET (pronounced "dot-net") framework is in a different classification from the above libraries. Instead of being linked to the application during the compilation process, .NET takes a different approach. In the previous chapter we briefly looked at the .NET definition. Now we will see if .NET should be considered for our user application development piece. There are several efforts underway to implement the .NET specification on several platforms. The most functional and recognized to date is the Microsoft implementation. While Microsoft is involved as a participant in defining the .NET architecture, there are others involved as well. In addition, the .NET architecture has been approved as a standard in Europe and the UK. The .NET specification defines the software equivalent of an electrical outlet and plug. Software developed for .NET is not compiled to native machine code but rather to an intermediate code that is tokenized. In order for this code to work, the .NET framework has to be installed on the target machine. Once installed, a program compiled to the intermediate language can be loaded and executed. Once loaded, the program is converted to machine language for the machine it is running on and then executed. This feature in and of itself isn't so remarkable since CPM BASIC was tokenized 26 years ago. But a compiled .NET program isn't just tokenized. The intermediate language file can be loaded on any .NET framework on any computer. This means the same program not only runs on Windows, but the same program image can be installed and run on Windows, Linux, UNIX, even IBM mainframes.

In the .NET environment, the user application is compiled to machine code after the program is loaded. The .NET framework becomes a part of the operating system and translates calls to the native API of the host system. The benefits here are very clear: .NET eliminates the need to develop multiple applications and the same executable can be run on any platform. The plug (application) now fits any wall socket (operating system). In the following illustration, the same user application is run on all three versions of the .NET framework.

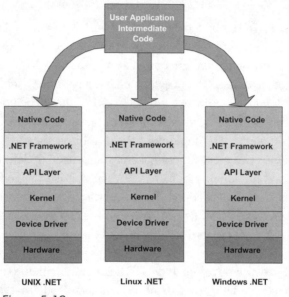

Figure 5-12

Including Microsoft, there are at least three .NET efforts going on. They are .NET from Microsoft, GNU.NET from The Open Group, and Mono, an open-source project sponsored by Novell. There are several private efforts also going on, but these three are the most widely available. The Microsoft implementation is complete and has been shipping for over two years. GNU.NET appears to be at the midpoint of development. While a lot of the core library is completed, not all of the functionality found in the Microsoft version has been implemented yet. So far GNU.NET is being developed and tested on Linux only. Mono is available on both Windows and Linux but again is not yet fully implemented.

While .NET should certainly be considered for the future, in its current state it doesn't meet our cross-platform requirements.

Cross-Platform Compilers

The next choice in cross-platform development is the compiler. Again we have a mix of commercial and free open-source products. In some cases, cross-platform compilers include a version of a cross-platform library. Before we get too far into this topic let me define what a cross-platform compiler is as it pertains to this project.

A cross-platform compiler includes a development interface that allows the developer to edit, compile, and debug a program using the same source code and with the same functionality in an identical fashion on all supported platforms. This does not preclude the fact that platform-dependent features are also included, but the same source must be compiled the same way to produce a same-looking application on all platforms from the user interface perspective. Database tools are not included since each platform has database systems available that are not cross-platform compatible. With these requirements in mind, the field of available products has been narrowed considerably. Let's look at the contenders.

Borland Products

Borland has several products that meet our requirements. This company has been developing commercial software products for over 20 years starting with Turbo Pascal. Over the years these products have evolved, and today Borland offers Pascal and C++ compilers that are cross-platform compatible. In fact, Borland is the only company to provide language-compatible compilers for Windows, UNIX/Linux, and .NET. Both C++ and Pascal are supported in the Windows and Linux markets.

Delphi

The flagship product of Borland, Delphi is what Turbo Pascal has evolved to be. Delphi has set the standard for adding object-oriented architecture to the Pascal language. I've use Turbo Pascal and Delphi since their inception and have always found both products to be of exceptional quality. The Linux version of Delphi is named Kylix. Delphi and Kylix have identical development environments. Figure 5-13 shows the Delphi 7 development environment for Windows. Notice the familiar Windows desktop.

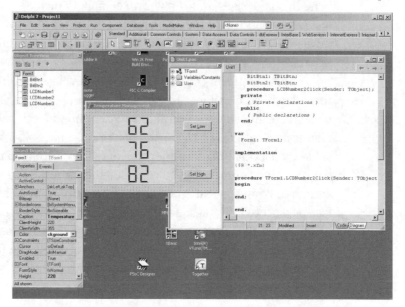

Figure 5-13: Delphi 7 version

Now take a look at Figure 5-14.

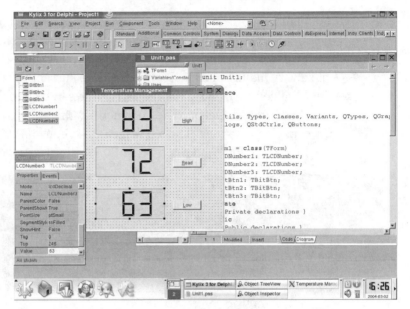

Figure 5-14: Kylix 3

This is Delphi Kylix running on Linux and KDE. The editor and visual designer are identical in functionality. While the Linux Desktop Manager looks similar, you'll notice the toolbar at the bottom is different. You'll also notice that both screens show the same application. While they look very similar, each is native to the operating system it is running on.

Delphi/Kylix meets the requirements of our project; however, our developers may not be completely comfortable with using Pascal. So let's move on to another commercial product.

C++Builder

Yes, another Borland product. I'm getting all the compilers from Borland out of the way before moving on to the next vendor. C++Builder began as Borland C and has evolved (like Delphi) into a very mature and stable compiler. The current versions of C++Builder are 6 and 2005; they share the same editor and visual designer as Delphi. The good news is that they are full C++ implementations. The following is a screen shot of C++Builder 6 for Windows.

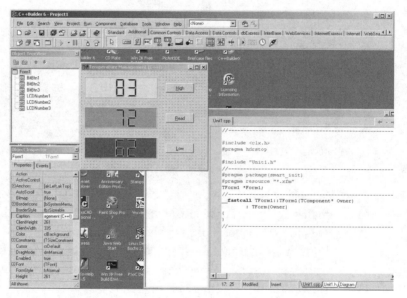

Figure 5-15

Like Delphi, C++Builder is also available for Linux. The following is a Linux image of C++Builder.

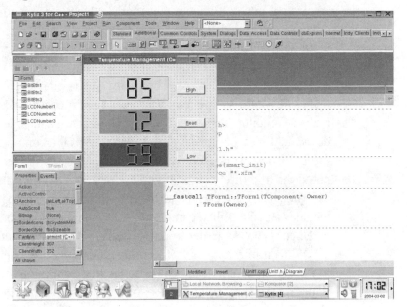

Figure 5-16

Again, except for the desktops, both the Linux and Windows versions of C++Builder look and function identically.

Our requirements call for the application to run on Linux, Windows, and UNIX. So far, Delphi and C++Builder have proven to work on Linux and Windows, but we haven't seen a UNIX version. Neither of these products has a native UNIX version. The version of UNIX we are using (FreeBSD 5.1) includes the ability to run a Linux binary. Rather than having three separate programs, we will install the Linux version of the application on the UNIX host.

Chapter 5

Intel C++

Intel is not new to the compiler market. Many years ago they developed and sold 16- and 32-bit DOS compilers that came complete with a DOS extender. Intel eventually sold that compiler off and stayed out of the compiler business for a while, but they have recently gotten back into the commercial compiler business. It makes sense for the people who make the processors to also make a compiler. The Intel C++ compilers are available for Windows and Linux platforms also. Like the Borland compilers, the Intel products work identically on both platforms. It should be noted that the Intel compilers do not include an editor or visual designer. They are command-line compilers only. The package includes a make utility, command-line compiler, linker, and debugger along with electronic versions of the documentation.

While it may appear that not including these items puts Intel at a disadvantage, nothing could be further from the truth. On Windows the Intel compiler is a direct replacement for Visual C++ 6 and the .NET compilers from Microsoft. On the Linux platform the Intel C++ compiler is a direct replacement for the GNU compiler, which is included with Linux. The Intel compiler package for Linux includes a make file utility, compiler, linker, and debugger.

The GNU Compiler Collection (GCC)

Next we have the GNU Compiler Collection, or GCC for short. The GNU compilers are free and have been around a very long time. Unlike the prior products, however, these compilers are supported strictly by volunteers. I submitted a question and was told that it could take up to two weeks to get a response. I never received a response to my question. Aside from support, the GNU compiler collection has several advantages over other compilers. First, the collection is available for many different processors other than Intel. Motorola, Hitachi, and many others are also supported. Second, the code is very mature and works well, and bugs are documented very well. The GNU compilers usually generate larger executables that run slower than commercial products. The GNU compiler collection also allows one platform to host a cross-compiler for another so at least in theory you can generate all your programs on a single machine. Now the downside: The GNU compiler collection has very scattered documentation and some of that documentation is wrong. When I had problems generating a cross-compiler, I found three different explanations for the cause of the problem, none of which was correct. This is the result of documentation on some of the more infrequently used functions not being updated. I used version 3.3.2 and the most recent documentation for cross-compiling I found was for 2.9.5.

Second, there is no visual designer for building a GUI, although there are many visual designers that support the GNU compiler. The GNU compilers run on Windows but require additional software that supports UNIX commands to operate. There are currently two of these UNIX shells available — Cygwin and MinGW. Either included or available for download are C, C++, ADA, Fortran, Objective C, Java byte code, and Java binary code compilers. Also included are all the tools for building, compiling, assembling, and debugging. The compiler suite includes source code so you can extend a language or write your own if you wish. The ability to build cross-platform compilers and create executable programs for a multitude of systems on a single host is a very big benefit. The support of some of the more obscure processors is another benefit. The GNU compilers generate professional-quality code and include a professional-quality debugger.

The biggest setback I had was finding a good editor that worked on all the selected platforms and the limitation of using visual designers that worked on all platforms (that were not dependent on a platform-specific framework). The next topic explores these types of utilities in more depth. If you choose to use the GNU compilers, I strongly recommend paying particular attention to available tools that support them. I also recommend doing a thorough evaluation of the available editors and visual designers before selecting one to use. It's easier to change those tools before spending the time to learn them and then throwing that time away.

Commercial Compilers in Comparison

There are several cross-platform compilers available to the development community. Borland and Intel are both first-class products. If you're developing a number of desktop applications, the Borland tools are a worthwhile investment for the time you'll save in designing interfaces. If you're not developing desktop applications, you may find the Intel compilers to your liking, but remember that they are command line only. The GNU compiler suite supports more platforms and supports hosting cross-platform code generation. I use all of these products and find each valuable depending on my objective. The following table gives a comparison.

Table 5-2: Comparing compilers

Product	Language	Forms Designer	Source Included	Open Source	UNIX/ Linux	Windows	Price
Intel C++ 7.0	C, C++	No	No	No	Yes[1]	Yes	$399
C++ Builder 6	C, C++	Yes	No	No[2]	Yes[1]	Yes	$399 to $2,999
Delphi 7	Pascal	Yes	No	No[2]	Yes[1]	Yes	$399 to $3,499
GNU C++	C, C++	No[3]	Yes	Yes	Yes	No[4]	N/A

Notes:
1. Runs on FreeBSD in Linux mode
2. Personal version available at minimal charge
3. Not included; third-party support
4. Cygwin or MinGW required to compile under Windows

There are several options available when it comes to compilers for cross-platform development. Determining factors are processor, integrated tools, visual designer, and platforms supported.

Cross-Platform Development Environments

This is our final category to examine before doing our final comparison. The reason for this category is twofold. First, there are cross-platform products that are neither compilers nor frameworks. Second, these tools are productivity enhancers that operate in a consistent fashion across multiple platforms. This category includes editors and development environments. Our first category is integrated development environments (IDEs). So let's get started with our options.

C++BuilderX

Here we go again. Now you may be asking why this wasn't covered above; that is a reasonable question. C++BuilderX is actually several products. It contains Borland C++ and the Intel C++ compilers for Windows and Linux, and supports the GNU C++ compiler and Microsoft Visual C++. It is also an open architecture IDE that works on Windows, Solaris, and Linux. Finally, the product includes the ability to do source level debugging on any of the supported platforms. It's not just a compiler suite but rather a complete architecture. While C++BuilderX does not currently include a visual designer, a preview version for Windows does include a visual designer for wxWindows. The following illustration shows the preview version running under Windows.

Chapter 5

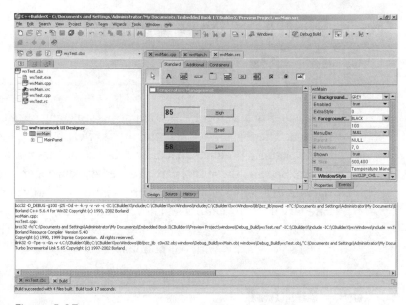

Figure 5-17

The visual designer is not available on the Linux or Solaris versions, but I think we can expect to see a cross-platform visual designer for C++BuilderX very soon. Since C++BuilderX is an open architecture, new compilers and tools can be added by the user. While it does include compilers and other tools, C++BuilderX is a development framework. The advantages are consistent user interface and functionality on all supported platforms. If you are already familiar with Borland products and want cross-platform compiler support for GNU in addition to the Intel compiler suite for both platforms, then C++BuilderX is a good addition to any toolbox. The following screen shot is C++BuilderX running on Linux.

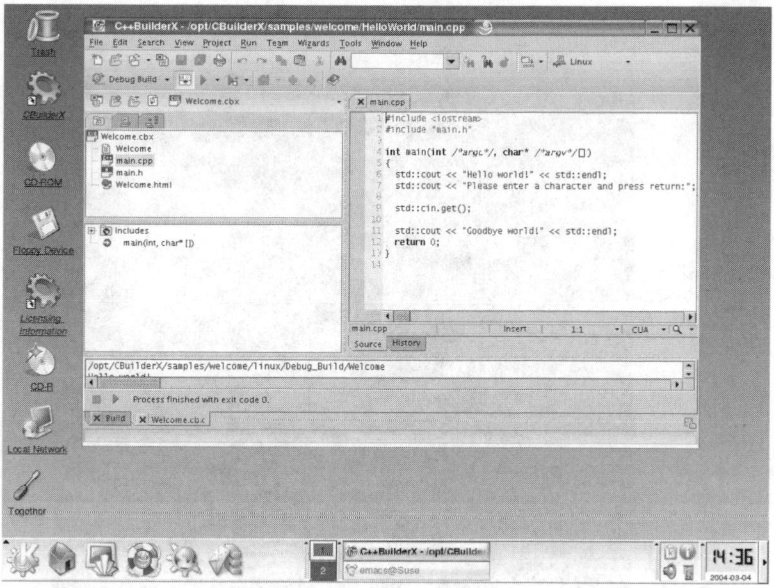

Figure 5-18

Even though there is no visual designer, the user interface is consistent and easy to use.

Emacs

Emacs is an open-source framework that has been around for many years. There are text- and GUI-based versions of the program available. Emacs is best known as a very flexible editor. It uses multi-key sequences to control the program, which is a carryover from the early days of WordStar. If you're accustomed to a menu bar, the Emacs learning curve may be a bit too much. Remembering multi-key sequences is no trade-off for a menu system. Emacs is very flexible so you can program it to compile within the editor and start the debugger. It is not an integrated IDE like C++BuilderX.

The following is a screen shot of Emacs running on Windows
in a Cygwin session.

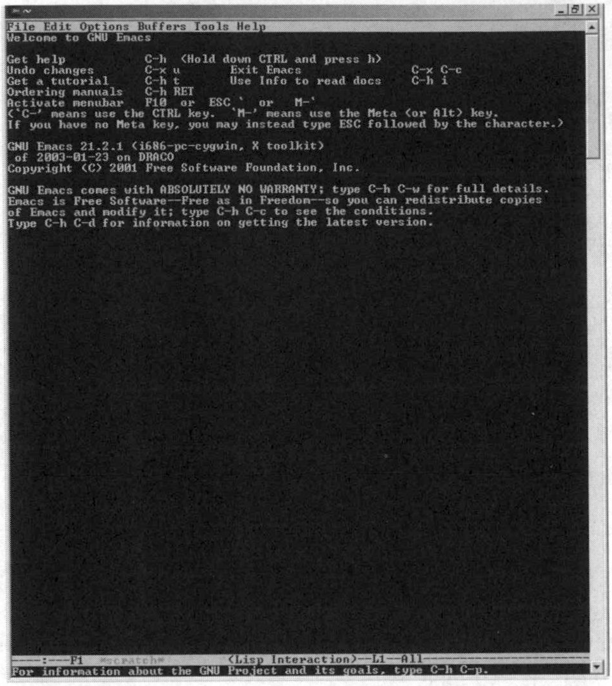

Figure 5-19

While Emacs is not as pretty as an integrated IDE, it is fully
configurable. As you can see in Figure 5-19, its many multi-key
sequences provide Emacs with flexibility. The GUI version is
more familiar to those who are using Windows or another desktop manager.

The following screen shot is the GUI version of Emacs running on Windows in a Cygwin session.

Figure 5-20

The familiar Windows Start menu is displayed at the bottom. Once a Cygwin session is started and running, X Windows is started. When X Windows is running, Emacs is invoked. While the mouse can be used for some features, Emacs is still heavily dependent on multi-key sequences. Even so, Emacs does work identically on all supported platforms.

Chapter 5

The following screen shot is Emacs running on a Linux desktop.

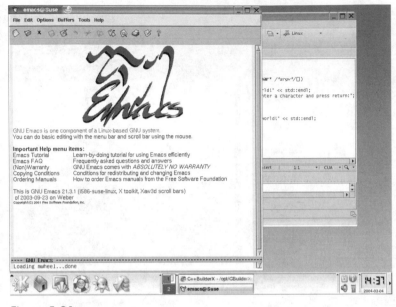

Figure 5-21

GDB

GDB is the GNU debugger. This is a professional-quality debugger that allows source line debugging, breakpoints, variable watches, and many other features. Some versions of GDB allow remote debugging through a serial line. You can modify GDB to suit your own needs since the source code is included. Emacs and C++BuilderX support GDB either directly or by invoking the debugger in a shell. C++BuilderX runs GDB within a window as seen in the following figure.

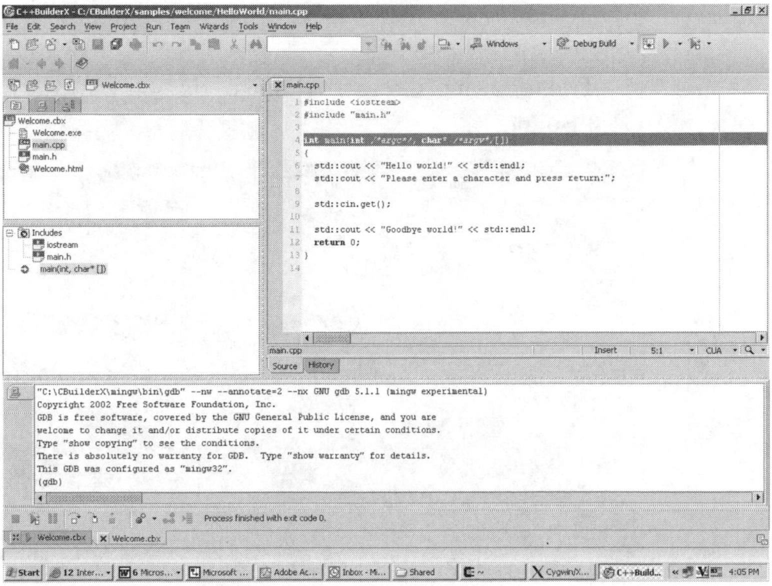

Figure 5-22

The GDB debugger is also supported in Cygwin as shown in Figure 5-24.

Figure 5-23

Regardless of how the debugger is invoked, it looks very similar and functions the same.

The following shows a debug session on Linux using C++BuilderX.

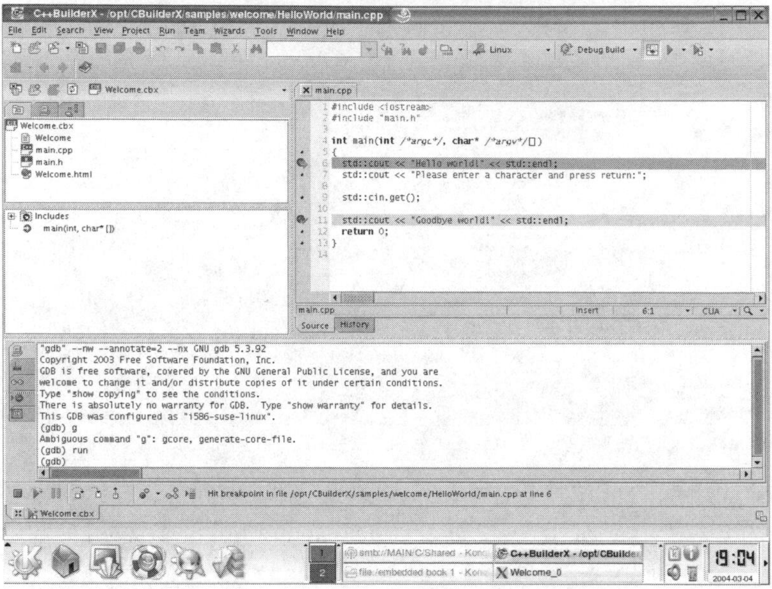

Figure 5-24

The debugging window is the center window on the right side. Two breakpoints are set and the program has stopped on break-point one. The bottom window is the direct command window for GDB. Commands can be entered directly or by using the mouse to select the debugging functions at the bottom of the C++BuilderX window. The red square and green arrow on the tab are debugger commands.

Choosing the Right Tools for the Design

As you can see we have a variety of choices and several ways to accomplish cross-platform compatibility. Our design calls for a single-source code base for cross-platform compatibility. Let's list our options explored thus far by category.

- Developer libraries:
  - GTK+
  - Qt
  - wxWindows
  - Zinc interface library
- .NET framework:
  - Microsoft .NET   (Windows only)
  - Mono   (Windows and Linux)
  - GNU .NET   (Linux only)
- Cross-platform compilers with IDE:
  - Borland Delphi/Kylix
  - Borland C++ Builder/Kylix
- Cross-platform compilers only:
  - Intel C++
  - GNU C++
- Cross-platform tools:
  - Emacs
  - GDB

Chapter 5

I've broken down the compilers into those with an integrated development environment and those without. We'll call our selected suite of tools our development workbench. To build a complete set of development tools we need the following:

■ Compiler

■ Editor

■ Debugger

■ Forms designer

Next, we'll build a matrix to see how a product or product combination fits our requirements. While product cost is an issue, the price of a product can quickly be overshadowed by poor documentation, long learning curve, or poor and inconsistent support. In the following table each row represents a bundled development solution for us to examine. Each bundle is rated by two factors — included tools and a rating of 1 to 5 on documentation, support, and available learning or tutorial tools.

Table 5-3

Compiler	Editor	Debugger	Form Designer	Doc	Support	Tutorial	Overall
Delphi Kylix	Included	Included	Included	Printed	Available[1]	Included	5
C++ BuilderX	Included	Included	Included	Printed	Available[1]	Included	5
Intel C++ 7[2]	Not included	Not included	Not included	Online	Web based	Included	3.5
GCC	Emacs	GDB	DialogBlocks[3]	Online[4]	Web based[5]	Available[6]	2.5
GCC	C++ BuilderX	C++ BuilderX	DialogBlocks	Online[7]	Available[8]	Included[8]	4.0
C++ BuilderX	Included	Included	DialogBlocks	Online	Available	Online	4.5
Intel C++ 7	C++ BuilderX	C++ BuilderX	DialogBlocks	Online	Available	Online	4.3
GCC	Zinc	GDB	Zinc	Online	None	Online	3.3
Intel C++ 7	Zinc	GDB	Zinc	Online	None	Online	3.8

Notes:

1. Installation support is free; tech support by phone has per-incident fee
2. Intel C++ is a replacement compiler for Microsoft and GNU
3. Third-party product
4. Online documentation may not be up to date
5. Email support may take several weeks for response
6. Independent web tutorials not part of product
7. Specific compiler documentation from GNU.org (see 4 above)
8. Provided by Borland

Overall ratings are based on a combination of experience and user comments. The ratings range from 2.5 to 5.0. As you might expect, commercial products carry a higher rating due to integration of editor and debugger, full-time support, and documentation. Let's examine the results from lowest to highest.

The GCC, Emacs, GDB, and wxWindows combination is a very solid workbench, but multiple sources for documentation and in some cases outdated documentation take the overall rating down.

Using the Zinc interface library scored a little higher because the Zinc documentation is complete. It consists of an installation manual, tutorial, and reference manual. The Zinc Designer provides the ability to visually develop an interface and edit the associated code. This combination didn't score higher because there is no ongoing development effort for Zinc. It is worth noting that the Zinc library is compatible with Microsoft C++ on Windows and GNU C++ on Linux. The Intel C++ compiler is compatible with both of these, allowing the Zinc library to be compiled on both platforms with the same compiler.

The Intel C++ 7 product scored lower by itself because it doesn't have an integrated editor or visual forms designer. It is compatible with Microsoft C++ and GCC, which means that any third-party tool that supports GCC also supports the Intel 7 C++ compiler. If you have Visual C++ version 6 or 7 on Windows, the Intel C++ 7 compiler can be used in its place. When we bundle the Intel compiler with C++BuilderX and the wxWindows library, its rating goes up. Most of this increase is due to the integration of the editor and debugger within the C++BuilderX product. It is worth noting that the Intel C++ compiler is included with C++BuilderX.

C++BuilderX scores slightly higher alone than when used with the Intel C++ compiler. This is due to the additional support for Microsoft C++ 6 and 7 and GNU C++ (3.2.3), and the inclusion of the Intel C++ compilers for Windows and Linux. In both evaluations we used wxWindows as the cross-platform GUI builder of choice.

We wrap the highest scores up with Delphi/C++Builder/ Kylix for Windows/Linux. These products work identically when using the CLX (Cross-platform Libraries) on Windows and Linux. No other tools include a compiler, debugger, visual designer, and visual libraries for both platforms with support for a single-source code base.

And the Winners Are...

We are going to take two different approaches for the prototype development. Our first approach is to use commercial products — the Delphi/C++Builder/Kylix combination. By using the visual design capabilities of these products and the cross-platform support for the visual components, the majority of our work has been greatly reduced. Our second approach is to use the personal version of C++BuilderX with the GNU compiler suite, and wxWindows. In deciding to use wxWindows there were several factors to consider. Qt, wxWindows, GTK+, and Zinc are all great tools. While Zinc is very well documented and mature, it is not currently being publicly supported and that means any problems encountered will be left to our developers to fix. Qt is also a great product with excellent documentation and support. If we needed support for the Macintosh, this would certainly give Qt an edge, but to produce the prototype we want to keep our costs down. Remember, we have not decided at this point if the same tools used in the prototype will also make the final product. If we choose to sell a prototype and use the noncommercial version of

Qt, we will end up violating the license agreement and be required to purchase the Qt libraries. wxWindows is available on all the required platforms. It also supports the Macintosh should support for that platform be added at a later time. While wxWindows does not include a visual forms designer, several are available for minimal cost. wxWindows is also included in the preview edition of C++BuilderX. This means in a short time there will be a commercial product that offers wxWindows support from both a visual design view and on the source code level. The personal edition of C++BuilderX allows us to sell a prototype without being in license violation. If we like the product we can simply purchase the product and enjoy the additional features and compilers included with the commercial license.

While GTK+ may work, the learning curve of the libraries and becoming familiar with the visual designer would take more time than the other chosen solutions. This is still a very good alternative to explore for future projects. While we are not officially developing for the .NET framework, we will explore whether a single application can be run in both Windows and UNIX. This information will be used for future development and would allow Internet integration of programs with minimal changes.

Chapter Summary

In this chapter we've examined our options for cross-platform development. Much to our surprise, we have found there are many options when choosing a cross-platform workbench. We've also learned that direct costs of a product can quickly be offset by support or documentation issues. If an average developer makes $20 to $30 an hour, it doesn't take long to recover the cost of a commercial product in support or documentations issues. Finally, we can see that product licensing can affect the end cost of a product development cycle by thousands of dollars. Project requirements play a big role in the tools needed to do the job right. Had our requirements been different, the tools selected for our workbench would also have been different. The next chapter is a recap of our design.

Final Design

Overview

Everything we've learned so far will be applied in this chapter. The result will be the master design document and master flowchart. This will serve as a summary of Chapters 1 through 5. The next chapter begins Part II, where we will build the embedded system and actually integrate it to the host systems.

Master Design Document

Purpose

This document will serve as the verbal road map through the development process. It provides the guidelines and standards to which the end product will be developed and measured. We will begin with the design definition of the embedded system, followed by the host interfaces, host integration design, user application design, and protocol design. Each interface will be covered in depth, as will hardware definitions and component selection for each chosen processor. The master flowchart will follow the design documentation.

Embedded System Final Design

Design Overview

This product is designed to monitor and control temperature and air flow within a given area. This area can be a room, a group of rooms, or a complete building. Each system will manage a given zone and control airflow and temperature through single or multiple temperature inputs. Each unit can perform alone or as part of a group, or interact with a host computer running Windows, Linux, or UNIX. This product will have the following features:

- Independent microprocessor control
- Remote temperature monitoring capabilities
- High and low temperature thresholds used as reporting triggers
- Multiple temperature sensor input
- Optional fan control outputs
- Network capabilities
- RS-232 serial interface support
- USB interface support
- Ethernet interface support
- Onboard time and date management
- Battery backup option
- Future expansion pins
- Optional software development kit
- Host integration software support for:
    - Windows 2000
    - Windows XP

- Linux
- FreeBSD (UNIX)

Our research indicates a wide variety of products are suitable for this type of system. Each component and tool has associated benefits and costs in terms of technology, time, and learning curve. After a close review of these components and tools we have decided to build three prototypes. Each will use a different processor, USB, and Ethernet interface. Each of these three prototypes will incorporate RS-232 serial interfaces, USB interfaces, and Ethernet interfaces. Three processor platforms have been chosen for the prototypes. They are:

- The BASIC Stamp 2p from Parallax
- The dsPIC from Microchip
- The PSoC from Cypress MicroSystems

These three processors offer a variety of cost and development benefits that range from high level language support and integrated interfaces to dynamically configurable hardware.

External Device Interfaces

Due to current market, legacy support, and emerging technologies, three different hardware interfaces have been chosen for host communications. They are:

- RS-232 serial communications
- Universal serial bus (USB)
- Ethernet

Each prototype will support each of these three interface methods. A wide variety of commercial products were evaluated. After a close inspection of cost and development effort, the following three products have been chosen for the prototype. They are:

- USB-232M from FTDI
- PIC 16C765 from Microchip
- EZ-USB from Cypress MicroSystems

Each of these devices has a different cost or development benefit associated with its use.

Three different approaches using two different types of Ethernet hardware will be used. They are:

- Ethernet Development System from NetBurner
- Embedded Ethernet from Systor

The NetBurner product uses an AMD Ethernet chip coupled with a Motorola Coldfire processor. While using a second processor may seem redundant, this does provide expansion capabilities. Again, we have chosen this as a launch pad for our prototype. There are several other microprocessor manufacturers that have embedded Ethernet. The choice was made by a combination of costs, functionality, and usable features for our product. We have consciously chosen to use microcontrollers instead of microprocessors due to pin count and intelligence. While microprocessors offer more in intelligence and expandability, they also contain much more power than needed in this project. Due to the added complexity, simpler products were chosen as a development platform.

Temperature Measurement

Since a major function of this device is temperature measurement and the ability to read multiple temperature sensors, the Dallas DS1822 1-Wire sensor was chosen for the prototype. This device was chosen because it is a part of the 1-Wire network product line that allows multiple devices to be attached to a single pair of wires. The 1-Wire scheme also allows additional sensors to be added on the same bus, conserving components and board space. While the 1-Wire protocol is complex, it is reliable and other device types that support the 1-Wire bus can be added without additional hardware. In short, the 1-Wire is mostly software dependent once the hardware interface has been refined. Other 1-Wire temperature sensors can replace the DS1822, providing higher temperature resolution without any hardware changes. This allows us to offer a variety of products with varying degrees of temperature accuracy without any hardware changes at all.

Output Display

The system communicates with the user through a 2-line by 20-character LCD display. A keypad is used to edit and update system parameters. There are also two LEDs for displaying temperature alarm and power conditions. A red LED is turned on when a temperature limit has been exceeded. A green LED indicates that external power is being provided to power the unit.

User Input

User input is accomplished via a seven-key keypad. There are three control keys and four cursor keys. The control keys are:

■ Function/Menu

■ Set/Select

■ Clear

The four cursor keys are defined as:

■ Up Arrow/Increase

■ Down Arrow/Decrease

■ Left Arrow

■ Right Arrow

Command Mode

To view or change a setting, the user will press and hold the Function/Menu key for five seconds. When command mode is entered the unit will sound a single beep through the internal speaker. Command mode is exited automatically upon 30 seconds of keyboard inactivity. Any changes not saved with the Set key are lost upon leaving command mode.

Menu Navigation

Once command mode is entered, a main menu will be displayed. Each menu selection is identified by a single uppercase letter. The currently defined selections are:

- **T**ime — Set time of day
- **D**ate — Set current date
- **I**nterface — Choose host interface
- **H**igh Temperature — Set high temperature alarm
- **L**ow temperature — Set low temperature alarm
- **E**xit Command Mode — Return to display mode
- **S**ensor Reset — Reset temperature sensor network
- Unit **R**eset — Reset entire unit

Cursor movement is obtained via the up, down, left, and right arrow keys as shown in Figure 6-1.

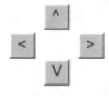

Figure 6-1

To change or view a specific function, press the left or right arrow keys to highlight the letter that identifies the chosen function and press the Set button. A new menu will be displayed with only function-dependent features.

Following is an illustration of the control keys.

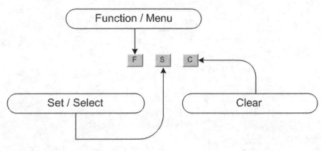

Figure 6-2

After entering command mode the display will look similar to the following:

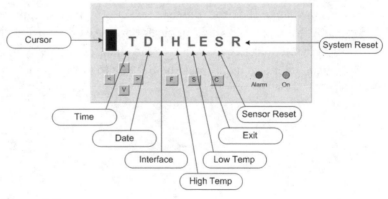

Figure 6-3

Once again, the left and right arrow keys move the cursor over the various selections. When the cursor is over the selection you wish to view or change, simply press the Set (or Select) button to display the menu for that selection. The following sections explain each menu selection and available choices.

Time – Set Time of Day

When the T menu option is selected the time display will appear as follows:

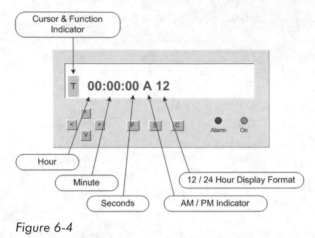

Figure 6-4

To change the time, the user selects the hours, minutes, seconds, AM/PM, or 12/24 hour indicator and uses the up and down arrow keys to make changes. Once the changes are ready to be stored, the user simply presses the Set key to store them permanently.

Date – Set Current Date

The following menu should be displayed after selecting the Date
menu item from the main menu:

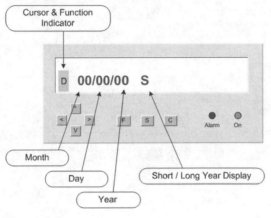

Figure 6-5

The D in the first column indicates the Date function is being displayed. By moving the left and right cursor keys, the user can
select month, day, year, and short or long date display. A short
date display shows only two digits for the year while the long
date display shows a four-digit year. The date display is numeric
only so marketing outside North America will require few text
changes.

Host Interface Type

Once selected, this menu should look as shown below:

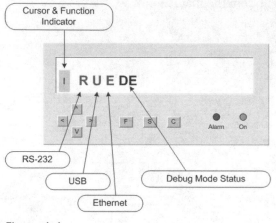

Figure 6-6

The interface menu is identified by the capital letter I in the left cursor column. The user can change the active interface by selecting the letter associated with that interface type. The choices are RS-232, USB, and Ethernet. A two-character debug status mode indicator allows debug mode to be chosen during the development cycle. Debug mode is only available if USB or Ethernet have been selected as the host interface type. When debug mode is on, the serial port shows all packet data going between the host and embedded system. The purpose is to do protocol debugging if necessary. This feature will allow the protocol to be quickly and efficiently implemented.

RS-232 parameters are fixed at 19,200 baud, 8 data bits, no parity, and 1 stop bit. Both the USB and Ethernet interfaces contain parameters that can be changed from either a remote terminal or a remote host system. In either case special administrative software must be used. In short, the end user application does not contain the ability to change these parameters.

High Temperature Alarm Trigger

It should be noted that supporting multiple temperature sensors and fan control is not implemented in the prototype. These features are not a part of the initial product offering. The only required support is for the temperature sensor onboard the circuit and the ability to control two fans, one for heat and one for air conditioning.

When selected, the menu should look as follows:

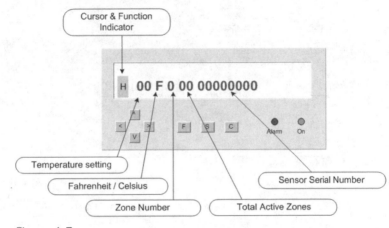

Figure 6-7

The H in the first column indicates we are setting the high temperature alarm. Only three of the displayed parameters can be changed. The user can move the cursor to the temperature setting with the left and right arrow keys. The temperature can be adjusted by using the up and down arrow keys, Moving to the English/Metric display and using the up and down keys will toggle between the Fahrenheit and Celsius scales for display purposes. As the logic is installed to support multiple zones, moving to the zone number will allow the user to select which zone to modify. The total active zone display shows the total number of active temperature sensors currently attached. Since each sensor has a unique serial number, the associated serial number is displayed. When the set temperature has been exceeded, the alarm LED will light and if a host is connected, an alarm condition will be triggered. The logic line for the air conditioning will be set to a logic level 1 to turn on air conditioning. Fan control will also be set to a logic level 1.

Low Temperature Alarm Trigger

The low temperature alarm trigger shares much in common with the high temperature trigger. When this menu item is selected, the following will be displayed:

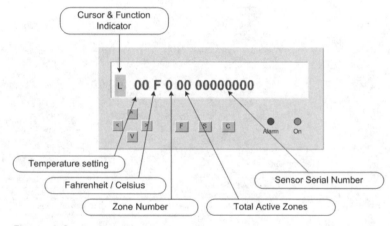

Figure 6-8

Functionally, both the high and low temperature sensors are identical in how they are handled.

Note:

There are several temperature sensor devices in the 1-Wire product line. The DS1822 is the lowest in cost at the time of publication. The accuracy of these devices varies depending on which part is used. The maximum high or low setting is determined by the sensor range. When using these sensors it always a good idea to be familiar with temperature range and accuracy to be certain the sensor matches the solution.

Exit Menu

Pressing the exit menu key will return the user to the main menu. If the exit menu key is pressed at the main menu, the display will go back to display mode.

Temperature Sensor Reset

When adding or removing 1-Wire devices, it is always best to reset the sensor bus. This will assure that all sensor serial numbers are read and each sensor is accounted for. This menu item resets the 1-Wire bus and scans for all available temperature sensors.

System Reset

The R option resets the unit from a power-up state, rescans for all temperature sensors, and sets the fan output to off. No stored parameters are lost.

Host Interfaces

Three types of interfaces are required to be implemented. Each interface needs to meet any national or international standards for communications and electrical interfaces. By default, IBM-type computers were originally designated as Data Terminal Equipment (DTE). In keeping with those original standards, the host system will be defined as Data Terminal Equipment (DTE) and the embedded system will be defined as Data Communications Equipment (DCE) where appropriate. Communications between the host and embedded system will be done via the proper cabling for the selected interface. For RS-232 that will be a 9-pin D shell female connector on the circuit board. This will allow a straight 9-pin D shell serial cable to be used with the RS-232 interface. The USB interface is a standard USB peripheral connector with a four-wire cable. The Ethernet interface uses a standard eight-wire RJ-45 female connector attached to the circuit board. The communications format of the data uses a custom protocol defined later in this chapter.

RS-232

The RS-232 interface will support a common signal ground, as well as one transmit and one receive line. Electrical handshake for the Request-To-Send (RTS) and Clear-To-Send (CTS) lines will also be supported. To facilitate proper voltage levels, a Max232 or equivalent component will be used. The RS-232 requires a total of four processor lines.

USB

Three different approaches are being tested during the prototype phase. The first is a serial to USB converter. This approach allows minimal code changes from RS-232 to USB, theoretically reducing development costs. The second approach combines the USB controller with the microcontroller, reducing code and components. The third approach is unique in that the USB device code is downloaded when the device is booted. This allows soft updates to the USB device by simply rebooting it. This approach also presents some other very interesting possibilities, one of which is building an onboard in-circuit serial programmer for making the microcontroller field-upgradeable.

Ethernet

The Ethernet approach is slightly different. This approach makes the Ethernet portion of the prototype an intelligent module. We have chosen a standalone Ethernet controller from NetBurner. This eliminates the microcontroller for the embedded system having to be involved directly with the TCP/IP functions or IP addressing. This approach allows the microcontroller to send and receive data serially from the Ethernet circuit without being concerned about IP address assignment or providing a TCP/IP stack. This approach allows the embedded system to immediately be put on a LAN or WAN. Using this approach will make the Ethernet controller a sub-assembly that is totally outsourced. While this may appear to increase the cost of the end product, that may not be the case. The reduced labor in board development, procuring and testing TCP/IP software, and support code in the microcontroller may make this a very cost-effective solution. The other approaches use a single chip Ethernet transceiver to convert the packet data to Ethernet packets but not using the TCP/IP protocol. For the prototype a separate Ethernet card will be installed in the host. This will allow direct communications with the Ethernet controller using the TCP/IP protocol. To make this approach work on a standard LAN or WAN, a TCP/IP protocol implementation will need to be provided. It is yet undetermined if there is available memory in the selected processors to implement this option.

Host Side Design

Device Layer

On the host side of this system the design calls for a single-source driver and user application. This is accomplished by developing a shared library or DLL that provides standard calls to the application layer and platform-dependent calls to the system layer. Essentially this middle layer code will handle all platform-specific driver issues. We can do this because no low-level device drivers are being created from scratch. We have chosen components that either include device drivers for the necessary platforms or can be addressed using standard OS drivers.

Application Layer

The end user application is required to use the same source code base across all chosen platforms. Several approaches are being tested to accomplish this requirement. The first approach is to use development tools that produce the same look and feel from the same source base on all chosen platforms. The first selected tool is the Borland compiler suite. This is a commercial product that provides a Windows and Linux development environment in the same box. The user interface and supporting logic will be developed using these tools and including the proper shared library for device access. The second approach will use a development framework or library to create the user interface component. By using a cross-platform compiler the accompanying business logic will be compiled for the specific target using a single code base. Using this approach two different types of development will be attempted. This first will use the GNU compiler tools for single-source business logic and wxWindows for the cross-platform user interface. The second approach will use the Borland C++BuilderX product, which provides a cross-platform compiler, editor, and debugging environment. The Borland product provides a tighter integration of these tools for the developer while the GNU approach has no dollar cost associated with it. Using the GNU approach the editor, debugger, and compiler will be obtained from several different sources and integrated on the development workstation.

Differences between Windows and UNIX

There are several differences between the Windows and UNIX (Linux) platforms. These systems are very different in design. In the Windows environment the graphical user interface (GUI) is an integral part of the operating system. It would appear this is done to provide tighter security and less chance of accidental system compromise. In both UNIX and Linux environments the

GUI is treated and executed as any other desktop application. This approach provides a wider array of available GUIs and tighter control over the task scheduler. This results in much finer control over how frequently the task scheduler can service a task. Several of the GUIs available for UNIX and Linux are also available on Windows. This is accomplished by providing a layer that goes between the Windows API and the desktop manager GUI calls. It should be noted that all of the prototypes use this middle tier of code for platform-specific code translation.

The Communication Protocol

To facilitate a platform- and interface-independent means of sending and receiving data, a custom protocol has been defined. The protocol definition puts each message into a wrapper that includes the following:

- Message Category — 1 byte
- Message Type — 1 byte
- Sensor ID — 1 byte
- Alarm Type — 1 byte
- Temperature — 2 bytes
- Message ID — 1 byte
- Message Size — 2 bytes

This allows for future expansion and variable length messaging without altering the original protocol.

Embedded System Flowcharts

The following flowcharts illustrate the functions of the embedded system.

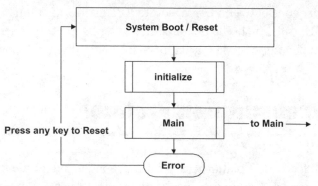

Figure 6-9

The above sequence is initiated by the following conditions:

- Applying power
- Pressing the System Reset key
- Pressing any key after a system error

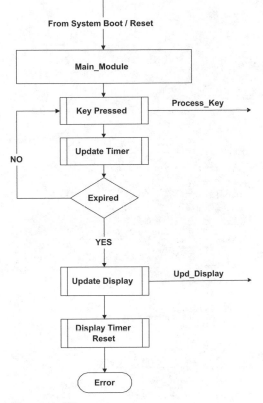

Figure 6-10

Once the system is initialized the main program loop starts. The main program is a simple timer-based loop. First, the keyboard scan routine checks for any pending command keys. If a key is detected, the Process_Key function is called. Next, a check is made to determine if the update display timer has expired. If it has, the display data is updated and the update display timer is reset. If the timer hasn't expired, the process starts over. If an error is encountered, the program terminates by displaying the error on the LCD and waiting for any key to be pressed to reset the unit.

Chapter 6

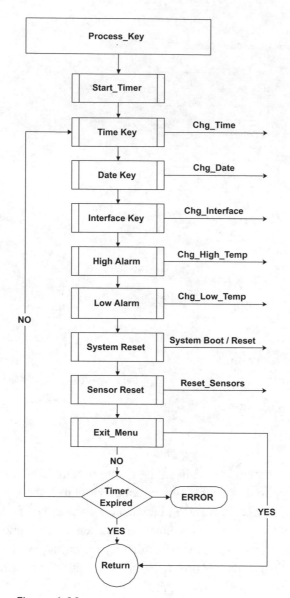

Figure 6-11

Upon entry a 30-second timer is set for reference. During that 30-second period the keyboard is scanned for a selected menu item. If a menu item is selected, the proper function is called. If the exit key is pressed, the timer is disabled and a return to Main_Module is made.

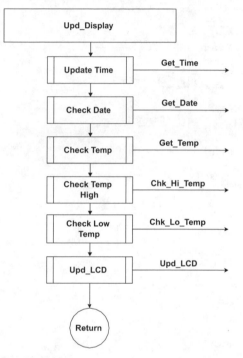

Figure 6-12

The Upd_Display function reads current temperature, alarm, time, and date, and then updates the LCD display with the new data.

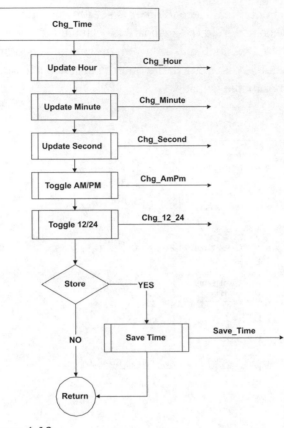

Figure 6-13

The Chg_Time function allows editing of the hour, minute, seconds, AM/PM, and 12-/24-hour display format. The values are changed on the LCD immediately but are only made permanent when the Save key is pressed. If the Save key is not pressed, the old parameters are restored when returning to the main display.

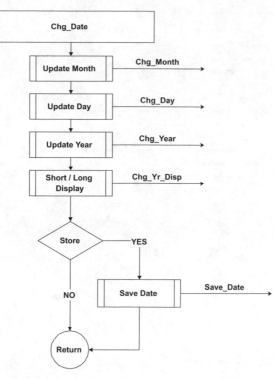

Figure 6-14

This function allows the day, month, year, and long or short year display to be changed. Again, the new settings are displayed immediately but lost unless the Save key is pressed.

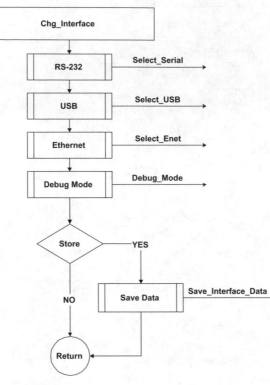

Figure 6-15

Each type of interface has different variables and parameters associated with it. Debug mode can only be turned on if USB or Ethernet is selected as the interface type. As always, the data is not stored unless the Save key has been pressed.

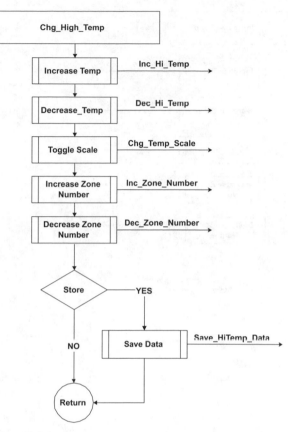

Figure 6-16

The Chg_High_Temp function allows the upper temperature
limit to be increased, decreased, and displayed in Celsius or Fahrenheit, and multiple zones to be edited. While there is no
requirement to support multiple zones in the prototype, the logic
is being included to see how much additional RAM will be available in a completely implemented system.

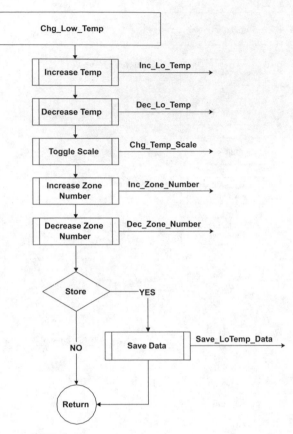

Figure 6-17

While the actual data stored and retrieved with the Chg_Low_
Temp function is different from the high temperature limit, much
of the functionality is shared with the Chg_High_Temp function.

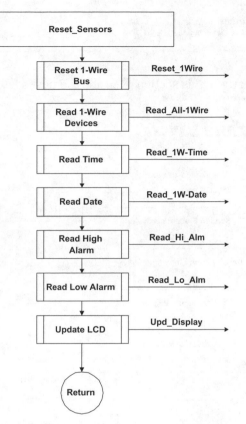

Figure 6-18

When the 1-Wire bus is reset, all 1-Wire devices are interrogated and accounted for. If a 1-Wire time and date chip is available, the time and date are read and stored. Next, the high temperature and low temperature sensor settings are read and stored. Before exiting the reset sensor function a call to Upd_Display is made. This displays the new readings on the LCD display.

This covers all the functions of the embedded system from a design point of view. Next we will cover the flowcharts for the host system.

Host System Flowcharts

The flowcharts in this section describe the host system.

Device Interface Layer

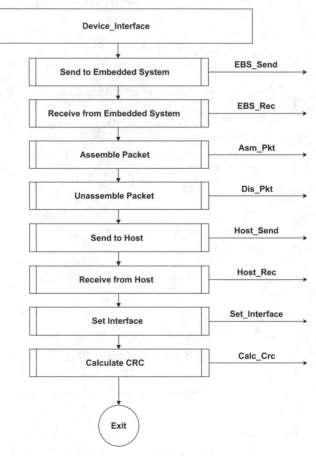

Figure 6-19

The primary function of the device interface layer is to provide
consistent send, receive, packet assemble, packet disassemble,

and interface routing on all supported platforms. All plat-form-dependent device driver code resides in this layer.

User Application Layer

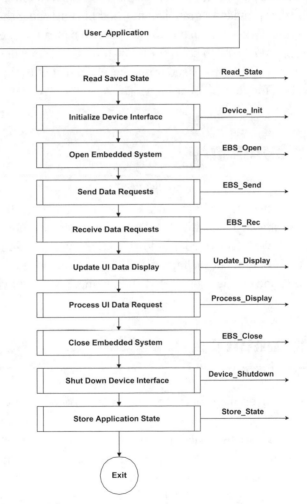

Figure 6-20

The user application serves three important functions on the host system. First, it provides an orderly communications channel to the embedded system. This allows the host system to both monitor and control the embedded system remotely. Second, it provides a means of controlling the embedded system remotely via a user interface that looks identical to the embedded system LCD display. Everything displayed on the embedded system LCD is also displayed on the user application display when it is active. Third, it provides a graphical method of controlling the embedded system. When a mouse is clicked over a control or the computer keyboard is used to control the system, those mouse clicks and keystrokes are processed immediately and sent to the embedded system for control processing.

Chapter Summary

In this chapter we have outlined the high-level functionality of the embedded system, host device interface, and host user application. We have not gotten down to the level of defining the actual contents of each function. That will be done as we develop and refine our designs in Part II, starting in the next chapter.

Part I Summary

We've covered an enormous amount of ground thus far: embedded system design, device drivers for USB Ethernet, and serial communications. Dallas 1-Wire network considerations and designing cross-platform applications are just a small part of what we've learned. No matter how many words we read or how many charts we review, the final challenge comes in the implementation of our system, which begins in the very next chapter. Use this chapter as a point of reference for Part II as we build, test, integrate, and write the host applications for our product.

Part II

Implementation

Hardware Development

Overview

If you made it this far, we are ready to start building the first prototype boards. This chapter begins by providing a list of required tools, and then takes the reader step by step through the building of several circuit boards that will be used by all the prototypes. Once the boards are completed, we will write test software for each board function to check our work. At the end of this chapter is a tutorial on how to make your own printed circuit boards and sources for the necessary materials, along with the artwork needed to build each board described.

I should note that wires were soldered on the top of the solder-type breadboards for illustration purposes. Normally the wiring would be kept on the bottom side of the board. This chapter provides step-by-step instructions for the beginner and schematics for the more experienced. For those who wish to make their own circuit boards, the full-scale artwork is at the very end of this chapter. It can also be downloaded from the Wordware web site at www.wordware.com/files/embsys or from my web site at www.time-lines.com.

Types of Prototype Circuit Boards

For those of you who have never built a prototype board, let's examine the most common methods of prototyping electronic circuits. There are several commonly used methods for starting the prototype cycle for an electronics board. They are:

- Solderless breadboard — Uses jumpers and predrilled insertion holes

- Soldered breadboard — Uses soldered jumpers and predrilled holes

- Wire wrap board — Can use a soldered breadboard or special wire wrap board

- Etched circuit board — Requires software and other materials

There are many factors to consider when determining which method of circuit prototyping is used. I use solderless breadboards to get portions of a circuit working first and then develop a schematic. Then I'll either use solderless breadboards or I'll make printed circuit boards for each functional section. This is my way of determining functional layout. Afterward I'll make a printed circuit board with all the functions on it. This technique allows my schematic to grow slowly as the project progresses with the end result being a completed circuit board. I always try to start with a single layer board even if it gets large. This allows me to resolve any problems by visual inspection if necessary, which can be impossible with multilayered boards. Once I have the final circuit design down, I'll send out for a couple of professionally made circuit boards from a board house.

Solderless Breadboards

There are many sources for solderless boards. If you can wait a few days and want to save money, I suggest you order them via mail order or the Internet. Figure 7-1 shows a small solderless breadboard. The two outside rows on each side are connected along the entire length of the board. These are usually used for power and ground connections. This allows power and ground connections to be accessed from any of the internal rows. The rows that are internal to the breadboards are connected together perpendicular to the power connections. The center breaks these into two sections. This allows for different types of components to be added and tested. The board pictured below will cost between $6 and $10 depending on where it is purchased.

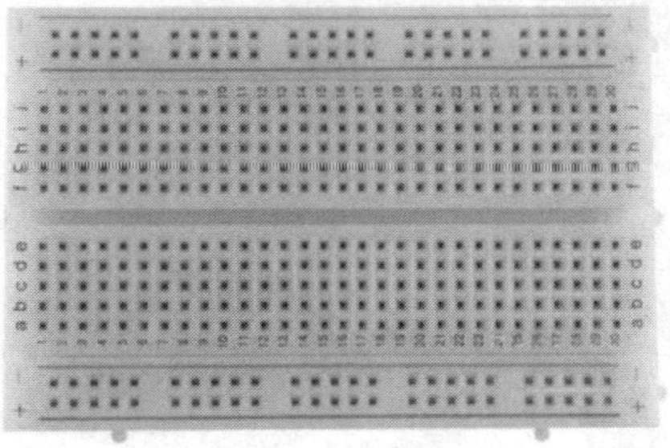

Figure 7-1

This board is the smallest board available. There are many sizes and some have power connectors on them. I keep a variety of these boards in my shop so I can prototype portions of a circuit before moving to a circuit board. One final note: When ordering these boards be certain to also order jumper kits; otherwise, you will be spending considerable time making jumpers for building your circuits.

Soldered Breadboards

There are several styles of solder type breadboards. The first style is laid out identical to the solderless breadboard mentioned above. If you're building a very simple circuit and want to finish it quickly, then by all means use this type of board. For our projects, however, we will use a grid-style solder type breadboard. There are numerous types and sizes of these boards available, but for our purposes we will use the Radio Shack 276-150. This particular board has two rows in the center of the board we will use for power. This is in contrast to the two outside rows on the solderless breadboard in Figure 7-1. Figure 7-2 shows the layout of the 276-150. Note the layout of the two center rows connected horizontally.

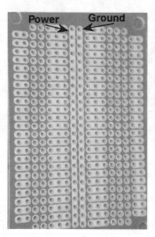

Figure 7-2

Wire Wrap Boards

The soldered breadboard can be used for wire wrapping or you can get a special wire wrap board. A real wire-wrap board doesn't have the connections joined together since every connection is jumpered. You can also use a soldered breadboard for wire-wrapping a circuit by soldering headers (at 0.1" spacing) to the main component connections. Wire wrap techniques require a very thin wire and a tool that is used for wrapping the wire around the components or wire wrap posts. This technique takes some getting used to. The benefit of wire wrap is that the circuit can be changed by simply unwrapping the wire and attaching it to a different lead or post. Doing this using a solder technique is more time consuming because you need a desoldering tool and a soldering iron to change connections. Since making changes on a soldered board is much more time consuming, you may be asking why we have chosen to use soldered breadboards. There are two reasons. The first is availability; soldered breadboards are available at any electronics store including Radio Shack. The second reason is because we don't need special wire wrapping tools and wire, which can be very expensive.

Required Tools

Now, let's talk about the tools we'll need. To build the circuits in this book an assortment of tools will be required. Some of these you may already have around the house or office; others you will need to purchase or borrow. Following is a detailed list of tools used:

- **Soldering iron** — A good 20- to 35-watt soldering iron is a must. I use a Weller that has replaceable heating elements and tips. I prefer a 25-watt element and a pinpoint tip for all but surface mount work. (I use a medium screwdriver tip for surface mount work.)

- **Rosin core solder** — I purchase one-pound spools of 60/40 rosin core solder, available at Radio Shack. In almost 30 years of working with electronics, I've used about five spools of solder. I also have a solder pot that I use for tinning the ends of stranded wires. I don't suggest you purchase a solder pot. They are expensive and can easily start a fire if left unattended for too long.

- **Desoldering tool** — I use a metal-barreled desoldering tool to fix my mistakes. There are many types of tools available from inexpensive bulbs (about $4) to desoldering irons (about $15). I also have a desoldering iron that I use if numerous parts are being desoldered.

- **Assorted stranded wire** — A good assortment of 22 and 24 gauge stranded wire is a must. I always have four or five spools of assorted colors in my toolbox. Stranded wire won't break as easily as solid wire and I put just a touch of solder on the end to prevent fraying (also known as "tinning" the end).

- **Assorted cutters and pliers** — I use small and medium ones for cutting wires and holding small parts. I also use a product called Miracle Point for grasping small parts. These little tools are springloaded and have attached magnifying lenses. I also find small cutters from Xcelite to be very useful. These tools are very sharp and maintain their sharp edges well.

- **Magnifying glasses** — When working with small parts a magnifying glass is a must. I use a product I found on the Internet called Helping Hands. It has a small metal base with two alligator clips and a magnifying glass and can hold small work pieces.

- **Small vise** — I use a PanaVise Jr., which is designed to hold small circuit boards.

- **Assorted screwdrivers** — Small and medium flat blade and Philips screwdrivers

- **Assorted tweezers** — A good assortment of stainless steel tweezers

- **Multimeter** — I have numerous multimeters that range in price from about $4 to over $60. Each has a purpose, with the most expensive meter having an RS-232 interface so I can do continuous recording. The least expensive meters I use to test components and low voltages.

■ **Oscilloscope (optional)** — An oscilloscope is a required piece of equipment if you're serious about getting into the electronics area. Oscilloscopes make measuring signals, signal timing, and debugging much easier. I own several oscilloscopes — one analog, one digital, and one USB digital scope. If you are just getting started and have never used an oscilloscope, I would recommend the Parallax USB oscilloscope. It comes with a book full of experiments to familiarize you with oscilloscope functions.

■ **Logic analyzer (optional)** — When developing any type of data communications product, a logic analyzer is almost a must. These devices capture electronic signals and reassemble them into readable data. While this can also be accomplished with a storage oscilloscope, a logic analyzer displays the bit patterns rather than just the signal transitions.

Soldering Techniques

I'm not going into tremendous details on how to solder because there are plenty of good sources of information on the subject already, so I'll just cover the basics. Make sure your work area is well lit and ventilated. This is a must if you're soldering for long periods of time or making printed circuit boards. If you're using a regular soldering iron, make sure you let the iron warm up to the proper temperature before using it. The key to a good solder joint is providing the right amount of heat to the right spot for the right amount of time and the right amount of solder. The higher the wattage of the soldering iron element, the hotter the tip will get. A 20- or 25-watt element provides enough heat to let the solder flow quickly. Do not heat the joint for more than a couple of seconds; applying too much heat for too long a period will damage components. If you're soldering surface mount devices you may want to use a soldering station with low resistance to reduce the risk of static damage. This prevents ground resistance from

finding a path to the component. I don't recommend you use surface mount devices (also known as SMDs) because they require
special consideration when soldering and are hard to work with
due to their small size. When soldering a joint, make certain that
solder covers the entire wire end, not leaving "holes" around the
connection. This will avoid a bad connection and uneven stress
on the wire.

Building the Prototype Circuit Boards

There are many functions of this prototype that are common to
all the microcontrollers we will use. We will start with the least
difficult and progress to the most difficult. Most of the parts we
will use can be obtained at the local Radio Shack store. Whenever
possible the Radio Shack part number will appear in parentheses.
Those parts that are not available at Radio Shack will be noted
along with a source and part number. A current list of resources
will also be available at www.wordware.com/files/
embsys and at www.time-lines.com. Since we have chosen to use
an intelligent LCD display our task has been made somewhat
easier.

To illustrate how we can build plug-compatible RS-232, USB,
and Ethernet interfaces, we will put the RS-232 circuit on a
separate board so we can create a true plug-and-play hardware
interface for our microcontrollers. The first and easiest board to
build is the RS-232 interface. The second board we will build contains the 1-Wire, 3-Wire, clock chip, temperature chip, and fan
relay. We are using a very small relay that has a low current rating. As a result, don't try attaching the fan blower on your
furnace to this as this design is for concept proof only. The third
and final board we will build has keypad functionality, power and
alarm functions, an I²C interface, and a power supply. The reason
we are providing power is because of the amount of current the
Ethernet interface can draw. Let's recap the purpose of each
board.

■ Serial interface board — This board uses just one IC and several capacitors to convert microcontroller signals to/from TTL to RS-232. It will be plug compatible with USB and Ethernet boards.

■ Clock/temperature sensor/1-Wire/3-Wire interface board — This board consolidates all Dallas components and interfaces. This board will illustrate how to build a simple yet reliable 1-Wire interface that can support devices up to 2 feet away. It can also be used later as a model for remote temperature sensors.

■ The LCD, keypad, LED, alarm, I²C communications interface, and power supply board — This board interfaces to our intelligent LCD and contains the keys, LEDs, keypad interfaces, alarm buzzer and LED, and power supply.

The RS-232 Interface Board

The RS-232 interface is well established, as the last technical specification change made to it was in 1991. The interface is defined by the Electronics Industry Association (EIA) and has been widely used for over 40 years. The RS-232 interface connects two devices directly and works by attaching a 9-pin cable between the two devices. In order to facilitate an orderly conversation two types of RS-232 equipment are defined. The first is Data Terminal Equipment, which is also known as DTE. A personal computer is defined as DTE (even though a computer is an intelligent device). In simple terms, DTE is always an origination point of data (and usually in control of the data conversation). The second type of equipment defined in the RS-232 standard is Data Communications Equipment, also known as DCE. DCE is always a data carrier or transport. Figure 7-3 shows a typical RS-232 application.

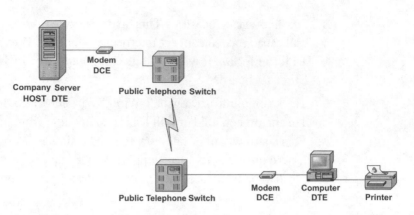

Figure 7-3

As you can see from this illustration, any data host or consumer is DTE and the modem or data communications equipment is DCE. This is the easiest way to remember how a piece of equipment should be defined. If it is a data source, it is DTE; if it is a data carrier, it is DCE. To non-communications engineers these definitions have been a source of confusion over the years simply because we think of a PC as a piece of communications equipment rather than a piece of terminal equipment. By applying these simple rules, the public telephone switch in the example above is used only as a data transport.

The RS-232 hardware interface originally used a 25-pin cable to connect devices, but in recent years that has been replaced by a 9-pin D-Sub connector known as a DB9. By standard definition, DTE normally has a male connector and DCE has a female connector (but only if DTE/DCE were fully implemented). Using the analogy in Figure 7-3, our embedded system will be DCE since the PC is defined as DTE. We could also make this determination because the PC is considered the host and in control of the communications flow. If we were to define our embedded system as DTE it would require using a null-modem cable and could cause potential problems in connecting it to a host system. In that case, either an extra adapter or jumper box would be needed to allow both sides to properly communicate.

Rather than defining a hybrid communications system, we will define the embedded system as DCE. Using these definitions the 9-pin cable definition of RS-232 is shown in the following tables.

Table 7-1: Data Communications Equipment (DCE) RS-232 pin definitions

Pin Number	Signal Name	Direction
1	Data Carrier Detect (DCD)	To DTE
2	Transmit Data (TX)	To DTE
3	Receive Data (RX)	From DTE
4	DTE Ready (DTE)	From DTE
5	Signal Ground	From DTE
6	DCE Ready (DCE)	To DTE
7	Clear To Send (CTS)	From DTE
8	Request To Send (RTS)	To DTE
9	Ring Indicator (RI)	To DTE

Table 7-2: Data Terminal Equipment (DTE) RS-232 pin definitions

Pin Number	Signal Name	Direction
1	Receive Signal Detect	From DCE
2	Receive Data (RX)	From DCE
3	Transmit Data (TX)	To DCE
4	DTE Ready (DTE)	To DCE
5	Signal Ground	To DCE
6	DCE Ready (DCE)	From DCE
7	Request-To-Send (RTS)	To DCE
8	Clear-To-Send (CTS)	From DCE
9	Ring Indicator (RI)	From DCE

RS-232 Signal Voltage Levels

Normal voltage levels range from 3 to 5 volts for today's microcontrollers. RS-232 voltage levels are different from the "normal" voltages. TTL voltages are in one of two states: high or low. A high TTL state is +5 volts. A low TTL state is +0 volts. These voltages are measured against the ground signal. RS-232, on the other hand, operates to a maximum of +12 and −12 volt signaling. The higher voltage levels allow an RS-232 signal to travel longer distances without additional devices needed to repeat the signal. In the early days of computing we designed line driver circuits that would boost the 5-volt signal level to the +12 and −12 levels. Over the years this method has been replaced with single chips that boost signals and handle the complete RS-232 TTL conversion to and from the host.

Note:

Many RS-232 circuits that appear in publications use +5 and −5 volts instead of +12 and −12. While it's true that in recent years many RS-232 drivers in PCs can operate fine at these lower voltage levels, not all types of equipment can operate at these lower voltage levels without modifications. In addition, using RS-232 at +5 and −5 volts over long distances can stress the communications interface components, causing premature component failure or erratic behavior.

The MAX232 Serial Interface Chip

One of the easiest and most frequently used solutions to the voltage differences for TTL and RS-232 is the MAX232 chip from Maxim Semiconductor. This chip converts 5-volt TTL signals to a minimum of +8 and −8 volts. There are several variations of these chips. The two biggest differences are the number of RS-232 interfaces and the use of internal or external capacitors. For our needs we will use the BASIC MAX232CPE chip, which has two TTL-RS-232 level converters. Each level converter handles the conversion of two TTL lines. We will use the first for data transmit and receive and the second for CTS/RTS handshaking. Over the years many other vendors have entered the market with their own version of the MAX232 chip. I happen to have several of the TI chips available so we will use that component for the heart of our circuit, but you can use any MAX232CPE-compatible chip as a direct replacement for the TI chip I'm using since they all share the same pinouts. If you decide to use a different chip, make sure the pinouts are the same or change your wiring to accommodate the new pinouts. Power and ground connections are not the same on all versions of the MAX232 chips. The MAX232CPE chip I am using requires a 1-microfarad capacitor. Some require only a .1-microfarad cap, so be certain you get the right capacitors if you choose a different MAX232 type component. The MAX232CPE is a 16-pin chip that has two complete RS-232 transceivers.

These chips work by using the capacitors to boost the signal voltage levels to operate within the RS-232 signal definitions. This type of circuit is known as a charge pump. The capacitor charges and when it reaches its discharge level, it pumps the higher voltage to the circuit. This chip comes in several different forms, but for our purpose we will use the 16-pin DIP, which is easy to work with and does not require surface mounting.

Note:

One of the biggest sources of errors in defining RS-232 electrically is made by not properly defining the DTE/DCE pins, which causes a hybrid to be developed. These types of errors lead to designs that are difficult to understand, wire, and debug. Avoid this problem by clearly defining the wiring between our embedded system and PC. Pay particular attention to the three different levels of handshaking available in the RS-232 standard. Two of these are hardware handshakes and the third is a software handshake. These handshake methods are defined as follows.

The DSR/DTR Handshake Described

The first handshake method we will cover is known as DTR/DSR, which stands for Data Terminal Ready and Data Set Ready. This handshake is generally used to let the data terminal or the data set equipment make itself known to the other. In short, looking at this signal tells if a matching piece of equipment is attached and powered up at the other end. It is not an indicator that the other piece of equipment is ready to accept data. For our purpose we will not use this handshake, opting instead to tie the pins for these signals together.

The RTS/CTS Handshake Described

The second handshake available is the RTS/CTS handshake, which stands for Request To Send/Clear To Send. This handshake is used to acknowledge it is OK to send data and/or data is ready to be sent. This handshake is also known as hardware flow control, since its primary use is controlling the flow or exchange of data.

The XON/XOFF Handshake Described

The third and final handshake is a software-only handshake. It can be used in addition to the RTS/CTS handshake or as its replacement. In this case, an XOFF character is sent to the transmitter notifying it to stop sending data. When the receiver is ready to accept data, an XON character is sent to start data flowing again. Again, this handshake is controlled by the host, which is defined as DTE.

Hardware and Software Handshake Considerations

If we choose not to use the handshaking, we may experience data loss. Remember that our protocol checks to see that only good data packets are accepted. If a bad data packet is received, the entire packet is thrown out, making the sender transmit the entire packet again and taking valuable time. While the amount of time this takes on a PC host is minimal, our microcontroller has better things to do than continuously ask for the same data over and over again. Also keep in mind that a new PC runs at upward of 2 gigahertz, whereas a microcontroller runs at from 4 to 50 megahertz, making a PC about 40 times faster. To prevent data transmission errors we will implement RTS/CTS hardware handshaking. This will cost us the use of two additional processor pins, but it will assure data integrity and notify the host if the thermostat goes offline for extended periods, which could be a symptom of other problems. If the thermostat goes offline, the CTS line will be low, telling the host no data can be sent. The CTS line will also be used to regulate the flow of data coming into the microcontroller, acting as a traffic cop. This hopefully will prevent buffer overruns and avoid unnecessary data retransmissions.

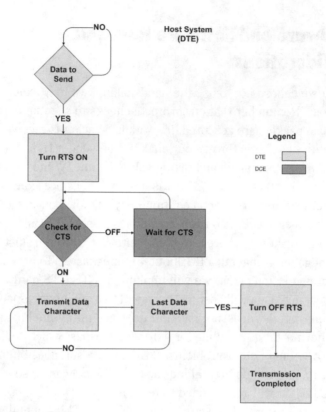

Figure 7-4

If the host system (DTE) has data to send, it first checks the Clear To Send (CTS) line to see if the embedded system is ready to accept data. If it is ready, the host will turn on the Request To Send (RTS) line, send a data character, check the status of CTS again (to see if the receive buffer on the DCE is full), and start the loop over again until the last character has been sent. The host will then turn off RTS. Remember that the host in this case is the Windows or UNIX system. In Figure 7-5 we illustrate how DCE handles the request from DTE.

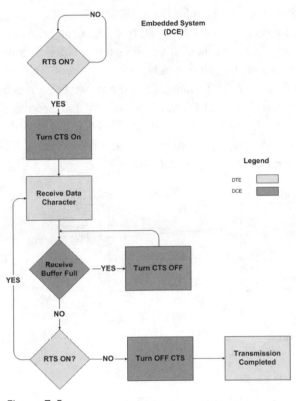

Figure 7-5

In Figures 7-4 and 7-5 we see how the DTE controls all data flow through the use of the RTS line. This is important because it means that DTE is being used as the RS-232 session manager. This is where many people get confused on how RS-232 communications works. The same signals exist on both sides of the interface. The difference is in where the pins get attached. In Figure 7-6 we have an RTS and CTS signal on both the DTE and DCE sides of the interface. At first glance it would appear that if pin 7 were RTS on the DCE, then pin 7 would be RTS on the DTE end. That assumption would be wrong.

This is one of the biggest areas of confusion when implementing a true RS-232 interface. Remembering how to properly implement this interface is both easy and straightforward. The signal pins are crossed for the CTS/RTS signals. This means that RTS at either end gets attached to CTS at the other end. If the RTS interface isn't used, it's always a good idea to connect the CTS/RTS pins together locally.

In Figure 7-6 RTS and CTS are crossed at both ends. In addition, please note that DTR, DTS, and Pin 1 are connected together. This indicates that the DTE/DCE interface is not used, and by tying the signals together they will always indicate ready if the handshake line is turned on.

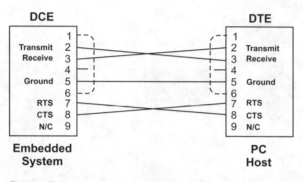

Figure 7-6

Figure 7-6 shows a top view of how our DTE and DCE will be connected. The embedded system end is a female DB9 connector since it is defined as DCE. This will allow any standard DB9 straight through serial cable to be used in connecting the two systems together.

To recap the RS-232 interface, we have three levels of hand-shakes. We have the DTE/DCE, which is really just an equipment handshake. It can only tell us if two mating pieces of equipment are connected and only if they are both turned on. Next we have the CTS/RTS interface, which is really a data traffic cop used to signal when data can be transmitted. Finally, we have the XON/XOFF interface, which is a software-only implementation of a data handshake.

Building the RS-232 Interface

The MAX232CPE serial interface chip can be broken into two different functional groups: power and data. The power management portion of the chip includes two charge pumps. Again, these are used to increase a voltage level through the use of capacitors. The first charge pump utilizes pins 1, 2, and 3 to provide a positive voltage of at least 8.5 volts. The second charge pump utilizes pins 4, 5, and 6 in providing a negative voltage of at least –8.5 volts. Both of these charge pump circuits claim to be voltage doubling, which means that +10 volts and –10 volts are provided; however, the chips are rated to provide at least 8.5 volts and RS-232 standards will work fine with these voltages. If we were going long distances, then we would want to consider increasing these voltages to +10 volts and –10 volts to provide adequate signal strength, but since we are only a few feet apart this isn't important.

The data portion of the chip is the RS-232 transceivers. Each transceiver uses four pins, two for TTL level I/O and two for RS-232 level I/O. The second transceiver uses pins 7, 8, 9, and 10. Pins 9 and 10 are TTL I/O, with pins 7 and 8 being RS-232 level I/O signals. Transceiver 1 is on pins 11, 12, 13, and 14 with pins 11 and 12 being TTL I/O, while pins 13 and 14 are RS-232 level I/O. You may have noticed the TTL pins are grouped together in pins 9 through 12. The remaining two pins are ground (pin 15) and power (pin 16), which carries +5 volts. Figure 7-7 shows how the functional divisions on the MAX232 chip are broken down.

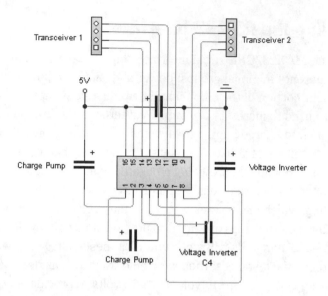

Figure 7-7

Let's go through the interface step by step. Take a look at Figure 7-8. First, you'll notice an absence of pins 1, 4, 6, and 9 being used on the DB9 connector. These pins aren't used in our application; however, pins 1, 4, and 6 get tied together just in case the host accidentally looks for DTR/DSR signaling. After tying these pins together we will assert the signals when the system initializes. Asserting those signals means they will be driven to a high state (+8.5 volts), which indicates a "ready" condition. Pin 9 was left off altogether since it isn't used at all in our design. I've tested the configuration on several systems and have not had any problems with it.

Next, you will note that the ground pin on the chip (pin 15) is connected to the ground on the DB9 (pin 5). This connection is very important since it equalizes the ground on both ends of the connection. If this ground is not connected or is improperly connected, the integrity of all the other signals will be compromised. This could cause all types of problems that would be all but impossible to diagnose, including erratic data.

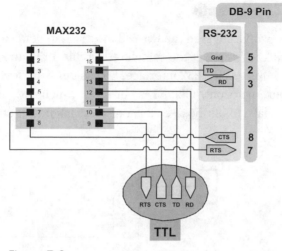

Figure 7-8

Finally, we have the DB9 connector as viewed from the front. In Figure 7-9 a standard DB9 is shown with the RS-232 signal definitions as we are looking at the front of the connector.

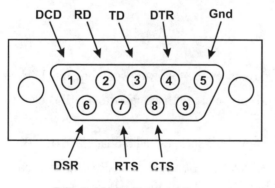

DB-9 Male Front View

Figure 7-9

Remember that DCD, DTR, and DSR (pins 1, 4, and 6) get tied together at both ends of the cable.

The RS-232 Schematic

Now that we've covered the RS-232 interface in detail and the handshake, let's look at the completed circuit. In Figure 7-10 we have a completed RS-232 interface. SV1 is our TTL level connection to our microcontroller. X1 is our DB9, which is the RS-232 level interface to our host. SV2 is our external power and ground interface.

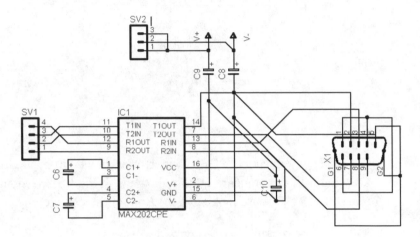

Figure 7-10

This board requires the following components. They are:

- One prototype board that supports a DIP socket (Radio Shack 276-159)

- One 16-pin DIP socket (Radio Shack 276-1998)

- One MAX232CPE or equivalent RS-232 transceiver (DigiKey Part #296-6940-5-ND)

- Four 1 µF electrolytic capacitors (Radio Shack 272-996)

- One DB9 female solder type connector (Radio Shack 276-1538)

- Assorted 22 gauge stranded wire (Radio Shack 278-1221)

- Two 2-wire terminal blocks (Radio Shack 276-1388)

To build this circuit, follow these steps:

1. Solder the 16-pin socket to the prototype board. Remember that the top of the socket is the end with the "U" recess in the center. When mounting the socket, leave the unused holes at the top of the board; we will use these for power connections.

2. Cut a 6-inch piece each of red and black 22 gauge wire and strip 3/8 inch of shielding from each end. Carefully apply a small amount of solder to each end of the wire to prevent fraying.

3. There are several additional solder pads not being used on the prototype board at the top. Solder one end of the red wire to the top leftmost hole.

4. Next, solder one end of the black wire to the top rightmost hole.

5. If step 1 was completed properly, there will be a second hole on the board directly beneath the two holes we just attached wires to. Using short pieces of red and black wires, connect the two holes and solder the jumpers in place.

6. Solder a capacitor across pins 1 and 3 of the 16-pin socket, making sure the + symbol is toward pin number 1.

7. Solder a second capacitor between pin 2 and the +5 volt supply, making sure the + side of the capacitor is toward pin 2.

8. Solder the third capacitor's – lead to pin 6 and the remaining lead to ground.

9. Solder the remaining capacitor's + lead to pin 16 and the – lead to ground.

10. Solder a jumper from the +5 supply to pin 16. This lead provides power to the chip.

11. Solder a jumper from pin 15 to ground. This will provide the ground to power the chip.

Note:

This jumper is in addition to the capacitor we attached above. The capacitors we used on pins 15 and 16 are filters to prevent noise from getting into the transceiver circuits. The chip will not work properly if pins 15 and 16 are not connected properly.

12. Cut four pieces of 22 gauge wire approximately 4 inches long and strip 3/8 inch of insulation off each end.

13. Solder one end of each wire to the solder pads attached to pins 9, 10, 11, and 12, leaving the other ends unattached. These are the TTL lines that will go to the microcontrollers.

14. Solder terminal blocks to the solder pads attached to pins 7 and 8, and 13, and 14. These are the RS-232 lines that will go to the DB9-F.

If you soldered the RS-232 wires as directed in step 14 your board will look similar to the photograph in Figure 7-11.

Note:

Figure 7-11 shows the board using tantalum capacitors instead of electrolytic. This was done to have plenty of room for labels in the photo. While you can use tantalum capacitors instead of electrolytic, tantalum capacitors cost much more than the equivalent electrolytic. The wires in the top of the photograph go to power and ground connections on the microcontroller. The resistor and LED provide a visual indicator that power has been applied. The lines marked 3, 4, 5, and 6 are the TTL lines that go to the microcontroller TX, RX, RTS, and CTS lines. Lines 1, 2, 7, and 8 are the RS-232 lines that get connected to the DB9-F.

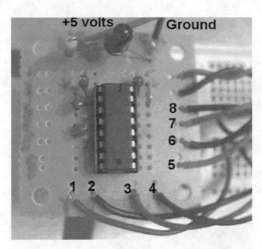

Figure 7-11

The data lines in Figure 7-11 are numbered as follows:

1) RS-232 RTS signal

2) RS-232 CTS signal

3) TTL CTS signal

4) TTL RTS signal

5) TTL TD signal

6) TTL RD signal

7) RS-232 RD signal

8) RS-232 TD signal

If you used terminals as directed in step 14, your board will look similar to the following.

Figure 7-12

Next, we will solder the wires to the DB9 so we can attach it to an RS-232 cable. This is very simple.

1. First, cut eight pieces of wire about 4 inches long and strip 3/8 inch of insulation from each end.

2. Now solder each wire to the DB9 by inserting the wire into the connector as far as it will go. Apply a small amount of solder around the joint where the wire and connector are joined. Do not use too much solder or apply the soldering iron for too long since the area around the connector is plastic. Solder all eight wires.

3. Apply a small amount of solder to the other end of each wire to prevent it from fraying. Just apply a small amount to change the color of the copper wire to silver.

4. Next, using either a wire nut or a small piece of electrical tape, connect the wires together that are attached to pins 1, 4, and 6. This will tie the carrier detect (DCD), data-terminal-ready (DTR), and data-set-ready together (DSR).

When the COM port on the PC brings DTR high, it will also raise DSR, thereby looping the signal back. This will fool the system into believing DTR/DSR is provided and eliminate any problems related to DTR/DSR availability on the embedded system.

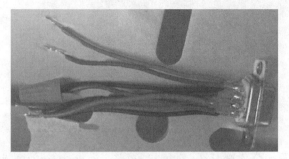

Figure 7-13

Remember to use a female DB9 connector!

Testing the RS-232 Interface

We have finally reached the point where we are ready to connect and test the RS-232 board. To do the testing I'm using the BASIC Stamp 2p Development Board, the RS-232 board, the DB9 connector we made, and a PC running Windows, FreeBSD, or Linux. At this point we will install and run MicroComm, a simple terminal program I wrote for this project RS-232 board.

Setting Up the BASIC Stamp Development Board

We will begin by setting up the jumpers on the BASIC Stamp Development Board. To allow plenty of space for your fingers, jumper BASIC Stamp pins 15, 14, 13, and 12 from the connector to the prototype area of the board as shown in Figure 7-14.

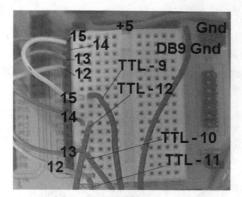

Figure 7-14

In Figure 7-14 the +5 and Gnd at the very top are connected to the power and ground connections on the RS-232 board. The DB9 Gnd connection is attached to pin 5 on the DB9 to provide a common ground. This connection is required to assure data integrity. On the far left side at the top are BASIC Stamp pins 15, 14, 13, and 12. They are connected to the MAX232CPE pins as follows:

> Stamp pin 15 → Max232 pin 9
> Stamp pin 14 → Max232 pin 12
> Stamp pin 13 → Max232 pin 10
> Stamp pin 12 → Max232 pin 11

With these four connections we have hooked up our TTL data and handshake lines. Next, we move on to the RS-232 board and hook up the RS-232 signal lines.

In Figure 7-15 we connect the RS-232 level signals to the DB9 as follows:

> Max232 pin 7 → DB9 pin 8
> Max232 pin 8 → DB9 pin 7
> Max232 pin 13 → DB9 pin 3
> Max232 pin 14 → DB9 pin 2

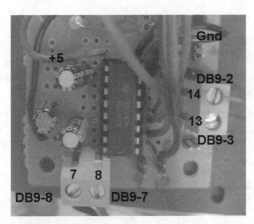

Figure 7-15

Troubleshooting

This is a very simple circuit. If it doesn't appear to be working, use a multimeter to check the DC voltage by touching the black lead to pin 15 and the red lead to pin 16. If you get a reading of 5 volts, the MAX232 chip is getting power. If you get a reading of –5 volts, you have the power and ground wires reversed. If you have the proper voltage but still can't send or receive data, then check your capacitors to be certain they have the + side positioned properly. If the polarity on the capacitors is reversed, the capacitors can explode, so be careful. Other problems that could cause the circuit not to work are listed below.

- Improper baud rate — This circuit relies on the baud rate being set to 9600 baud, 8 data bits, 1 stop bit, and no parity. In the code in Listing 7-1 that follows, this is defined by the number 110. If the second parameter is not 110, you need to change it so you will see good data.

- Improper handshake — Check to be certain the handshake lines are properly connected; otherwise, you may not be able to send data at all. The uComm window (described next and shown in Figure 7-16) will display CTS and RTS if properly connected. Check the data line with an oscilloscope. Connect a channel 1 probe to the transmit data line and attach the ground to pin 5 on the DB9. Set your voltage levels to at least 2 volts (preferably 5) and your timing to 5 ms. If data is being sent, the data bits should be able to be disguised at this speed. If no state transitions are seen, then go back and check your circuit to be sure everything is connected properly, power is properly connected, and a good ground connection has been made.

Finishing Touches

To finish our RS-232 hardware setup, connect a serial cable between a host PC and the BASIC Stamp board. Apply power to the board and start the BASIC Stamp Editor program. To test our RS-232 board, enter the following program into the editor:

Listing 7-1

```
//
// {$PBASIC 2.5}
//

// Test Program for RS-232 output using MAX232 with RTS/CTS Handshaking
// for Embedded Systems Desktop Integration
// Copyright 2004 - Oliver H. Bailey
//
// Pins are assigned in the following order:
// Pin 12 - Transmit Data    (TX or TD) =>
// Pin 14 - Receive Data     (RX or RD) <=
// Pin 13 - Clear To Send    (CTS)      =>
// Pin 15 - Request To Send  (RTS)      <=
//
// This program uses the FPin variable on SerIn and SerOut commands. Example follows below
// Serout 12\15, 110, "Mary had a little lamb" CR, LF
InData VAR Byte
OutData VAR Byte


LOW 14                                  // Set RD Low
LOW 15                                  // Set RTS Low

Main:
```

```
SERIN 14\13, 110, [InData]              // 14=RD,13=CTS,110=9600,N,8,1
OutData = InData                        // Assign to output variable
IF OutData = 13 THEN                    // Turn CR into CRLF
   SEROUT 12\15, 110, [CR, LF]          // Echo Back to Terminal
   DEBUG CR, LF                         // Echo to Debug port
ENDIF

SEROUT 12\15, 110, [OutData]            // Just Print the RAW data
DEBUG OutData                           // Echo to Debug Port
GOTO Main:                              // Start Again
```

The above program reads the data coming into the RS-232 port and echoes it back unless it's a carriage return, in which case it adds a line feed before echoing the data back. Once you've typed the program in, run it. You will see a debug window open if the program downloaded and started successfully. If you want to see the debug data, connect another serial cable to the DB9 we attached to the RS-232 board and install uComm as shown below.

Running uComm

To see if the RS-232 board is working properly, I wrote a small terminal program that I call uComm (u = micro, hence microComm). uComm is a very small program (350 K) that opens a communications port, sets up hardware handshaking, and starts a terminal window. uComm is very basic. It only supports communications ports 1 and 2, and is limited in baud rate, data bits, and parity selections. To change uComm settings, drag the cursor over the terminal portion of the display and right-click your mouse. A popup menu will appear. You'll notice many features are grayed out. Those features are available in the full uComm product, which is available from the downloadable files (see www.wordware.com/files/embsys or www.time-lines.com/embedbk1 for more information). Figure 7-16 shows the uComm display.

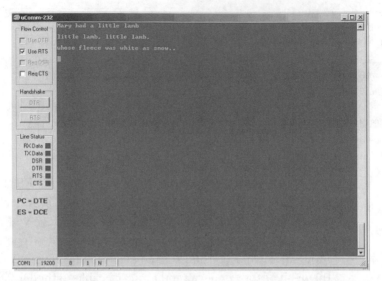

Figure 7-16

If everything is wired correctly, anything you type in the terminal window will be echoed in the terminal. The uComm program is set to full duplex. This, combined with the fact that both SERIN and SEROUT in the above Stamp program use hardware handshake lines, causes the characters to be echoed when typed. When uComm starts, the Use RTS option is unchecked. If you move the cursor to the terminal window and begin typing, you will see the TX Data LED turn red but nothing typed will be echoed back. The reason for this is because the RTS line has not been used to handshake with the Stamp. Type a few characters and then check the Use RTS box. Now you should see the characters you type displayed as you type them. This means the CTS/RTS handshake is working; otherwise, nothing would be displayed. If you checked Use RTS and still don't see any characters that were typed, try checking your wire connections to be certain everything is connected properly.

The Time and Temperature Board

The Dallas 1-Wire Protocol

Now that we have a working RS-232 interface, let's move on to our time and temperature board. If you've never worked with the Dallas 1-Wire interface, it is a variation on serial communications. 1-Wire devices can operate in one of two modes. The first mode requires a separate 5-volt power supply line. To operate a 1-Wire device in this mode actually requires three wires: +5 volts, data, and ground. The second mode of operation is known as parasitic mode. Parasitic mode consolidates power and data into a single wire by using a capacitor (like the charge pump used in the previous circuit). In parasitic mode the data response from the device is powered by the data inquiry from the master, thus eliminating the need for a separate power wire. For simplicity and educational purposes, we will use the first mode, which has separate power, data, and ground wires. The 1-Wire network has some similarities to an Ethernet-type LAN in that multiple hubs can exist and have multiple devices attached to each hub. I wouldn't recommend putting large numbers of 1-Wire devices on a single data line because the data rate can be slow if the accuracy for time and temperature required is high. Even so, the 1-Wire network can operate very well hundreds or even thousands of feet from the network master.

1-Wire networks are broken into three categories: light duty, medium duty, and heavy duty. What makes these categories different is the distance from the network master (hub) at which a remote device can successfully be operated. A light-duty network is considered effective to three meters or less (about 11 feet). A medium-duty network is effective to over 100 meters, or about 330 feet. A heavy-duty network operates at distances greater than 200 meters. Even though we are building a standalone device, we do have a requirement that allows expansion of the 1-Wire network. For that reason we will design, build, and test both a simple, light-duty 1-Wire network and a medium-duty 1-Wire network. Before continuing I should note that operating 1-Wire devices over long distances should be done using Cat 5 Ethernet cable, which is the same cable used in computer LANs. Cat 5 cable offers the best choice of line resistance over long distances.

There are many types of 1-Wire devices but for our purpose we are concerned with just four types, discussed in the following sections. In order to make effective use of a single wire for data these devices are broken down into device families, each with a unique family code or family ID. In addition to the family codes, each 1-Wire device has a unique address (or serial number) that no other 1-Wire device has. This address can identify a location, a specific device, a board, or even be used for a product serial number. Depending on the device type, each device also has a set of commands to read, write, and perform other tasks associated with the functions of that particular device family.

When using a 1-Wire temperature chip, there are commands for converting and returning the current temperature, setting high and low temperature alarm level, and reading temporary memory. On the 1-Wire switches and variable potentiometers there are commands for opening and closing switches, and setting and reading the potentiometers. Devices like the DS2404 also support multiple interface protocols at once, which allow them to be used as a data drop station for a local processor. This means the clock function could be addressed using the 1-Wire interface while the onboard static RAM could be addressed using the 3-Wire interface for higher speed memory access by a local processor. This is how dual-port RAM works.

The DS1820 and DS1822 Temperature Chips

The DS1820 temperature chip is a high-resolution temperature chip. It utilizes the 1-Wire network and is used where accurate and high-resolution temperature tracking is required. The DS1822 is a very cost-effective digital thermometer and temperature conversion chip. The DS1822 is less expensive but offers lower resolution of temperature readings. The DS1822 has programmable temperature resolution from 9 to 12 bits with the default being 12-bit resolution. That means the chip has a maximum resolution of +–0.0625 degree Centigrade or about 2 degrees Fahrenheit. This chip also offers high and low temperature alarm settings. The alarm feature allows a trigger to be set at high and/or low temperature readings. Once the trigger temperature is reached, an alarm condition is set and will remain until it is reset by the 1-Wire master. This is one way of logging temperature extremities.

The DS2404 Time/Date/Static RAM Chip

The DS2404 chip is also known as the EconoRam chip since it offers 512 bytes of static RAM in addition to time and date functions. It can easily be battery backed up. The time and date functions are free running counters, so date and time comparison variables need to be provided to set a base date and time reference point. The static RAM and counters are kept in adjacent memory locations. One other feature of the DS2404 is the ability to keep a counter of power brownouts or outages. This feature can only be used when battery backup is provided, as it is dependent upon the battery voltage.

The DS2890 Potentiometer

This 1-Wire device allows the potentiometer to be read and set using the 1-Wire network. For our purpose this chip could offer one solution for variable speed fan control. The data line allows the potentiometer's wiper to be set or read via the 1-Wire network.

The DS2406 Digital Switch

The DS2406 is a digital switch. This could be used in conjunction with the DS2890 to provide fan power control. It could also be used to turn an alarm on or off in the case of a temperature alarm.

Combined, these devices offer a wide variety of options for our embedded system. We will not implement all of these devices at once, opting instead to develop the 1-Wire network interface and add the temperature sensor, real-time clock, and digital switch functions as needs require.

The Dallas 3-Wire Protocol

The 1-Wire protocol trades speed for distance. Before we continue, let's briefly discuss the Dallas 3-Wire protocol. Our clock chip is the DS2404 and supports two methods of access. The first is the 1-Wire interface, which we examined above. The second method of access to this chip is the Dallas 3-Wire protocol. The benefit of the 3-Wire protocol is speed. Unlike the 1-Wire protocol, this protocol allows us to access the chip at much higher speeds. The three wires are defined as:

- Reset line
- Clock line
- Data line

Using the 3-Wire protocol, the reset line is used to turn communication on and off. If the reset line is low, then no 3-Wire communications can take place. If the reset line is high, the next step in communicating is to place the clock in the proper state and send the data bytes. Once the data has been sent, the clock line is changed back to an idle state. What makes this dual interface interesting is that in addition to the time, the DS2404 also has memory and both the 1- and 3-Wire interfaces can be used so long as you can handle contention issues. This means that the 1-Wire could be used for exchanging data over long distances with a master while the 3-Wire is used to communicate with a local processor that collects and stores data. Before the 3-Wire protocol can be used, the 1-Wire interface must be initialized and reset.

A Light-Duty 1-Wire Network

There are several different ways to implement the 1-Wire protocol. Which method you use depends on the overall distance you
need the network to operate within. Let's first explore a
light-duty 1-Wire interface. The Dallas documentation defines a
light-duty interface as one that operates at distances no longer
than 3 meters. Now you may be asking why anyone would want
to implement a 3-meter interface, so here is one example of
where this would work very well. If you had a walk-in freezer
control accessible on the outside of the freezer, you could attach
the sensor inside the freezer by simply drilling a hole to the
inside area. You could also keep track of a room's temperature by
having multiple sensors on different walls. In either of these situations, a light-duty 1-Wire interface would work just fine and is
inexpensive to implement.

This interface requires only one resistor (2.2 kOhm resistor
(Radio Shack 271-1121)), a +5 volt power supply, and a ground
wire. While we are using the BASIC Stamp for developing this
interface, it can just as easily be implemented with the PIC or
PSoC.

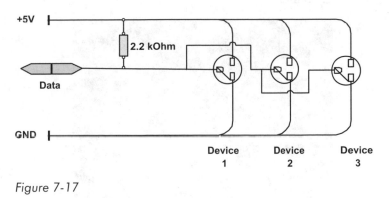

Figure 7-17

As you can see from the figure, only three wires are needed to build this interface and only one processor pin is used. Implementing this circuit takes only a few minutes and a 2.2 kOhm resistor. In Figure 7-18 the circuit has been implemented on a solderless breadboard.

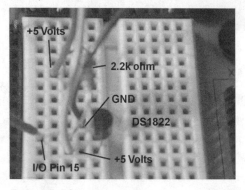

Figure 7-18

The power pin of the DS1822 is always located on the left with the flat side of the device facing up. In Figure 7-19 you can see how few components are in this circuit and how easy it is to implement.

Figure 7-19

The schematic in Figure 7-20 illustrates how our completed circuit will be assembled. Since this board does not have its own power supply, both power and ground must be provided from an external source. Since the 1-Wire interface requires +5 volts and ground, +5 is supplied through pin 1 on either JP8 or JP1, and ground is provided on pin 3 of the same connectors. Pin 2 of JP8 and JP1 is connected to the 1-Wire data line of the DS1822. To provide better 1-Wire communications, R4 is a 2.2 K resistor between +5 volts and the 1-Wire data line.

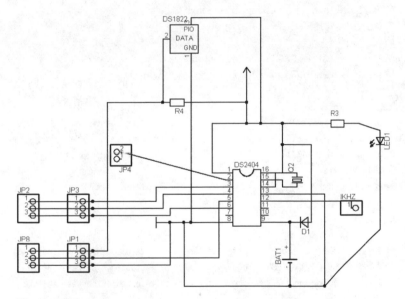

Figure 7-20

The DS2404 has both 1-Wire and 3-Wire I/O. Headers JP8 and JP1 are the 1-Wire interface, while headers JP2 and JP3 interface to a 3-Wire bus. Jumper JP4 is the interrupt output. The jumper marked 1KHZ is actually a 1-kHz output and is strictly for test purposes. BAT1 is the CR2032 holder for battery backup.

A Simple 1-Wire Test Program

To test this circuit, start the BASIC Stamp Editor and type in the following program:

Listing 7-2

```
// {$STAMP BS2p}
// {$PBASIC 2.5}


// Test Program for Dallas 1-Wire Thermometer
// for Embedded Systems Desktop Integration
// Copyright 2004 - Oliver H. Bailey
//
// This program uses PIN 15 for both Input and Output
// Pin 15 - Transmit/Receive 1-Wire Data      <=>
//
Temp VAR Word                          // Temperature Storage Variable
TempLo VAR Temp.LOWBYTE                 // Temperature Low Order Byte
TempHi VAR Temp.HIGHBYTE                // Temperature High Order Byte
TempSign VAR temp.BIT11                 // Temperature Sign Bit
signBit VAR Bit
tempCel VAR Word                        // Centigrade
tempFar VAR Word                        // Fahrenheit
ChkLoop VAR Byte                        // Three attempts


// This is a very simple program for testing a DS1822 Temp sensor.  Rather than using
// the traditional Read ROM command we simply make an attempt to read the temperature.
// If a device is present then the temperature is returned; otherwise it is assumed
// no DS1822 is attached.

ChkLoop = 0                             // Set to Zero Tries


Main:
  GOSUB ChkDev                          // Check for DS1822
  // Reaching this line requires a response from the DS1822
  tmpLoop:                              // Read temperature loop start
    GOSUB Read_Temp                     // Gosub read temperature
    DEBUG HOME, SDEC tempCel, " C", CR  // Display Centigrade
    DEBUG SDEC tempFar, " F", CR        // Display Fahrenheit
    PAUSE 500                           // Wait
  GOTO tmpLoop                          // Start again
```

```
// If the code reaches here, it was by mistake.
GOTO forever                              // Loop forever


// Check Device Subroutine
ChkDev:
  OWOUT 15, 1, [$CC, $44]                 // Check for temperature
NotDone:
  PAUSE 25                                // Wait for response
  OWIN 15, 4, [Temp]                      // Check Status
  ChkLoop = ChkLoop+1                     // Increment Loop Counter
  IF ChkLoop = 100 THEN no_Dev            // Max Tries then Stop
  IF Temp = 0 THEN                        // No Response
    GOTO NotDone                          // Otherwise Try Again
  ENDIF
  RETURN                                  // Return if Found


// Read and Convert Temperature
Read_Temp:
  OWOUT 15, 1, [$CC, $44]                 // Check for temperature
  notReady:                               // Start completion loop
  PAUSE 25                                // Wait for response
  OWIN 15, 4, [Temp]                      // Check results
  IF Temp = 0 THEN notReady               // Not done, start again
  OWOUT 15, 1, [$CC, $BE]                 // Read Scratchpad Temp
  OWIN 15, 2, [TempLo, TempHi]            // Get Temp Bytes
  signBit = TempSign                      // Get sign bit (0 = +, 1 = -)
  tempCel = Temp                          // Store to variable
  tempCel = tempCel >> 4                  // Store Temp to variable
  IF (signBit = 0) THEN PosCel            // Shift to get actual temperature
    tempCel = tempCel | $FF00             // Check for sub-zero
                                          // Adjust if below zero

  PosCel:
    tempFar = tempCel */ $01CD            // Positive Temperature
    IF signBit = 0 THEN PosFar            // Adjust for display
      tempFar = tempFar | $FF00           // Check for sub-zero
                                          // Adjust Fahrenheit scale

  PosFar:
    tempFar = tempFar + 32                // Not sub-zero
  RETURN                                  // Add 32 for Fahrenheit display
                                          // All Done, return


  no_Dev:
```

```
DEBUG "No DS1822 Device Found", CR      // No response at startup so display
                                        // message
forever:                                //
  GOTO forever                          // and loop forever
```

This code listing performs the following functions:

1. Tests for the existence of a DS1822.

2. Runs in a continuous loop, taking a new temperature reading
    every 500 milliseconds. This value could be lengthened but
    at half a second any temperature changes will be displayed
    quickly.

3. A safety "loop forever" routine if something goes wrong.

That's all the code needed to check out our circuit. If it works,
you will see a screen similar to the one in Figure 7-21.

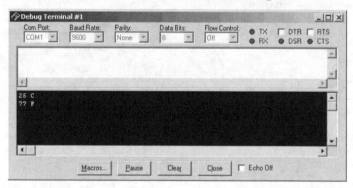

Figure 7-21

This is a very simple test. The first line displays the temperature
in Celsius and the second line displays the temperature in Fahrenheit. This procedure confirms that our circuit works just fine.
While we haven't added the DS2404 yet, we now know the circuit will read the DS1822 temperature chip. Next, we'll add the
DS2404 time and date chip before building the main I/O board.

Adding the DS2404

Your circuit would be complete if you only wanted to watch the temperature rise or fall, but we need to add support for the date and time. The temperature sensor looks like a transistor; this is called a TO92 case. It is round with a flat spot on the face of the part that has the part number inscribed on it. Mounting this type of component is very easy and the holes can be close together (0.1"). The DS2404, on the other hand, does not come in the same style case. The DS2404 has three packaging options but for our purpose we will use the standard 16-pin dual inline package (DIP). This will make handling the chip easier and prevent us from having to worry about surface mount parts. The DS2404 is a very versatile but complicated part. The following list shows the major features of this device:

- 1-Wire interface
- 3-Wire interface
- Reset input
- Timer interrupt
- 1 Hz output
- ROM serial number
- 512-byte battery-backed RAM
- Time and date counters
- Power cycle counter
- External battery backup

There are two voltage connections for power and battery backup connections to keep the clock running if power goes down. Figure 7-22 shows the DS2404 16-pin DIP layout.

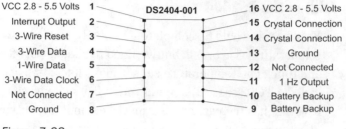

Figure 7-22

Of all the 1-Wire products this device is one of the most complicated. Since this is a book about communications, we will
implement both the 1- and 3-Wire interfaces even though we are
interested only in the timekeeping, battery backup, power cycle
counter, and memory functions. The main reason we've selected
this device is for the 1-Wire network access. This device can be
added to our existing 1-Wire network with no additional usage of
microcontroller pins, but utilizing the features of this chip will
require some software development. For this chapter, however,
we only want to build and test the circuit to be certain the device
is working and the circuit design is sound. Figure 7-23 illustrates
the 1-Wire side of the DS2404.

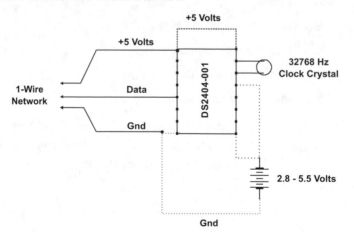

Figure 7-23

The only components required to make this circuit work is a clock crystal and battery (CR2032 type). Our test circuit will look similar to Figure 7-24.

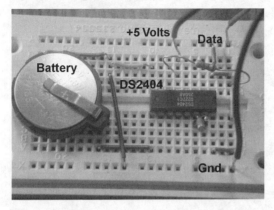

Figure 7-24

Note:

This chip has a built-in cycle counter. The battery-backed functions of this chip work across a pretty wide voltage range. This means you could set a voltage filtering system that would report voltage drops based on the battery value. This could be used to track brownouts or power surges.

Test Software for the DS2404

Now it's time to see if our circuit works. Testing the device consists of detecting the presence of the device, writing a few bytes of data to the device's scratchpad memory, and then reading the data back. This will prove the device has power and the 1-Wire network is working properly. The following program will accomplish this task.

Listing 7-3

```
// {$STAMP BS2p}
// {$PBASIC 2.5}


// Test Program for Dallas 1-Wire Time/Date Chip DS2404
// for Embedded Systems Desktop Integration
// Copyright 2004 - Oliver H. Bailey
//
// This program uses PIN 14 for all I/O. It should be noted that all communications with
// the DS2404 memory functions on the 1-Wire bus are done using bit I/O
//
// This is a very simple program for testing a DS2404 Time chip.
// ChkDev Variables
ChkLoop VAR Byte                        // Loop Counter for Reset
TmpByte VAR Byte                        // Presence Pulse Indicator

// Write_SP_Mem Variables
TA CON $0077


TA VAR Word
TA1 VAR TA.LOWBYTE                      // Target Address 1
TA2 VAR TA.HIGHBYTE                     // Target Address 2
EADDR VAR Byte
tempVar VAR Byte(8)
index VAR Nib
TestByteOne VAR Byte                    // First Test Ram Location Byte
TestByteTwo VAR Byte                    // Second Test Ram Location Byte
TestByteOne = %01010101                // Byte One is 01010101
TestByteTwo = %10101010                // Byte Two is 10101010
TA1 = $26                              // Hex 26
TA2 = 0                                // Hex 00

// Read_SP_Mem Variables
SA1 VAR Byte                           // Storage Address 1
SA2 VAR Byte                           // Storage Address 2
LEN VAR Byte                           // Data or Offset Length
ByteOne VAR Byte                       // Test Byte 1
ByteTwo VAR Byte                       // Test Byte 2
SA1 = %00000000                        // SA1 = 0
SA2 = %00000000                        // SA2 = 0
Len = %00000000                        // Len = 0
ByteOne = %00000000                    // ByteOne = 0
```

```
ByteTwo = %00000000                          // ByteTwo = 0


// Misc. Variables                           // For Bit Bang Mode
// CurBit VAR Byte                           //
TA=$0000                                     // Target Address is Page 0, Byte 0


PAUSE 1000                                   // Wait for Debug



Main:
  ChkLoop = 0                                // Set to zero again
  GOSUB ChkDev                               // Check for DS2404
  // DEBUG DEC ChkLoop, CR                    // Debug Display
// Reaching this line requires a response from the DS2404
// DEBUG HOME, "DS2404 Device Found..", CR
// Write to RAM Locations 0026H and 0027H. Write binary 01010101 and 10101010 to check
// RAM locations
  GOSUB Write_SP_Mem                         // Write to scratchpad memory
  FOR index = 0 TO 3                         // Loop through variables and
    tempVar(index) - $95                     // write asterisks * to data area
  NEXT
  PAUSE 100                                  // Wait for 3ms.
  GOSUB Read_SP_Mem                          // Read scratchpad memory
  // PAUSE 1000                               // Wait
  // GOTO Main                                // Start all over
  // If the code reaches here, it was by mistake.
  GOTO forever                               // Loop forever


// Check Device Subroutine - This subroutine looks for a presence pulse to determine
// if a 1-Wire device is a available. There are a couple of things to be aware of here.
// First, the normal state of the line is high since a pull-up resistor is used. This
// means that with ChkLoop being 0 upon entry at least one state transition is needed
// to determine a 1-Wire device is available. Without at least one state transition
// there is no way to determine if the line was pulled low after the inquiry was done.
  ChkDev:
    OWOUT 14, 1, [$CC]                       // Read Memory Page
  NotDone:
    OWIN 14, 0, [TmpByte]                    // Check Status
    ChkLoop = ChkLoop+1                      // Increment Loop Counter
    IF ChkLoop = 100 THEN no_Dev             // Max Tries then Stop
    IF TmpByte = 0 THEN                      // If no Response
    GOTO NotDone                             // Otherwise Try Again
```

```
      ENDIF
      IF (ChkLoop <> 1) THEN no_Dev            // State Change was detected
      RETURN                                   // Return if Found


// WRITE Scratchpad Memory
Write_SP_Mem:
  DEBUG CLS, "***** Sent Data Info *****", CR
  FOR index = 0 TO 3                           // Loop through 4 Bytes
    tempVar(index) = index + $30               // Write 0, 1, 2, & 3
  NEXT                                         // Write next number
  DEBUG "Data Sent:", STR tempVar\4, CR        // Send debug string to terminal

  DEBUG "TA:", HEX2 TA2, HEX2 TA1, CR          // Print Settings to Debug Terminal
  OWOUT 14, 1, [$CC, $0F, TA1, TA2, STR tempVar\4]  // Setup Address & Length
RETURN                                         // Return to Caller


PAUSE 5000


// Read Scratchpad Memory
Read_SP_Mem:
  OWOUT 14, 1, [$CC, $AA]                      // Read Scratchpad Function
  OWIN 14, 2, [TA1, TA2, EADDR, STR tempVar\4] // Read Address, Length, and Memory Contents
  DEBUG "***** Received DATA Info *****", CR
  DEBUG "Target Address:", HEX2 TA2, HEX2 TA1, CR // Send Target Address to Debug Terminal
  DEBUG "End Address:", HEX2 EADDR, CR         // Send End Address to Debug Terminal
  DEBUG "DATA Received:", STR tempVar\4, CR    // Send Received Data Bytes to Debug Terminal
RETURN


no_Dev:
  DEBUG "No DS2404 Device Found", CR           // No response at startup so display message
forever:                                       //
  GOTO forever                                 // and loop forever
```

This program will write the numbers 0123 to scratchpad memory, write asterisks (*) to the local variable, and then read the scratchpad memory locations back and display them. While it's a simple program, it tests the network and memory functions. Later we will implement the time, date, and cycle counter functions.

From Solderless Breadboard to Circuit Board

Now that we've gotten our design working on a solderless breadboard, let's make a real soldered version. To make this board we will use a grid-style PC board from Radio Shack (Part 276-150). If you look at this board you will notice two lines of white markings that run the entire length of the board as shown in Figure 7-25.

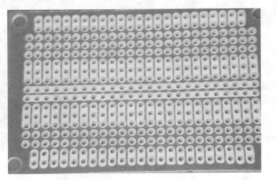

Figure 7-25

Those will be used as our power strips, just like our last board. The first step in building this circuit is to solder two terminal connectors to each end. One will supply power to our board and the other will feed power to another board. We will solder these to each end. Next, we will solder a 16-pin socket at the top left of the board. This will be for the DS2404 chip. Below the socket we will solder our battery holder. This will hold the CR2032 battery for backing up our RAM if we lose power. At the bottom we will solder one 3-Wire connector for our 3-Wire interface, and two 3-Wire connectors for our 1-Wire interface. By using two connectors we can continue to extend our 1-Wire network without additional components. At the bottom on the right side we can mount our DS1822 thermometer chip. I added an LED at the top left just to be certain that power is not a problem. If you decide to add an LED, a 1N914 diode should be used to prevent draining the battery if the power goes off. This allows the LED to double as a visual indicator that external power is being supplied.

In Figure 7-26 the LED is at the upper left. Going clockwise is the DS2404, battery holder and backup circuit, 3-Wire interface, 1-Wire interface, and DS1822 thermometer chip at the lower left. The thermometer has been mounted away from the other components to avoid false readings due to heat. There is plenty of room left on this board for a 1-Wire switch or pot and relay for fan control. Power is supplied to the center rows and all 1- and 3-Wire interfaces are located at the lower right of the photo. Note the power connectors attached to the center rows of the board.

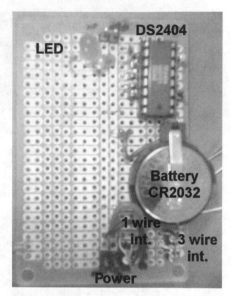

Figure 7-26

The Keyboard, Alarm, and Power Supply Board

The third and final board contains the keypad, alarm buzzer, alarm LED, power LED, and power supply. We've decided to use the Matrix Orbital LK202-25 LCD display. This display is an intelligent device that has support for six general-purpose outputs, a 5 row by 5 column keypad, and text and graphics display capabilities. It can be addressed via the RS-232 port or through the I²C protocol. Using this board requires only two processor data pins, a +5 volt supply, and a ground. The LK202-25 offers the following functions:

- A 2 line by 20 character backlit LCD display
- Bidirectional serial or I²C interface
- Programmable baud rates (serial interface only)
- Keyboard inputs for a 5x5 keypad matrix
- Six general-purpose I/O lines
- Programmable startup screen
- Programmable serial number
- Software controlled LCD backlight

Because of the long feature list, the LK202-25 has several connectors on the back for different purposes. For our prototype we will use the I²C interface. I²C was developed by Phillips Electronics. It utilizes four pins: +5 volts, SDC (clock), SDA (data), and ground. To use this interface we need to locate the 4-pin connector at the bottom left side of the LK202-25 as the back is facing up.

Figure 7-27

The connector shown in Figure 7-27 contains all the power and communications lines needed for using the LK202-25. In addition to the I²C interface, the LK202-25 has six general-purpose I/O lines. We will use two of these I/O lines, one for the alarm buzzer and the other for the alarm LED. The connections for these I/O lines are at the far left side of the board as the back is facing up. Figure 7-28 shows the I/O pin connections.

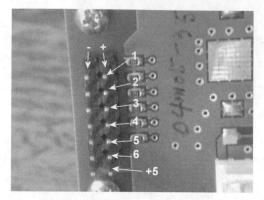

Figure 7-28

When connecting a device directly to the I/O pins, only devices with current requirements of 20 mA or less can be used unless the resistors (on the right) are bypassed. Both our alarm buzzer and alarm LED will work fine within the 20 mA current rating, so they will be directly attached to the top two posts (pins 1 and 2). The LK202-25 also supports standard RS-232 I/O. There is a DB9 connector on the back of the unit on the lower right side as shown in Figure 7-29. While we could use the RS-232 interface, I have chosen the I²C so you can gain experience with this method of communications. In addition, I²C is faster than standard RS-232.

Figure 7-29

Our final connection is for the keyboard. This connector, located in the center at the bottom of the LK202-25, is shown in Figure 7-30.

Figure 7-30

The connector has a total of ten pins. With the connector face up and looking from left to right, the first five pins are for connecting the keyboard columns 1 through 5. The next five pins are for connecting rows 1 through 5. The LK202-25 can handle a keyboard with five rows of five keys for a total of 25 keys. The keyboard interface is fairly simple to implement and is what we call a matrix type keyboard. Figure 7-31 illustrates exactly how we will implement this keyboard. Using this type of interface seems more confusing than it really is. When a key is pressed, two pins will sense the closure. Those two signals combined indicate which single key was pressed.

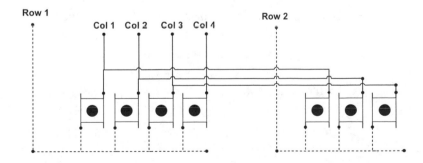

Figure 7-31

Our keyboard matrix contains two rows and four columns for a maximum of eight keys. The first row has the direction keys on the left side of the unit with each key being part of a separate column. The three function keys on the right are row 2. Each of the function keys is also connected to columns 1 through 3 from row 1. We could add one more key to this matrix to fill it out, but for now we don't need an additional key. Figure 7-32 shows the front of our I/O board. Clockwise starting on the left, we have the following connections:

■ +5 volts — Power connection

■ Ground — Common ground connection

■ I²C data line — Exchange data with embedded processor

■ I²C clock line — Synchronize data stream

■ Column 1 connection — Keyboard input

■ Column 2 connection — Keyboard input

■ Column 3 connection — Keyboard input

■ Column 4 connection — Keyboard input

■ Alarm LED — Visual alarm display

■ Power LED — Visual power display

■ Alarm buzzer — Audible alarm warning

■ Function keys — Store and clear parameters

■ Menu keys — Select menu items

■ Microcontroller I²C connections

Building the keyboard matrix requires only seven momentary push buttons (Jameco PN: BTS-1102B-2) and several lengths of 22 to 24 gauge stranded wire. The three pieces of unshielded wire just above the buttons are for test purposes. These allow each row and column to be tested for proper layout and continuity.

Figure 7-32

This board requires a little patience to build. With the exception of the power, ground, and I²C interface leads at the bottom of the figure, everything else connects to the LK202-25. That's right — only two pins are used on the microcontroller. There are several different functions the I/O board performs. First, it contains the keyboard matrix that has already been explained. This board is also the connection point for the data and power connections to the LK202-25. Figure 7-33 illustrates the four-pin power and data communications connector. Since we have chosen I²C, the center two pins of that connector will be used for data and the data clock.

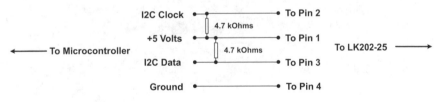

Figure 7-33

Again, these are the only four wires required from the microcontroller. Following is the parts list for this portion of the circuit.

■ Two 4.7 kOhm resistors (Radio Shack 271-1124)

■ One four-pin male connector 0.1" centers (Jameco PN: 114930)

■   Four crimp type pins for the above connector (Jameco PN: 114921)

Next, we have two LEDs on the I/O board to connect. The first is a power LED used to simply indicate external power present. This requires only two components. Figure 7-34 illustrates how this circuit is connected.

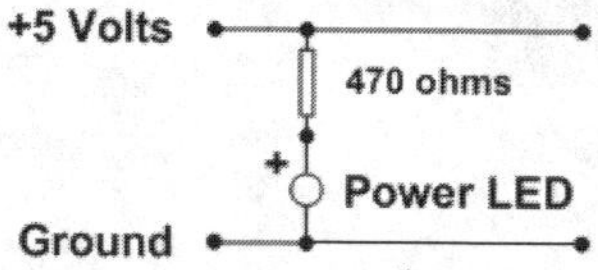

+5 Volts ───┬────────●
　　　　　　　□ **470 ohms**
　　　　　　　+
　　　　　　　○ **Power LED**
Ground ●───┴────────●

Figure 7-34

This circuit contains only two components. They are:

■   One 5-volt green LED

■   One 470 ohm resistor (Radio Shack 271-1115)

The next LED will be attached to the general-purpose I/O pins on the LCD display (see Figure 7-28). This circuit is illustrated in Figure 7-35 and again uses only two components.

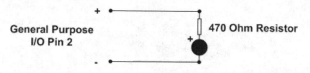

General Purpose
I/O Pin 2

470 Ohm Resistor

Figure 7-35

The following parts are required for the alarm LED circuit:

■   One 5-volt red LED

■   One 470 ohm resistor (Radio Shack 271-1115)

The last component we will install on the I/O board is the temperature alarm buzzer. The alarm is connected to I/O pin 1 on the LK202-25. Figure 7-36 illustrates how the circuit works.

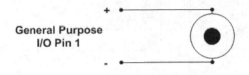

**General Purpose
I/O Pin 1**

Figure 7-36

This circuit again requires only minimal parts, in this case a piezo buzzer. I used the Radio Shack part number 273-065. This is a small buzzer rated at 70 dB and is rated for 3 to 16 volts.

While I put all of these circuits on a single board, you may wish to instead put them on separate boards. Keeping everything on a single board is easy and convenient, and once working and tested frees us to concentrate on the communications in upcoming chapters.

The final addition to this board is the power supply. This consists of an LM7805 voltage regulator. This device is rated at 1 amp, which will provide plenty of power for our circuit. Until now we have used the power from the regulator on the BASIC Stamp, but since that component is surface mounted the current rating is about half of this component's current rating. The smaller the package the less current the component can handle, so we will add the supply to avoid any problems. Once we attach the Ethernet controller our current usage will go up and probably exceed the regulator on the Stamp. Our completed schematic for this board is shown in Figure 7-37.

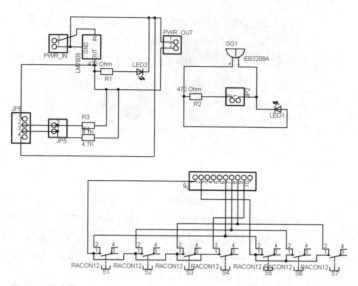

Figure 7-37

The first thing you will notice is that this board has three separate sections that do not share a ground wire — or at least it appears that way. In truth, the circuits do share common voltage and ground but in a different way than our previous boards. Let's start with the upper-left circuit, which is our power supply. That circuit uses a 9- to 12-volt input and provides a 5-volt output at the connector PWR_OUT. Connector JP6 is a four-pin connector that provide the power, ground, data, and clock for the LCD display. JP5 is the I²C interface to a microcontroller. You will notice that both the clock and data lines get connected to the +5 volt supply through a resistor. There is also an LED connected through a 470 ohm (R1) resistor. This is the power indicator.

As we move clockwise, the next circuit is the alarm circuit. This circuit is connected to output pin 2 on the LCD display. Both the power and ground are provided by the LCD, but the power and ground originate from our power circuit.

The final circuit is our keyboard interface. This interface gets connected to the keyboard input on the LCD as we discussed earlier. Again, the original power was provided by our power circuit.

Testing the LCD and I/O Board

Once all the functions have been added, the program in Listing 7-4 will run the board through its paces. Once completely wired you can test the functionality of the LK202-25 with this program.

Listing 7-4

```
// {$STAMP BS2p}
// This program will test the Matrix Orbital LCD Display
// It is a very simple program to use.
// The Matrix Orbital LCD contains a 2 x 20 LCD display
// 6 general-purpose I/O lines, and keyboard support for up to 25 keys.
// The keyboard scan routine is interrupt driven so keystrokes are captured
// when they are pressed.
//
KeyChar VAR Byte                        // Holder for Keystrokes
LastKey VAR Byte


PAUSE 1000                              // Wait for System Start


Main:                                   // Main Program
  GOSUB StartMsg                        // Show StartMessage
  GOSUB SoundBuzzer                     // Sound Buzzer
  PAUSE 1000                            // Wait a Second
  DEBUG CLS                             // Clear Debug Screen
  I2COUT 8, 80, [254, 88]              // Clear LCD Display


KeyLoop:                                // Start Keyboard Polling
  I2CIN 8, 81, [KeyChar]               // Read Key Character


  IF (KeyChar = 0) THEN KeyLoop        // If 0 No Key Pressed


  IF (LastKey = 0) AND (KeyChar = 0) THEN KeyLoop

                                        // If LastKey and ThisKey are Zero
                                        // then no key was pressed
  IF (LastKey <> KeyChar) THEN ClearKeyDisp

                                        // If they are not equal then
                                        // clear the display and show the keys

  IF (LastKey = KeyChar) THEN ShowKeyState

                                        // If they are equal display then
```

```
  GOTO KeyLoop                                    // Scan for another key

ClearKeyDisp:                                     // Clear the Debug Display
  DEBUG CLS                                       //
ShowKeyState:                                     //
  LastKey = KeyChar                               // Assign OldKey = Current Key Character
  DEBUG BIN8 KeyChar, " ", DEC2 KeyChar, CR

  I2COUT 8, $50, [DEC KeyChar]                    // Print 1st Text line

  GOTO KeyLoop                                    // Loop again


// Display Message
StartMsg:
I2COUT 8, $50, [254, 88]                          // Clear Display
I2COUT 8, $50, ["Embedded Systems"]              // Print 1st Text Line
I2COUT 8, $50, [$A]                               // Carriage Return
I2COUT 8, $50, ["Desktop Integration"]           // Print 2nd Text Line
PAUSE 5000                                        // Display for 5 seconds
I2COUT 8, $50, [254, 88]                          // Clear Display again
I2COUT 8, $50, ["Copyright 2004"]                // 1st Text Line
I2COUT 8, $50, [$0A]                              // Line Feed
I2COUT 8, $50, ["Oliver H. Bailey"]              // 2nd Text Line
PAUSE 5000                                        // Display for another 5 seconds
RETURN


// First Test the Piezo Electric Buzzer
SoundBuzzer:
I2COUT 8, 80, [254, 88]                           // Clear Display
I2COUT 8, 80, ["Alarm Start"]                     // Print 1st Line of Text
DEBUG CLS, "Alarm Start", CR                       // Show Debug Message
I2COUT 8, 80, [254, 87, 1]                         // Turn on Alarm
PAUSE 5000                                        // Wait 5 seconds
I2COUT 8, 80, [254, 86, 1]                         // Turn off Alarm
I2COUT 8, 80, [$0A]                               // Send Linefeed to display
I2COUT 8, 80, ["Alarm Stop"]                      // Print Line Feed
DEBUG "Alarm Stopped", CR                          // Debug Display End Message
RETURN                                            // Return to caller


Forever:
  GOTO Forever
```

There are a couple of items to keep in mind when using this design. First, the BASIC Stamp 2p allows only pin combinations of 0 and 1, or 8 and 9 for I²C communications. By default, the lower numbered pin of the pair is the data pin and the higher numbered pin of each pair is the data clock. Listing 7-4 uses pins 8 and 9 for I²C communications. Addressing the LK202-25 is not difficult. By default, the I²C device address is 50 hex (80 decimal). While this can be changed, the default address is suitable for our needs.

Unlike RS-232, I²C supports multiple devices on the same address and clock pins. As you can see from Listing 7-4, addressing the LK202 is very simple. We will use some of the additional features of this device in later chapters.

Design Considerations

Using an intelligent LCD display like the LK202 shifts some of the processing burden from the embedded processor to the LCD display processor. This makes the LCD much more expensive than its non-intelligent counterparts. The fact that this display can perform many other tasks needs to be considered when designing a device of this type and expense. Even though the LK202 is a more expensive device, it offers features and expansion capabilities that may more than justify the additional cost. By using this device in our design we have effectively moved the tasks of managing alarm functions (LED and buzzer), keyboard input, and display output to this device and with the logic to control all of these functions squeezed into a very small space.

How to Make Your Own Printed Circuit Boards

The last topic we will cover in this chapter is how to make printed circuit boards and avoid the expense of using photosensitive boards. Recently I began using the toner transfer system and have found that I can make a board in under 20 minutes and with resolution good enough to allow pads for surface mount components. Let me cover this process because we will be making a few circuit boards as we continue. To make your own boards using this process you will need the following items:

- Laser printer or photocopier
- Toner transfer paper
- Blank circuit board material
- Clothes iron
- Small tray of water (at room temperature)
- Pint size bottle of ferric chloride (board etchant)
- Sponge
- Disposable rubber gloves
- Acetone or nail polish remover
- Full-scale board image in printable format

Now let's cover the process.

1. Print a mirror image (or "flipped" image) of your full-scale (1:1) PCB layout on regular paper. (This will be your "carrier" sheet to hold a small piece of TTS paper that will be run through your printer a second time.)

2. Cut a piece of toner transfer paper equal to the size of the circuit image with about a 1/2" border all around.

3. Position the blank TTS paper directly over the printed circuit image shiny side up. Using a laser-type label (e.g., Avery brand), secure the TTS paper to the "carrier" at the leading edge (the edge that will be heading into the printer).

4. Place the sheet into the manual-feed tray and print. You will now have a perfectly printed image on the small piece of TTS paper.

5. Perform the simple iron-calibration procedure as outlined in the TTS paper instructions to be able to apply the proper pressure and temperature to get a perfect transfer.

6. Prepare the copper surface of the blank PCB using a Scotch-Brite or similar scrubbing pad and a drop of dishwashing soap. The copper surface will have a layer of oxidation and fingerprint oils that must be removed. Wet the board and scrub the surface well with a circular motion. Wash under running water and dry.

7. Place the TTS paper over the circuit board image-side down.

8. Place the TTS paper over the board and cover both with a clean sheet of white paper. Carefully apply the iron so as not to move the paper. Apply heat evenly to the entire image for 20 to 25 seconds, then remove the iron. Wait another 30 seconds or so for the toner to dry to avoid any smearing. Discard the white paper covering the assembly.

9. Put the circuit board with the attached TTS paper into the water bath until you see the paper start to float away (about 2 minutes). Do not "help" the paper to separate.

10. Lift the board and paper out of the bath and slide the slippery side of the paper over the circuit image. This will break the surface tension where some of the dissolved glue will sit inside doughnut holes and between tightly spaced traces. Now wash in a sink to remove all glue residue. Discard the paper.

11. Inspect the board for missing areas of black toner. If there are small gaps, you can use any waterproof permanent marker to fill in voids.

12. Dry the PCB by gently patting the board with paper towels to absorb the water.

13. Cut a piece of green TTF paper the same size as the toner transfer paper in Step 2.

14. When the board is completely dry, place the TTF paper over the board and repeat Steps 8 through 12.

15. Again pat the board dry with a paper towel.

16. Put on the rubber gloves and soak the sponge in ferric chloride until wet.

17. Evenly rub the circuit board with the wet sponge. Immediately you will see the etchant over the copper turn very dark. That is the copper ions being removed. Depending on the amount of copper on your board (0.5, 1, or 2 oz.), your etch times will vary greatly. The thin layer (0.5 oz.) should etch completely in 45 seconds to 1 minute and proportionally longer for thicker copper boards. Your aggressiveness of rubbing over the copper has a direct effect on total time to etch.

18. Flush the board with fresh water to neutralize the etchant and dry with paper towel. The board must be COMPLETELY dry before the next step. (Dispose of the ferric chloride soaked sponge in an EPA approved manner.)

19. Wet a dry piece of paper towel with acetone and rub over the board. Both the green TRF and black toner will liquefy on contact; however, if there is any water present, this will not work. A second fresh wiping will remove all residue.

20. Rinse the board under water and pat dry.

21. Tin plate the copper surface if desired.

22. Solder components and assemble the board.

Circuit Board Artwork

This chapter concludes with the artwork for each of the boards made thus far. The artwork for each board contains two images. Only image titles appear on the page as the details were covered earlier. If you are making boards using the methods outlined earlier in this chapter, then use the inverted images. This will be correct after it has been printed and transferred to the board. If you are using a photo-sensitive method, use the normal image.

The artwork for the boards in this section do not have ground planes. The reason for this is due to the number of colors available when exporting the original circuit. When the colors are reduced to black and white some of the traces disappear. If you wish to use a ground plane, see the artwork in the downloadable files.

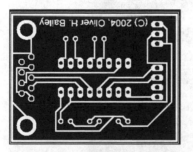

Figure 7-38: Inverted TTL-RS-232

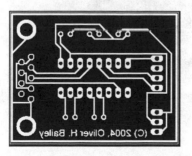

Figure 7-39: Normal TTL-RS-232

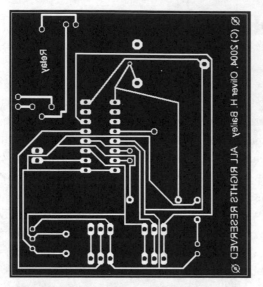

Figure 7-40: Inverted 1- and 3-Wire

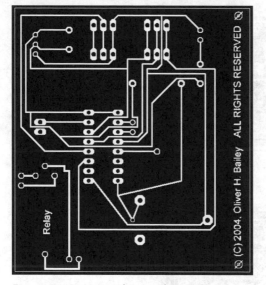

Figure 7-41: Normal 1- and 3-Wire

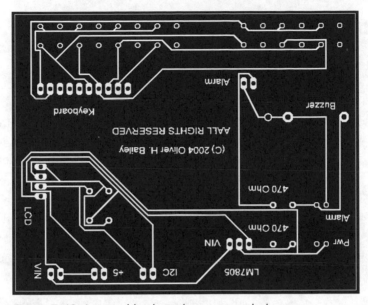

Figure 7-42: Inverted keyboard, power, and alarm

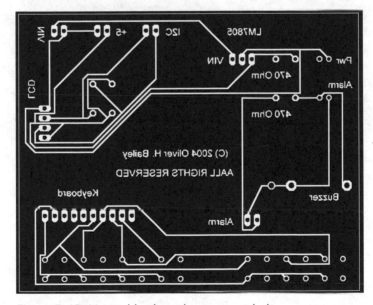

Figure 7-43: Normal keyboard, power, and alarm

Chapter Summary

In this chapter we have built the foundation for our embedded system. We now have boards that provide power, alarm capabilities, LCD interface, keyboard interface, temperature, time, and Dallas 1- and 3-Wire interfaces. You've been introduced to the BASIC Stamp microcontroller to understand how this device can be used to quickly test a circuit board and its functions. We have also learned how to make a circuit board from scratch using commercially available materials and a little elbow grease. In the next chapter we will add the BASIC Stamp board and build a completed prototype using the boards we have built here.

Chapter 8

The BASIC Stamp 2p Prototype

Overview

It's time to complete our first prototype. In this chapter we will use the BASIC Stamp 2p microcontroller to complete our embedded system. We will implement our firmware in PBASIC, the free BASIC development system included with the Parallax products. In Chapter 7 we built several boards that will provide the needed functions for our prototypes. So we will begin this chapter with a road map of how our implementation will proceed. Once we have our strategy developed, we will build a BASIC Stamp prototype board so we can connect and test each of our components as we integrate the system.

> **Note:**
> Only code snippets that illustrate how to interface each device are provided in the text. Complete program listings can be found at www.wordware.com/files/embsys and at www.time-lines.com/embedsys1.

Our Development Road Map

Since the BASIC Stamp provides a high-level language interface and doesn't support true interrupts, we need to choose devices that will work within these design considerations. This means we need to choose components that are intelligent and easy to interface since the program running on the Stamp will be infinitely polling for activity. While we have already developed some of the circuits, we still need to determine the best design for communicating to our host systems. The functional aspect of this system has been predetermined in the design, so we are only concerned with the implementation in this chapter. Before we begin to develop the order in which the functions will be implemented, let's first look at the host interface components that have been chosen.

The Ethernet device we have chosen is the NetBurner SB72. This is an economical board designed to provide either true RS-232 or TTL level RS-232 signals to a microcontroller or other serial interfaced device. It has full support for all Ethernet protocols including standard sockets (TCP/IP), secure sockets (SSL), email (SMTP), and web services (HTTP). This version of the prototype will only be using basic TCP/IP functions, but the expansion possibilities for future revisions are endless. Since expansion capabilities are already in the hardware, we need to only write or update the software to expand the system capabilities. This product also interfaces to the BASIC Stamp using the same interface pins as the RS-232 host connection. This means we can share BASIC Stamp I/O pins and design our prototype board to use either or both RS-232 and Internet interfaces at the same time for debugging purposes. We also have plenty of RAM and program space on the SB72, allowing us to set up large buffers if necessary so the chance of losing data is minimal. In order to effectively use the SB72 we will need to familiarize ourselves with the C language, the GNU C/C++ compilers, and the SDB debugger. We will also need to become familiar with the uC/OS, which is the real-time OS running on the SB72. The uC/OS is a multitasking system, so we can have multiple tasks running at once.

There is a wide selection of USB devices to choose from. We will implement two different types of USB interfaces that both use the FTDI serial-to-USB chip set. The first of these devices is from Parallax and is the SER2USB product. This is a very small and inexpensive product that uses transmit, receive, attention, and ground pins. As an alternative, we will also use the DLP Designs DLP-232BM product, which is a pin-for-pin replacement for RS-232 signals. Both of these choices use the same serial commands as the RS-232 and Ethernet interfaces but have different handshake requirements.

The DLP-232BM device provides us with the ability to simply swap the RS-232 interface for a USB interface at the embedded system side. This means that we can swap RS-232, DLP-232BM, or the SB72 with complete software transparency from the BASIC Stamp. There are no tricks here, but both the DLP-232BM and SB72 are intelligent, programmable devices. This gives us a lot of flexibility and additional functionality for this particular prototype. The SER2USB device from Parallax is a simple replacement for an RS-232 that has no onboard intelligence other than programmable baud rates and handshakes. The SER2USB, like RS-232, is strictly a protocol converter. Now you may be asking why we would use such a device. The answer is cost and board space. The SER2USB is the cheapest prepackaged TTL serial-to-USB device around for the BASIC Stamp. Because it simply converts RS-232 to USB, it also has the smallest footprint. If board space is at a premium or you want a very quick USB interface for data I/O, this device makes perfect sense. There are some differences at the software level that we need to consider for interface purposes; we will explore these later in this chapter.

Since we have already developed and tested our RS-232 level interface in Chapter 7, we can now move on to listing the required functions to make our prototype complete. The following functions are needed to complete our prototype using the BASIC Stamp:

■ Display output — Formatted time, temperature, and error messages

■ Keyboard input — Function selection, menus, and variable storage routines

■ 1-Wire functions to read and set date, time, and high and low alarm thresholds, service a temperature alarm, read/write to 1-Wire memory, read/display power outage and brownout counter, and read/display the current temperature

■ 3-Wire interface to provide high-speed memory and clock access

■ High and low temperature alarm routines

■ Develop the host protocol to communicate with a desktop system

■ Implement RS-232 communications with a desktop computer

■ Implement USB communications with a desktop computer

■ Implement Ethernet communications with a desktop computer/LAN/WAN

■ Develop a device interface layer that will work on Windows, Linux, and UNIX to support a single-source code solution for all supported platforms

■ Develop a desktop application that will work on Windows, UNIX, and Linux using the same source code

■ Implement automatic fan control

Note:

The Dallas 1-Wire interface is very flexible but with that flexibility comes a level of complexity when adding devices while the network is in operation. To keep the 1-Wire interface simple we will add device IDs and types manually. There are plenty of resources that explain how to build more complex 1-Wire networks.

Using the BASIC Stamp 2p24

We used the BASIC Stamp 2p24 device in the last chapter for testing but did not cover the specifications, so here are the highlights. The BASIC Stamp Professional starter kit contains most of the components we need for this chapter. The kit includes a BASIC Stamp 2p (with program memory, power regulator, and BASIC interpreter), a Windows versions of a BASIC editor and tokenizer (Linux users can find resources and resource links at the Parallax web site), serial cable, miscellaneous support components, and several Dallas 1-Wire components. Figure 8-1 shows the contents of the starter kit.

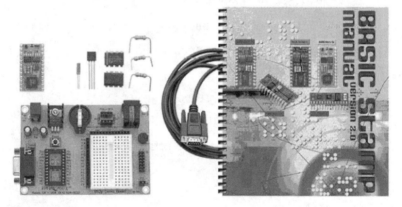

Figure 8-1

Starting from the upper left and going clockwise we have the BASIC Stamp 2p24, clock crystal for Dallas 1-Wire devices, Dallas DS-1822 sensor, Dallas timekeeping chip, resistors, serial cable, manual and CD, and development board, which includes a prototype area.

Implementation Strategy

The first step is to break down our task list into manageable
pieces. To do this we will first take a look at all of the tasks
needed to accomplish our end goal. The following list accounts
for all the pieces that make up the temperature sensor and controller that have remaining work to be completed.

- Display output
- Keyboard input
- 1-Wire communications
- RS-232 communications
- USB communications
- Ethernet communications
- Desktop/host communication protocol
- Read temperature
- Set low alarm threshold
- Set high alarm threshold
- Temperature alarm detection and action
- Fan control logic

Note:

Fan control is not required but for the experience we will
examine how to control the fans. This would be required
before the product goes to market.

The BASIC Stamp 2p24 provides us with 16 general-purpose I/O
lines, unregulated voltage in (6 to 30 volts), regulated voltage out
(+5 volts), ground, serial in, serial out, and one handshake line
for programming.

Developing Our BASIC Stamp Board

You're probably wondering why we are making a BASIC Stamp board since one is included in the BASIC Stamp development kit. The board included in the development kit is a prototype board that is great for testing and debugging portions of a circuit. But as we progress through this chapter we will be interconnecting the modules together, and if we don't make secure connections we will find ourselves in a bowl of spaghetti fixing broken wires. By developing our own BASIC Stamp board we will be using solder instead of wire-wrap or jumpers, making things much easier as we get closer to completion.

We will use off-the-shelf components whenever possible. Most of the components we use can be purchased at your local Radio Shack store. For those who wish to make a circuit board I will provide artwork at the end of this chapter just as I did in the previous chapter.

We will start by using another prototype board (Radio Shack 276-150). This board will provide enough space for the BASIC Stamp 2p24, our serial interface to the host, power LED, and Stamp reset switch. We will place a 24-pin socket (Radio Shack 900-7249) almost in the center of the prototype board so each row of pins is within a three-column contact. This will allow use to solder additional wires without the worry of overheating the parts. When completed your board should look similar to Figure 8-2.

Figure 8-2

Power Sources

In Chapter 7 we used the built-in voltage regulator on the BASIC Stamp itself. That works for applications that have low current requirements, but since we are adding Ethernet we need a little more current than the Stamp can provide. If you made your own circuit boards using the artwork in Chapter 7, then you need only the 7805 voltage regulator and power connector. If you haven't made those boards, then the following instructions will provide you with the information necessary to build a +5 volt supply.

Building a +5 volt supply requires only four components. They are:

- Power supply 7.5 V (Radio Shack 273-1696)
- Power supply connector (Jameco 216451)
- Voltage regulator (Radio Shack 276-1770)
- Capacitor 220 μF (Radio Shack 272-1017)

This is a very simple circuit. Figure 8-3 is a diagram of how the circuit is built. The LM7805 is on the left and the capacitor is on the right. The capacitor is optional. The ground and +5 out connections are attached to the center rows on the prototype board we are building.

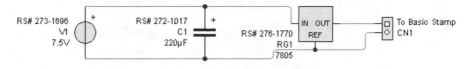

Figure 8-3

Changing the power source to the BASIC Stamp requires no modification because the same 5-volt regulator output on the Stamp can also be used for +5 regulated input. This isolates our other power circuit, and we can power everything by simply connecting the output from the above circuit to the +5 and ground connector on the keyboard.

Connecting the Reset and Host Communications

We need to be able to reset the Stamp so we will solder a normally open push button to pin 21 on one side and ground on the other. When the switch is pressed, the momentary grounding of pin 22 will reset the BASIC stamp. A normally open board-mounted push button switch (Radio Shack 275-1571) can be used as shown.

Note:

Be sure you use a normally open push button (NO). If you use a normally closed button, your stamp will always be in reset mode and never execute a program.

Now we need to connect our programming and debugging lines to be able to start using the Stamp. Figure 8-4 shows how our regulated power in, reset, and programming/debugging lines are

Chapter 8

attached. Pins 1 through 4 are attached to data in, data out, attention, and ground.

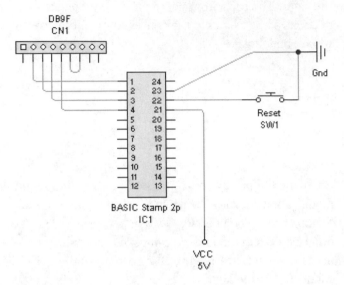

Figure 8-4

Now insert a BASIC Stamp 2p into the socket with pin 1 inserted into the side with the notch in the middle. Your board should look similar to Figure 8-5.

Figure 8-5

Notice the RS-232 programming interface is the four wires on the left. The reset button is at the upper left, and the power is at the lower portion of the board, out of view.

Remaining I/O Pin Requirements

Before we begin connecting the remaining I/O devices and pins, let's see what our needs are if we choose not to share I/O pins among devices.

- I^2C — Two I/O lines, +5 volt supply, ground
- Dallas 1-Wire interface — One I/O line, +5 volts, ground
- Parallax USB — Three I/O lines, ground
- Ethernet — Four I/O lines, ground
- Dallas 3-Wire interface — Two I/O lines, +5 volts, ground
- DLP 232BM — Four I/O lines, ground
- Non-Host RS-232 — Four I/O lines, ground

This list is in order of importance. We need I^2C for display output, keyboard input, alarm function, and fan control. The Dallas 1-Wire interface is required to gather temperature and temperature alarms. We need at least one USB and Ethernet interface. We also need one RS-232 interface for the finished product. If we look at just the I/O pins required in this list, we have a total of 20 I/O lines. Since we have 16 I/O lines available, we will have to drop some devices or find creative ways to make this work. The good news is that we have plenty of I/O pins available to meet our minimum requirements. With this in mind, we will begin implementing our final functionality in order of importance and see how we can modify our design to allow the extra I/O devices to be supported.

The LCD Display

The I²C Communications Interface

The I²C interface was developed by Phillips Electronics to allow multiple slave devices to communicate with a master device via a single serial interface. This form of serial communications has similarities to RS-232, RS485, and USB; however, it is designed for use only over short distances (although there are ways to obtain greater distances). It has two wires for communications just like RS-232, RS485, and USB, but it does not use differential signaling like USB and it has only one data line, unlike RS-232. The other line is used for the data clock to synchronize the data bits. Like USB, all communications are initiated by the master, which in this case is the BASIC Stamp, and the master always provides the data clock signal since it initiates communications. Each device has a unique ID that it responds to. In the case of the LCD display, the default device ID is the decimal number 80 (or 50 hex).

BASIC Stamp I²C Communications Support

Of all the BASIC stamp products, only the BASIC Stamp 2p series has built-in support for I²C communications, and those communications are limited to only two sets of I/O pins. Those are pins 0 and 1, and 8 and 9 with the even-numbered pin carrying the data and the odd-numbered (or higher) pin carrying the clock signal. Before we begin writing code to support our LCD we should attach the device to our BASIC Stamp board. We will use pins 8 and 9 for our prototype. These two pins are located at the very bottom of the right-hand side of the Stamp with pin 8 at the bottom and pin 9 the next pin up. We will solder a four-pin header to the top right side of our Stamp prototype board. The top pin of the header will be attached to +5 volts. This will provide power to the LCD. The next pin will be attached to Stamp pin 9 for the clock signal. The third pin will be attached to pin 8, the data line, while the fourth and lowest pin will be attached to ground. The following schematic shows our current circuit.

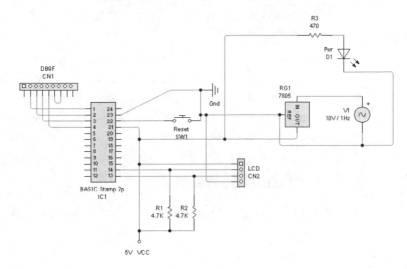

Figure 8-6

There are only two commands in PBASIC to manage I²C: I2COUT and I2CIN. The slave device address is used to send data to the proper device. To receive data we must add 1 to the slave device address as illustrated in the following code snippet.

```
I2COUT 8, 80, ["Temp"]          ' Send the string "Temp" to the LCD
I2CIN 8, 81, [KeyChar]          ' Read Key Character
```

The first command outputs the string "Temp" to the LCD display after the last cursor position. No formatting commands were used in this case so the text will be output as typed. The second command reads a keyboard character from the LCD and stores it to the variable KeyChar, which is defined as a byte. If no key has been pressed, a zero will be returned. Using a keypad with the LK202-25 LCD gives us flexiblility. We can program auto repeat and duration, and even transmit the characters without being polled. For this prototype we will use the default values that come standard from the factory. I've explained how to send display data and receive keystrokes, but one question remains: How do we toggle the I/O lines available on the LCD? There are two commands that deal with general-purpose outputs. Both are shown below.

```
I2COUT 8, 80, [254, 86, 1]          ' Turn off Output #1
I2COUT 8, 80, [254, 87, 1]          ' Turn on Output #1
```

The state of an output cannot be read, so it's up to the developer to keep track of outputs in the software or to always set outputs to a known state based on program inputs. We have covered all the information needed to use the LCD display, key scan, and outputs, so we can now begin developing our prototype software.

LCD Command Software

The LCD command functions we need to implement for our project are:

- Clear Screen
- Display Time
- Display Date
- Display Temperature
- Display Menu
- Display Error
- Turn Backlight On
- Turn Backlight Off
- Read Keyboard
- Turn Alarm Buzzer On
- Turn Alarm Buzzer Off
- Turn Alarm Light On
- Turn Alarm Light Off

These 13 functions cover our needs for finishing the prototype. None of these functions alone are complicated, but combining some of these functions may prove tricky or create unexpected results. The LK202-25 uses control codes mixed with command codes to alter the appearance of the display. Some of the functions we need are simple command codes sent to the LCD, but others require data or text to execute. Of the above functions, the following can be handled by simply sending control codes to the LCD display. The PBASIC command is shown to the right.

- Clear Screen   I2COUT 8, 80, [254, 88]

- Turn Backlight On   I2COUT 8, 80, [254, 66, Delay]

- Turn Backlight Off   I2COUT 8, 80, [254, 70]

- Read Keyboard   I2CIN 8, 81, [Key]

- Turn Alarm Buzzer On   I2COUT 8, 80, [254, 87, 1]

- Turn Alarm Buzzer Off   I2COUT 8, 80, [254, 86, 1]

- Turn Alarm Light On   I2COUT 8, 80, [254, 87, 2]

- Turn Alarm Light Off   I2COUT 8, 80, [254, 86, 2]

When turning on the backlight we can turn it on indefinitely by setting Delay = 0, or we can set a time delay in minutes. We will set Delay to 3 so the backlight will turn off after three minutes. This will give the user enough time to make changes and save them.

    We could use a single I/O pin on the LCD for both the buzzer and LED, but to give us flexibility we will use two different I/O pins. The alarm buzzer will use I/O pin 0 and the LED will use I/O pin 1 on the LCD display.

    The above eight functions have completed almost 75 percent of our work for the LCD. The remaining functions are:

- Display Time

- Display Date

- Display Temperature

- Display Menu

- Display Error

These remaining functions require formatted data output. We have several options available to us here, as we can clear the display and repaint both lines each time an update is needed or we can position the cursor and update only those areas that need to be changed.

We have 20 characters on each display line. If we display the time in 24-hour format we will use eight characters for the time, a blank space, and eight characters for the date, which is a total of 17 characters. If we use AM/PM indicators, our time field is expanded to use 11 characters, bringing the total characters for line 1 to 20, the exact number available. This leaves us 20 characters on line 2 for menu items and the temperature display. We want to remain as flexible as possible so we will allow Fahrenheit and Celsius to be selected from the menu. Our temperature display will show the minus sign, three digits, and the Fahrenheit or Celsius character for a total of five characters. This leaves us 15 characters for displaying navigation and error messages for the first-level menus. On the far right of line 2 we will display an asterisk if a host system is connected and communicating with the thermostat. That will leave us 14 characters for our first-level menu or error message display.

Creating Formatted LCD Output

If we store all the text in memory for a full line display, it will take 40 characters. This is a lot of memory for the BASIC Stamp. If we use cursor positioning, we won't have to redraw the display each time it needs to be updated. Based on our calculations above, our display routine would look something like this:

```
I2COUT 8, 80, [254, 71, 1, 1, Time]    ' Display time @ column 1, row 1
I2COUT 8, 80, [254, 71, 13, 1, Date]   ' Display Date @ column 13, row 1
I2COUT 8, 80, [254, 71, 1, 2, Temp]    ' Display Temperature @ column 1, row 2
I2COUT 8, 80, [254, 71, 6, 2, Menu]    ' Display Current Menu @ column 6, row 2
I2COUT 8, 80, [254, 71, 20, 2, Connected] ' Host Connection @ column 20, row 2
```

This method requires that we have five preformatted variables that each contain display information. These commands can be written as a subroutine that simply displays the information from each stored variable.

Alarm, LED, and Fan Control Outputs

As we've seen earlier, using the outputs on the LK202-25 is not difficult from a software point of view. We do need to review the electrical current requirements of our devices to be sure we don't overload the outputs. This could result in, at the very least, destroying an output, or, at the very worst, destroying the LCD completely.

The I/O pins on the LK202-25 have current-limiting resistors of 240 ohms attached. They can sink 20 mA of current. Our LEDs require 2.6 volts and the buzzer operates on as little as 3 volts, so neither of these will be a problem. The alarm buzzer uses about 4 milliamps, which leaves us 16 milliamps for the LED; this is more than enough.

Fan control is another story. We will isolate the fan circuitry by using a low-voltage relay with a diode and capacitor to prevent voltage spikes from damaging our I/O pins on the LCD. The voltage that controls our fan is then physically isolated from our control circuit. We can use 110 or 220 relays, allowing us to control fans of various sizes depending on the need. This is a very simple method of isolation and requires only three components. They are:

■ One 1N4001 diode (Radio Shack 276-1101)

■ One 50 µF electrolytic capacitor (Radio Shack 272-1018)

■ One 5-volt relay (Radio Shack 275-232)

The use of this circuit requires a separate power supply for the fan. Figure 8-7 illustrates how the circuit is constructed. The output pins on the LCD are shown at the top of the image.

This circuit prevents damage to the LCD output pin by creating an electrical shock absorber. Current surges are typical when relay contacts change positions. These surges can destroy electrical equipment. The capacitor absorbs voltage spikes and discharges them slowly through the

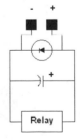

Figure 8-7

circuit. The diode prevents the electrical charge from reaching the voltage source. I added this relay circuit to the time and temperature board we built in Chapter 7. Figure 8-8 shows where the circuit was placed on the prototype board.

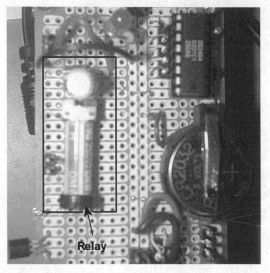

Figure 8-8

The two pins on the left edge of the board connect the relay to the output pins of the LCD. The coil we have chosen provides 250 ohms of resistance in the circuit. According to Matrix Orbital documentation if 240 ohms or more resistance are provided, then the 240 ohm resistor should be bypassed. See Figure 8-9.

Figure 8-9

The same power used for the LCD is also used to power the I/O pins on the LCD, so no additional connections are needed. The following PBASIC program will alternate the relay on and off every 5 seconds.

```
TestRelay:
I2COUT 8, 80, [254, 87, 6]        ' Turn Fan Relay On
PAUSE 5000
I2COUT 8, 80, [254, 86, 6]        ' Turn Fan Relay Off
PAUSE 5000
GOTO TestRelay
```

Enter this program into the BASIC Stamp editor, connect the Stamp to the host via the RS-232 cable, apply power to the Stamp by attaching a 9-volt battery, and download and run this program. If you cannot feel the relay switching, set your multimeter to continuity or buzzer and attach the leads to the fan control termi-nals. You should get a tone or see the LED continuity light for 5 seconds and then go off for 5 seconds, then repeat the process. Once you've tested the circuit, disconnect the power as this will drain a 9-volt battery pretty quickly.

Note:

Earlier we defined fan control using a 1-Wire switch. Since we have chosen a smart LCD display that provides us with outputs that can drive a relay, this approach makes sense and saves the engineer the additional cost of a 1-Wire switch.

Wiring the Alarm LED

The alarm LED is connected to I/O pin 2 on the LCD display. Since we have a resistor already connected to the LED we need to bypass the current limiting resistor as we did on pin 6. Once this modification is completed, attach a wire between the + side of the I/O pin to the resistor for the alarm LED. To complete the circuit, add a second wire from the –I/O pin to the ground lead on the LED. Use the same software we developed for testing the fan control except change pin 6 to pin 2. The LED should flash on and off at 5-second intervals.

Wiring the Alarm Buzzer

We have worked our way back to I/O pin 1 on the LCD. The buzzer we installed in Chapter 7 will operate on voltages from 1.5 to 12 volts. Since we are outputting +5 volts, we are well within the ratings of the buzzer. As a result we can connect the + and – leads directly to the buzzer terminals.

Keyboard Wiring

The keyboard is the last item on the LCD to wire. The LK202-25 supports five rows of five keys for a total of 25 keys. We have seven keys, which is too many for one row or column. To make interfacing with the keys easier we will define two rows of keys by function. The first row will contain the four menu keys and the second row will contain the remaining three function keys.

Keyboard Codes

The following commands are useful when doing keyboard scanning or control. The following command will read the current key being pressed or zero if no key is pressed.

```
I2CIN 8, $51, [KeyChar]        ' Read Keyboard = 0 if no key pressed
                               ' or key code
```

We covered this command earlier. Remember to add 1 to the base port number to read.

```
I2COUT 8, $50, [254, 126, 2]   ' Set Auto-Repeat mode to send
                               ' press/release codes
```

This is the default mode for the I²C interface. When a key is pressed, no other codes are sent until the key has been released. The release code is the key code + 32 (20 hex).

```
I2COUT 8, $50, [254, 96]          ' Turn off Auto-Repeat mode
```

Auto-Repeat is initiated by holding down the key just as with a PC keyboard.

```
I2COUT 8, $50, [254, 69]          ' Flush Keyboard buffer.
```

This empties the keyboard buffer of any remaining keys that have not been received. This is useful when the time between fetching keyboard code is lengthy and multiple keyboard characters may be in the buffer.

We have not implemented all of the functions on the keyboard/alarm board we built in Chapter 7. The remaining fuctions are discussed next.

Menu Functionality

We have considerable flexibility in how we implement the menu details and menu navigation. Earlier we determined how our LCD display would be designed. Now, we will provide the details of how our menu should look. We have 12 characters to display our main menu. Following is a description of the needed menu items, the LCD display message, and the message length.

Table 8-1

Menu Item	LCD Display	Length
Set Date	Set Date	8
Set Time	Set Time	8
Set Time Format	Time Fmt	8
Set Temperature Display (Celsius or Fahrenheit)	Temp Fmt	8
Set Ethernet Address	Net Addr	8
Set High Temperature Alarm	High Temp	9
Set Low Temperature Alarm	Low Temp	8
Set Fan Temperature	OnΓan On	6
Set Fan Temperature Off	Fan Off	7
Reset Temperature Network	Reset Temp	10
Reset Unit	Master Reset	12

The longest message length is 12 characters, the exact maximum we have. To add flexibility we will store the message strings in the EEPROM so they can be easily maintained. At this point our BASIC Stamp board is connected to the LCD and the alarm/keyboard is also attached. Your system should look similar to Figure 8-10.

Figure 8-10

Here we have the BASIC Stamp board, keyboard/alarm, power LEDs, and LCD mounted to a 0.25" backer board (you can purchase this at any art supply store for about $3). Now, let's move on to integrating the time and temperature.

Using the DS2404 Time and Memory Chip

Now it's time to integrate the Dallas 1- and 3-Wire components. Our design calls for a Dallas 1-Wire interface to be implemented. Earlier we built a board that has both the 1- and 3-Wire interfaces and here's why. Accessing our temperature chip is fast since we are not sending or receiving large amounts of data. We have 512 bytes of RAM that is battery backed up. This is a great place to store nonvolatile information we want to retain. If we read and write large amounts of data using the 1-Wire interface, it will certainly slow things down. In addition, we can use the memory in the DS2404 as dual-port RAM, meaning it can be read from one interface and written to by the other. This has promise for future projects, so we will implement and test the 3-Wire interface even if we don't use it in the final prototype right now.

The DS2404 Timers

Just as the DS1822 can tell us when a temperature threshold has been reached, the DS2404 can tell us when a timer has expired. The DS2404 time functions are simple free-running counters. We can set timed events; when they are reached, a bit in the corresponding status register is set. The DS2404 timers can trigger interrupts, but since the BASIC Stamp can't process those interrupts, this feature is of little use to us right now. We can still set the interval timers and look for a change in the status register that indicates the event time has been reached. Let's examine how the DS2404 timers work and how we can put them to effective use. First, the timing functions of the DS2404 don't really store the time and date but are free-running elapsed counters. The DS2404 data sheet tells us there are three timers. They are:

■ Real-time clock — A 5-byte binary counter updated 256 times each second. The least significant byte contains a count of fractional seconds and the remaining four bytes holds the total seconds since the clock was started.

- Interval timer — A 5-byte counter incremented 256 times each second. The least significant byte again holds fractional seconds while the remaining four bytes provide the interval counter in total seconds. This timer has two modes of operation: automatic and manual.

- Cycle counter — A 4-bit binary counter. This counter keeps track of the number of times the unit has gone into backup battery mode.

If the interval timer is set to automatic mode, it is started by holding the data line for a predetermined time period. It will stop when the data line has been held low for that specified time period. Both time periods are controlled by the data select bit (DSel) in the control register. If the interval timer is set to manual mode, then it is started and stopped by the start/stop bit in the control register.

The cycle counter is incremented when the I/O line goes low if the proper timing requirements have been met. Again, timing is set by the DSel bit in the control register. The cycle counter is a very easy way to determine if a power outage has occurred and power has been restored. All the time functions mentioned here are available from either the 1- or 3-Wire interface.

The DS2404 Alarm Time Registers

In addition to the three timer registers, the DS2404 has an alarm register for each of these timers. To use the alarm registers, load the value of the alarm into the proper register. When the associated timer reaches that value, the appropriate flag bit is set in the status register. This feature is accessible for both the 1- and 3-Wire interfaces.

DS2404 Interrupt Registers

In addition to the alarm registers, there are interrupt enable flags for each of the three counters. If the associated interrupt bit is set, an interrupt is generated when the event occurs. It's important to note two items: First the interrupts are only available on the 1-Wire interface and second, they only fire once. The good news is that even though we may miss the actual interrupt, the interrupt bit for the associated timer will remain set until it is manually cleared. This means that if we enable the interrupt for the Stamp, we will have to read the status register and test to see if the interrupt was triggered.

Timers and the BASIC Stamp 2p

There are two ways to test if a timer has expired. The first is to create an endless program loop that continuously polls for keyboard input, updates the display, checks for host communications, and reads the 1-Wire and 3-Wire networks. This is a classical way for a developer to handle what we call "the do forever loop" and it works just fine. The only drawback to this technique is that we will never reach power conservation mode. That's not a big issue right now since are keeping the clock going with a battery backup circuit. In the lab, the CR2032 3.3-volt battery has kept the timer going for well over a week with no external power. Figure 8-11 illustrates our flowchart for how the BASIC Stamp code will manage our thermostat. The emphasis is on how we will process temperature and time.

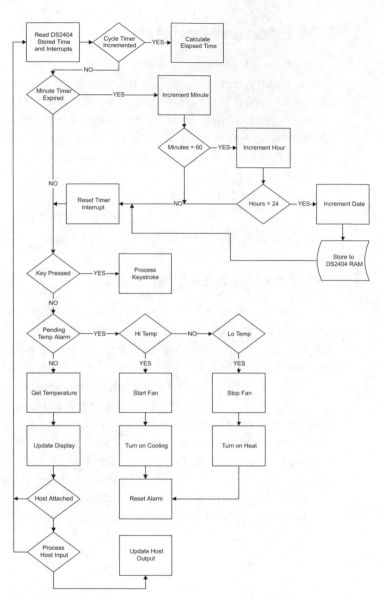

Figure 8-11

First, we check the cycle counter to see if a power outage has occurred. If it has, we recalculate the elapsed time. The next thing we do in the loop is check to see if our minute timer has elapsed. If it has, we check and update minutes, hours, and date accordingly. You've probably noticed we are not checking seconds; the reason is simple: If the system gets busy, it is too easy to miss more than one second, thereby putting our second counter out of sync. We should be able to check the minute interrupt with ease and keep the display updated. Additionally, if we trigger on each second we have to add the logic to check if seconds equals 60. If we lose track, our minute counter may be off so we will stick with a minute display for now.

Static RAM vs. EEPROM

At this point we need to consider where our data is stored. You'll notice the date, hours, and minutes are read and stored back to the DS2404 battery-backed RAM. This assures we always have a copy of the current date, hours, and minutes images as they were last updated. If we lose power, the counters in the DS2404 will continue to run but we have no reference counter to check it against. The solution to this is simple: We retain the cycle coun ter copy in the DS2404 RAM to compare against. If the cycle counter has incremented since it was last stored, we know that a power outage has occurred. In that case we will compare the counter values to the last counter values read and adjust our minutes, hours, and days accordingly.

We haven't discussed using the static RAM area of the BASIC Stamp (EEPROM). Since we have battery backed-up RAM in the DS2404 and there is a limited number of times we can write to the EEPROM on the BASIC Stamp, we've avoided having to use the EEPROM. The EEPROM could be used but we would need to rotate locations to extend the life of the part. We would also need to check each write with a read to verify the data was written to a good location. Rather than add those routines, we've chosen instead to use the battery-backed RAM, which does not have those limitations. We can use the EEPROM for storing our menu strings, since it won't need to be updated very frequently. Reading the EEPROM has no effect on its life; only writing to the EEPROM is limited.

So now we've added the time, temperature, and relay board to our prototype even though we haven't completely wired the 1- and 3-Wire interfaces to the Stamp. Now your prototype should look similar to Figure 8-12.

Figure 8-12

Communications Selection Options

Now that we have our keyboard, LCD display, temperature, time, and alarms all working it's time to implement the communications interface. As you may recall, we have a design requirement to provide RS-232, USB, and Ethernet for our prototype. Our requirements call for only one active interface at a time and we have enough BASIC Stamp I/O pins available to accomplish this task. This means we have two options in how we implement our communications interface. The first is to use the available pins and implement all three interfaces separately, and at the same time. If we do this, we can share the handshake lines, thus reducing the total number of pins we need to eight total.

The second option for the BASIC Stamp is to build an interface that is functionally identical from a hardware interface point of view and implement all three interfaces using either a switch,

DIP switch, or jumpers to select the active interface. If we take this approach we will need a total of four pins for the data and handshake lines and two additional pins for a switch for a total of six pins. This approach does save two processor pins. We could also make the interface software switch selectable through the menu, reducing the total pins needed to four. This is a very good solution but there are two concerns. First, if a default interface isn't chosen, the board may not communicate at all. Second, the BASIC Stamp interfaces to the board in a physically different way and at a different level then a PC. While an inexperienced user might place a call to customer service, the manual with the board clearly shows how to interface a TTL serial device such as a BASIC Stamp. Those who are not as comfortable with technology will call for support. In the final product, marketing has decided that a switch or automatic method of detection is preferred over a software menu item.

There are benefits and drawbacks to both approaches. If we have enough processor pins available there is no reason to add additional switch circuitry other than for future expansion, which isn't needed right now. This also provides us the flexibility of using multiple interfaces concurrently for debugging purposes. On the other hand, if we don't have enough processor pins already, then changing interfaces may be more efficient by using a switch instead of software. If we are switch selectable, we limit our available software expansion capabilities and make adding future interfaces a hardware task. On the other hand, if switch settings are left in a state unknown to the embedded system, we run the risk of disabling all interfaces. Remember, if we have to change hardware, we have to make circuit board changes and inevitably our costs will increase for each change, not to mention that field upgrades will become a requirement.

We have a third alternative that combines both of the above approaches. Since we are using two handshake lines for the RS-232 and USB interfaces, both can use the same four BASIC Stamp I/O pins. This would allow us to have a single hardware switch to select RS-232 or USB and would reduce the number of processor pins required by four pins. Since RS-232 and USB are both forms of "serial" communication it would consolidate the serial communications hardware interface.

Now you may be asking how we would make this work and still use a menu selection, so here is the logical thinking behind this approach. To add the capability to switch select between RS-232 and USB, we would add a single switch that would electrically switch between the interfaces. By utilizing one processor pin we could read this switch to display the currently selected serial interface in use on the LCD. If we choose to use this approach it will be designed in after implementing all the interfaces to see how many processor pins are left unused.

Ethernet for the Embedded Developer

Let's get started with the Ethernet interface first. Ethernet differs from RS-232 and USB because it communicates through a network backbone rather than a direct host connection. This means that the host doesn't need to be physically nearby and any host that supports TCP/IP either in hardware or software can attach to the embedded system. In fact we could even use an embedded wireless Ethernet connection to eliminate cables completely. Today, Ethernet is the most common and widely used network interface in the world. For the embedded systems developer Ethernet offers many benefits that allow it to compete favorably with USB and RS-232. Over the last few years Ethernet has become very price competitive with USB as a high-speed interface.

Additionally, many microcontroller manufacturers now include Ethernet as a standard option. Maxim/Dallas Semiconductor and Zilog both include Ethernet hardware interfaces in their products. Go into any local store and you'll find Ethernet cards for PCs for a little as $10 per card.

So, you ask, what about TCP/IP software? Well, there are many sources of embedded Ethernet software. The Maxim/Dallas Ethernet controllers have the TCP/IP protocol embedded right into the chip. Zilog provides the protocol in software, and there are many TCP/IP software packages that range in price from free to thousands of dollars. There is really something for everyone.

Embedded systems developers have as many choices for Ethernet interfaces as PC users.

Ethernet interfaces operate at 10 to 100 MPS (megabits per second). Assuming a 10-bit frame per character (including overhead), that's a full 1 to 10 million characters per second. Hook that up to the Internet over a high-speed connection and you are moving at a very fast pace that allows huge blocks of data to be moved very quickly. In fact, combining high-speed Ethernet cards with a broadband connection comes much closer to the speed of a dedicated T1 line than dial-up or DSL provide, and usually for a much lower cost than a T1.

Taking your Ethernet interface from being LAN to WAN accessible is a simple matter of providing a cable or hardware link to the WAN and possibly changing the IP address. To go from WAN to Internet access means adding accessibility to the outside world and possibly making some Ethernet address and port changes. The point is that the basic hardware connection doesn't change. If you're connected to a single system and want to connect to the LAN, it's a simple matter of changing cables and possibly making some IP address changes. Here are the benefits that Ethernet provides for the host:

- Cost — Ethernet chips and cards are inexpensive.

- Wide platform support — All major host operating systems have built-in support for the protocol.

- Expandability — Widening the availability of your device is fast, inexpensive, and easy once the initial development has been completed.

- Speed — Ethernet is fast when compared to RS-232.

- Provides a many-to-many connection — Ethernet can broadcast messages to a single user or a group at the same time.

Okay, Ethernet has some great benefits, but how easy is the software to implement on the embedded systems side? That depends on several factors. Ethernet is scalable from the hardware perspective and implemented in software through multiple layers. A LAN becomes a WAN by scaling the network up in size as opposed to a complete software/hardware reconfiguration. Software is implemented in a similar fashion with different protocol layers to meet memory and protocol needs.

At the foundation of the software protocols is TCP/IP. This protocol provides endpoint connection identifiers called *sockets* (named after the old telephone switchboards where a plug had to be inserted in a socket for a call connection to be complete). TCP/IP is necessary for communication on LANs, WANs, and the Internet. Even though TCP/IP is widely available from many sources, it may not be implemented or fully implemented for your processor, so you may have a considerable amount of work to do. There is also a possibility that the Ethernet chip you have chosen (assuming you've chosen to build the Ethernet interface from scratch) has TCP/IP partially or fully implemented in firmware right on the chip (like the Maxim/Dallas components). As you can see, when it comes to implementing an Ethernet interface we have several options that require from little or no development to a full-blown hardware/software development project.

The trade-off is cost. The less hardware or software you'll need to develop in-house, the higher the cost of the hardware interface (typically). Having said that, it can be more cost effective to use an off-the-shelf hardware/software solution in some cases depending on what (if any) special protocol/communications needs are required. Consider the human resources needed to build a custom Ethernet interface and the experience they will need to do it right. Developing a high-quality working Ethernet interface could cost hundreds of thousands of dollars, and that money is spent before you even know if the design works.

Remember that on the host side TCP/IP is handled by the operating system, but on the embedded system side the chances of Ethernet being a part of your microcontroller depend on several factors of which the two biggest are available memory and EEPROM space. No matter how you look at this topic, there are three ways for an embedded developer to implement TCP/IP.

The first is to write, purchase, or obtain a TCP/IP software toolkit, making certain it supports the Ethernet chip or microcontroller you have chosen. Most of the products offered in this category either target specific processors and charge a per-unit license fee or come with generic TCP/IP protocol handlers and drivers that require the developer to customize it to the chosen platform. Again, costs can vary widely using this approach.

The second implementation method is to purchase a packaged Ethernet system that contains the necessary hardware and software. There are several excellent products that provide a standalone Ethernet module designed to be used with embedded systems. Usually these products include an Ethernet controller and processor along with software to customize the module and add application-specific functionality.

Note:

All devices used as controllers in these prepackaged Ethernet kits are intelligent. That is to say they have I/O capability and are programmable just as the BASIC Stamp. How much of this functionality is accessible to the developer is up to the manufacturers of these kits.

The third Ethernet implementation method is to purchase a processor that already has TCP/IP embedded in the silicon or has software support from the manufacturer. More and more processors are offering built-in Ethernet capabilities as you enter the 16- and 32-bit microcontroller markets.

Note:

A lot of factors need to be considered when implementing an Ethernet interface in an embedded system. Each project has different requirements and different areas where development is needed. All of these approaches to implementing Ethernet have their place, and under the right design circumstances are cost effective. As an engineer I too often see an approach eliminated early in the review process because of perceived costs. First perceptions are not always what they seem when development alternatives, ongoing maintenance costs, licensing fees, and integration costs are considered. As we move on we will see how using the NetBurner product with the BASIC Stamp will pay off in several ways.

The NetBurner SB72

For this prototype we have selected an out-of-the box hardware solution that provides a full software implementation and software development environment for enhancing or modifying the TCP/IP environment. We've made this choice because it allows us to immediately use the hardware and simply develop the needed software changes to communicate with the desktop systems. Since Ethernet will be an option for the finished product, we could purchase Ethernet interfaces for only those units ordered with that type of host interface. This can be very cost effective since it allows us market entry with a fully functional interface that has a minimal investment in staff and engineering costs.

Building the Ethernet Circuit

The NetBurner SB72 Ethernet kit includes the following components:

- SB72 serial to Ethernet board
- SB72 adapter development board
- Software CD

- Serial cable
- SB72 to Ethernet hub cable
- SB72 to computer cable
- 12-volt power supply

The software on the NetBurner CD contains of the following components:

- TCP/IP stack
- Web server
- Real-time operating system based on uC/OS
- GNU C/C++ compiler and linker
- GDB debugger (the GNU debugger)
- IPSetup configuration utility
- Auto-update Flash update utility
- User manuals and documentation

Figure 8-13 shows a picture of the full kit.

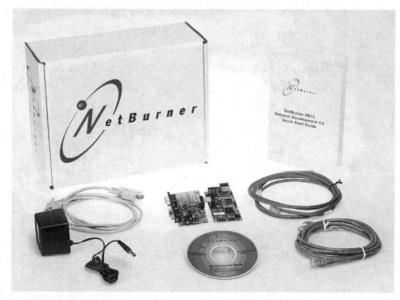

Figure 8-13

The SB72 uses the Motorola Coldfire processor as the brains of the system. The processor and Ethernet interface are contained on one board while the second board provides various types of serial communication to an embedded system. These include RS-232, RS485, SPI (3-Wire), and TTL. The Ethernet board is shown in Figure 8-14 and the serial communications board in Figure 8-16.

Figure 8-14

The main processor/Ethernet board has several jumpers and interfaces. For our use we are concerned with only two of these connectors. They are J4, which is at the center top of Figure 8-14, and J8, which is the three-pin connector located just above the Ethernet connector and behind the second and third LED.

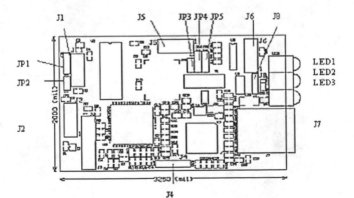

Figure 8-15

Connector J4 contains the RS-232 TTL interface for two serial
ports. J8 has +5 on both outside pins and GND on the center pin.
The second board contains connections for two RS-232 PC ports
and power. Figure 8-16 shows the second board.

Figure 8-16

In Figure 8-16 RS-232 port 1 is at the lower left with RS-232 port
0 on the right. Power may be connected either by a terminal
block located at the upper right of the board or a regular power
connector just below the terminal block. The connector at the
center top of the board has a 10-pin ribbon connector that attaches it to the processor board.

Figure 8-17 shows the complete assembly with both boards
attached.

Figure 8-17

In Figure 8-17 the processor board is located on the left side with the I/O card on the right. Notice the 10-pin ribbon cable that connects both boards. For our use we want to use the TTL RS-232 port that would normally be connected to a PC. We can simply disconnect the ribbon cable and attach the TTL level signals to the BASIC Stamp; however, in doing so we will eliminate our ability to do source code debugging since the second RS-232 port is used for that purpose. So to allow our debugger to work and still connect to the TTL RS-232 of the BASIC Stamp we will need a second 10-pin cable and two 10-pin headers that we will attach to our Stamp prototype board. Figure 8-18 illustrates what I'm talking about by simply adding a "tap" between the boards to which we can connect the BASIC Stamp.

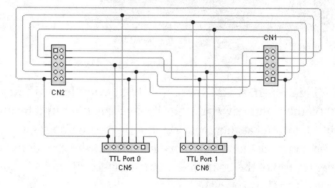

Figure 8-18

This will allow us to use either or both RS-232 or TTL level RS-232 without losing our ability to debug. Table 8-2 shows the pin outs for the J5 connector.

Table 8-2

Pin	Signal
1	(VSS) Ground
2	CTS1
3	TX1
4	RX1

Pin	Signal
5	RTSI
6	RTS0
7	CTS0
8	TX0
9	(VCC) +5 Volts
10	RX0

Setting up the SB72

The SB72 is a very complete product that includes its own operating system, compiler, and programs. The product includes
GCC, the GNU C Compiler, the SDB debugger, and a graphical
front end to the SDB debugger, which provides source level
debugging for the board. The SB72 also includes a developers
manual in PDF format that is over 60 pages long and includes
setup, debugging, and step-by-step instructions on using each of
the available protocols. The developers guide is very complete
and easy to understand, so setting up a development system and
getting your first working program should not take long (assuming you're familiar with the C language). Software for the SB72 is
written in C. While we won't cover the C language here, we will
go through a list of things you should do before and after the
installation.

Before the Installation

Before installing the SB72 kit review the README file. If you
already have a Cygwin or MSYS installation, this file will explain
how to migrate the SB72 developers kit into the existing installation. This could save you considerable time in fixing a broken
Cygwin or MSYS installation.

After the Installation

Once the SB72 kit is installed, review the quick start guide to make sure the installation was done correctly. Within the NetBurner NNDK program group there are several programs and manuals. The quick start guide explains how to use the C IDE and create C projects. Also review the NNDK programmers guide (NNDKProgMan.pdf) and work through the first sample application. This will give you some first-hand experience in setting up the debugger, creating a project, saving the project, compiling, downloading, and debugging. Once this step is completed and working, you will know your installation is set up correctly. Then I would suggest reading the developers manuals that cover TCP/IP and uOS, the operating system used in the SB72. The SB72 compilers and IDE are open-source products that have been enhanced by NetBurner. The IDE is Dev-C++ and is available from SourceForge.net. The compiler is GCC and is available from www.gnu.org. SDB is also available from www.gnu.org.

Testing the SB72 Setup

Now let's test our SB72 installation and see if it works. Once we complete this step, we will attach our BASIC Stamp and write a short program to see if the Stamp can send and receive data via the NetBurner connection.

The SB72 can be connected directly to a PC or to an Ethernet hub. The kit includes two cables, one red and one blue. If you're connecting the SB72 directly to your computer, use the red cable; otherwise use the blue. Connect the Ethernet cable and make sure the cable that connects the SB72 and the I/O board together is in place. Plug in the transformer and connect power to the SB72 I/O board. The green LED next to the Ethernet connect should light immediately, indicating the power is connected. After a few seconds the remaining two lights should come on to indicate a good Ethernet connection has been made.

If you installed the NetBurner tools to the default path, then you should have a directory on your C drive named Nburn. Navigate to the PCBin folder and run the IPSetup program. You should see a screen similar to Figure 8-19.

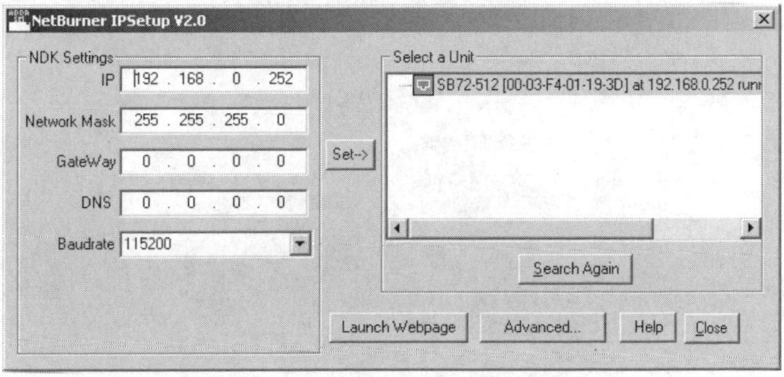

Figure 8-19

If you're unfamiliar with Ethernet let's walk through the information you're looking at. The first address is the device address of the SB72, which in this case is set to 192.168.0.252. This is the device address and has to be unique to the LAN or WAN it is attached to. The second address is the network mask. This can be used to define a workgroup or location within a company or region. The gateway address is set to 0.0.0.0, which means the IP address in line 1 is static or set manually. We could have a DHCP server assign the IP address, in which case we would input the address of the DHCP server in this line. The final IP address is for the domain name server, or DNS. Again, if we had a resident domain name server we would put that address here. The last entry is the serial baud rate for the RS-232 debug port.

If an SB72 is detected when IPSetup starts, it will be displayed in the window to the right of the IP addresses, which in this case is true. If the application running on the SB72 supports a web page the Launch Webpage button will be active. If you wish to set up TFTP, then click the Advanced button to see or change current TFTP settings. Since the SB72 has an application running that does support a web page, let's click the Launch

Webpage button. Your default browser should start and a page similar to Figure 8-20 should be displayed.

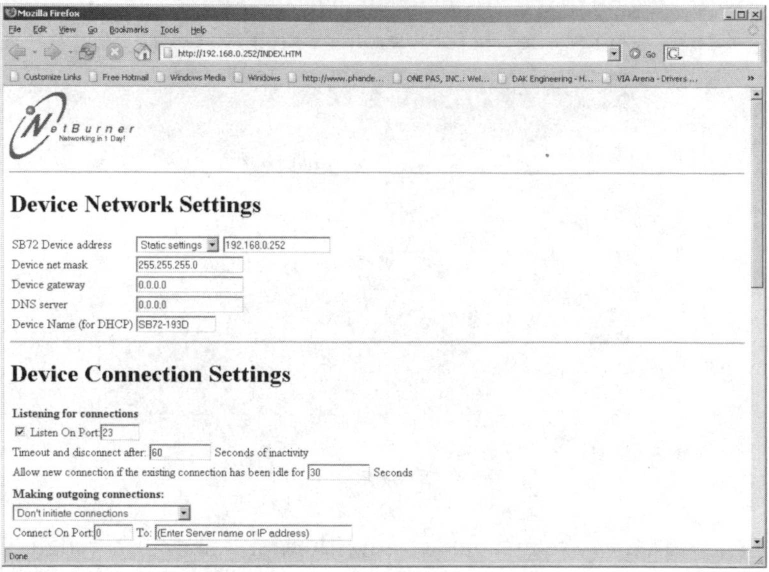

Figure 8-20

Some of the information displayed also appears in IPSetup but other information does not. For example you can change the device name and submit the change to the SB72 by clicking the Update button at the bottom of this page. You can also configure the other serial port that will be attached to the BASIC Stamp from this page.

Let's download and run a simple test program. We will walk through the steps necessary to write, download, and test a simple program. In the process we will take a look at what needs to be done to utilize the Ethernet interface with minimal code changes to the BASIC Stamp code. Remember that the BASIC Stamp views the SB72 as a serial I/O device. This means that the SB72 will be responsible for the session management to the host and serial data I/O to the Stamp, and properly packetizing the data into our message protocol. While Ethernet allows us to have a many-to-one relationship, we will implement a simple TCP/IP program without the frills for the prototype. The SB72 has a multitasking supervisor that allows many tasks to run at one time by dividing the available time by priority. Let's take a look at how the finished Ethernet interface will integrate to the BASIC Stamp.

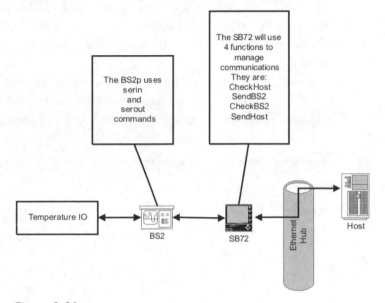

Figure 8-21

Right now we are dealing with the embedded side; we will cover the host development in Chapter 11. We will set up the SB72 as a TCP/IP server that listens on port 3675. Port 3675 is allocated by IANA to another product I developed and sell for the telephony industry so we aren't stealing someone else's port number. (Please don't use this port in your production products; you can apply for a port number at www.iana.org.) This test will require one Ethernet port and two serial ports. As we complete the SB72 interface we will eliminate the need for one serial port since we will move that I/O data to the BS2, but this test is just to get us started.

We will write a template that will be used for the rest of this chapter. Using the template we will then write our test program, which will evolve into our Ethernet handler for the BS2. Currently we are using the SB72 serial port and power board. By using the same port and data configuration for our test we can get our software working. Then we will connect the port to connector J6 on the SB72 and our BS2 will be connected to J5 (which is the TTL serial). Finally, we will supply +5 and GND to connector J8 on the SB72. Those three connections will allow us to eliminate the SB72 I/O board, power connection, and second serial port.

To write our template let's go the Nburn\devcpp folder and run devcpp. When the program starts, there are no open files or projects. To create our base template, select File | New | Appwizard.

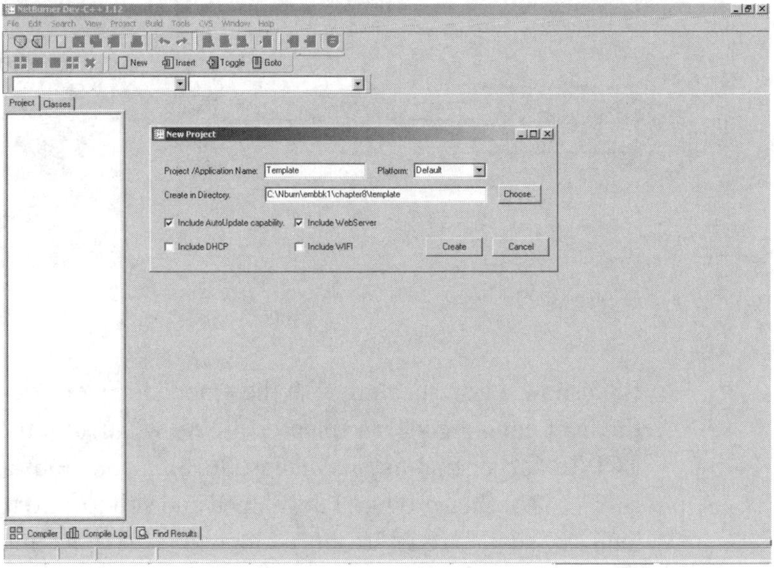

Figure 8-22

Enter Template for the application name. Leave the platform set to Default. Create a path to Nburn\embbk1\chapter8\test1 and use this as the target folder for the template project. Uncheck Include DHCP and WIFI but leave the WebServer and AutoUpdate boxes checked. Click the Create button. We now

have a project named template that has one source file named
main.cpp, a makefile named dcpp_makefile, and a subfolder
named HTML. The HTML folder is where our web server files
would be stored if we choose to use the web server later.

The source file, main.cpp, is open in the editor window and
just a few lines of code have been added to initialize the SB72 and
start the task manager and web server. The following code lines
are created by the Appwizard.

Listing 8-1

```
#include "predef.h"
#include <stdio.h>
#include <ctype.h>
#include <startnet.h>
#include <autoupdate.h>


extern "C" {
void UserMain(void * pd);                      // Main Task Definition
}

const char * AppName="template";               // Application Name
void UserMain(void * pd)                        // Main Task Function
{
  InitializeStack();                           // Initialize TCP/IP Stack
  OSChangePrio(MAIN_PRIO);                      // Highest Useable Priority
  EnableAutoUpdate();                          // Auto-update Code in SB72
// StartHTTP();                                 // Start Web Server (Currently Not Needed)

iprintf("Application started");                // Print to Terminal Port
  while (1)                                      // Do Forever
  {
    printf("Hello from Embedded Systems!\r\n");
    OSTimeDly(20);                             // Sleep for 20 Clock Ticks, then wake up
  }
}
```

This program will compile and run just fine but it doesn't do very
much other than sit around and look for events every 20 clock
ticks. Let's compile, download, and run this program to see
exactly what it does. First, let's select the Build menu and

choose the Make Clean option. This will erase any temporary files and get the environment ready for a clean build. When complete, a progress window will remain on the screen like the one in Figure 8-23.

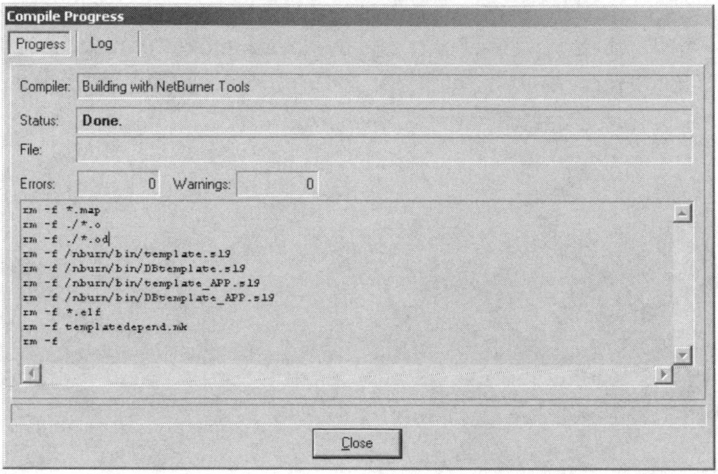

Figure 8-23

When all the files have been removed, the Progress button will change to Close; just click Close to continue.

Next, we will compile, link, and download the program to the SB72. This is where the AutoUpdate selection comes into play. AutoUpate will download the code and start the program automatically. This allows you to see the results of your program immediately. If we wish to debug we need to make a few changes, but for now let's see what this program does.

By default the program will output any information via the printf statements to port 1, so make sure you have a DB9 cable attached to serial port 1 on the SB72 and attached to a COM port on the host. After you've connected the serial cable we need to go to the Nburn\pctools directory and run the MTTY application. Select the proper COM port and choose a baud rate of 115200, leaving all the other options unchanged. Now press the Connect button. If the port was properly opened, Connect will change to

Disconnect; otherwise an error message will be displayed after a timeout period has elapsed.

Now we will compile, link, and download the program to the SB72. Again, choose the Build menu but this time select the Compile and Download selection or simply press the F9 key. A progress dialog will be displayed such as the one in Figure 8-24.

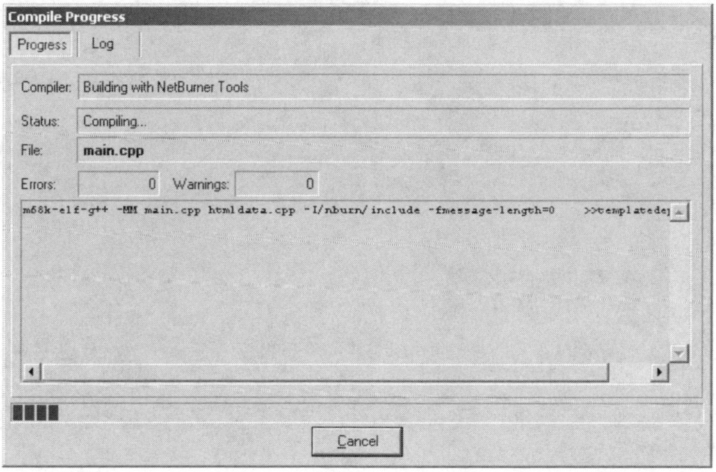

Compile Progress

| Progress | Log |

Compiler:	Building with NetBurner Tools
Status:	Compiling...
File:	**main.cpp**
Errors:	0	Warnings:	0

```
m68k-elf-g++ -MM main.cpp htmldata.cpp -I/nburn/include -fmessage-length=0  >>templatedej
```

[Cancel]

Figure 8-24

If the program compiled and linked correctly when the auto update program is executed, a download progress bar will be shown as in Figure 8-25.

Program Netburner [x]

Percent Complete

[Cancel]

Figure 8-25

Once the download is completed the progress bar will disappear automatically. After the program is downloaded successfully, the SB72 will automatically be reset. Once the application is running, an "Application started" message will be sent to the terminal port

that is connected to the MTTY program. Running the program
template without modification should produce output in MTTY
similar to that in Figure 8-26.

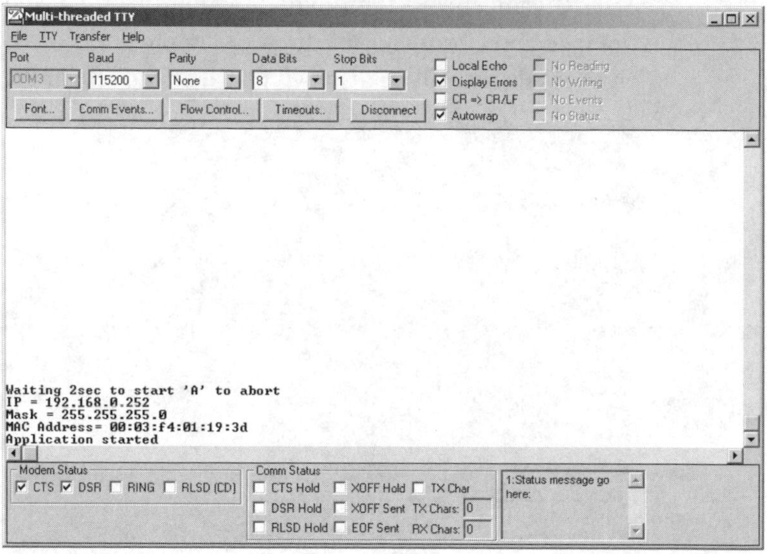

Figure 8-26

As you can see, there is information sent to the terminal we
didn't print so let's examine each line. The first s printed after
the reset command has been issued to the SB72. This gives us
two seconds to interrupt the start of execution. If we don't interrupt the program, the IP address and network mask will be
displayed. The next line prints the MAC address, which is a
unique address assigned to each and every network card or chip
used. Every Ethernet interface must have a unique address! The
last line prints our "Application started" message, so all of the
preceding information is from the boot program prior to passing
control to our application.

Debugging an SB72 Program

Debugging a program on the SB72 takes a slightly different process. Let's add one line to our program and then compile and debug it. Add the following line just above the OSTimeDly(20) line in the program:

```
printf("Hello from Embedded Systems!\r\n");
```

This one line will simply print the message "Hello from Embedded Systems!" every 20 clock ticks. After you have added the line of code, select Build | Make Clean again to remove the old code files. This time we will select Build | Make Debug Version to compile and link the debug version of the code. We have not downloaded the finished program this time because we load and execute through the Insight debugger, which is started by selecting Tools | GDB INSIGHT from the menu bar. The Insight debugger will open with an empty source window. Choose File | Open, navigate to the Nburn\embbk1\Chapter8\test1 folder, and choose the DBTemplate.elf file. When we compile for the debugger the letters DB are prepended to the filename. The elf extension is the excitable code that the debugger will associate with the source file. Once the selection is made, the source code is loaded into the source code window.

Our next step is to connect to the SB72 board. We do this by selecting Run | Connect to Target.

The following screen will be displayed.

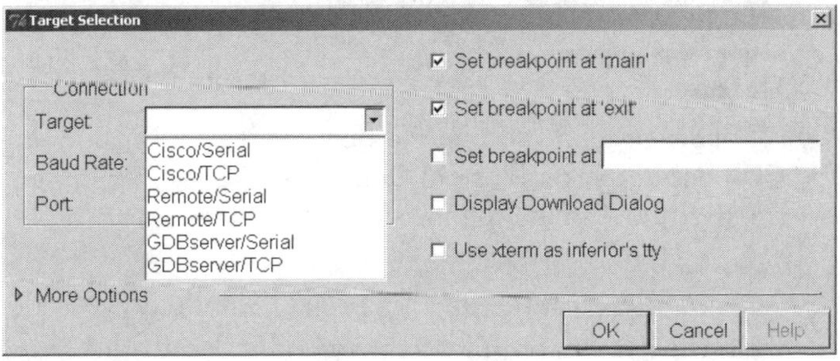

Figure 8-27

To connect properly, the target, baud rate, and port selections must be set correctly. The choices for Target are:

- Cisco/Serial — Cisco Serial Protocol
- Cisco/TCP — Cisco TCP Protocol
- Remote/Serial — GDB Direct Connect Serial
- Remote/TCP — GDB Direct Connect TCP
- GDBServer/Serial — GDBServer Serial Connection
- GDBServer/TCP — GDBServer TCP Connection

Since we are using the AutoUpdate utility, the Dev C++ IDE will automatically load the compiled program using TCP/IP to the SB72 board. Since we are using the SB72 TCP/IP protocol for our main program, we will choose Remote/Serial as our connection. This allows us to do real-time debugging of the Ethernet program while it is running.

Our Baud Rate selections are 9600, 19200, 38400, 57600, and 115200. While 38400 is the default selection, the NetBurner COM port defaults to 57600. The COM port list should show the available COM ports for your machine. Choose the port connected to the SB72 board. If your choices are correct, you will be connected to the SB72 and the breakpoint will rest at either the program's main function or the breakpoint line you've chosen, depending on the status of the Set Breakpoint at Main check box. You can now step through the program and display variables, buffers, etc., without affecting the program operation.

Note:

I strongly suggest reading the documentation for both the GDB debugger and Insight Debugger IDE to both understand and utilize the full feature set of these tools.

The complete source for this project can be downloaded at www.wordware.com/files/embsys or at www.time-lines.com/embedbk1/source.

Testing Ethernet Communications

We are now ready to test our Ethernet interface. This will be a two-stage process. The first stage is to test the connection between the Ethernet board and the BASIC Stamp. Once we have that working, our next task will be testing the Ethernet to network connection.

To test the connection between the BASIC Stamp and SB72 TTL serial connection we will need a Windows 2000 or Windows XP machine with the following:

- Serial port to connect the console program to the SB72

- Serial port to connect the SDB Debugger to the SB72

- Serial port to connect SB72 to TTL pins in BASIC Stamp

- The SB72 development kit installed on the Windows machine

- The BASIC Stamp Editor and Debugger installed on the Windows machine

- An Ethernet card installed and working in the Windows machine

- An Ethernet hub with at least two available ports

- Two Ethernet cables to connect the SB72 and Windows machine to the hub

If you have already installed and tested the SB72 development software, then you are already familiar with installing the serial cables and starting an mtty terminal and debugger session. Running both of these at the same time normally requires two serial cables, or USB to serial cables. You can install the Ethernet cables to the hub now or wait until we complete our first test.

To understand how the communications between the SB72 and other microcontrollers work requires reading the NetBurner NNDK user manual, which is provided in a Windows help file format. The getting started section, titled "Networking in 1 Day," helps the user implement a network interface in one working day. If you want to understand more about how Ethernet and Internet protocols work, I would strongly suggest spending some time working through this section of the manual. Another section of interest for our purpose is "The NetBurner Cookbook," which is a very detailed set of instructions on installing and troubleshooting your development system. For software development purposes we will utilize the chapters on uC/OS and NetBurner System I/O libraries for our first test.

Establishing communications between the SB72 and BASIC Stamp is done through the use of the NetBurner System I/O routines. The debugger is attached to serial port 1, and the mtty terminal program is attached to serial port 0. As we walk through these short but informational listings, our objective is to reach three goals. First, we need to be able to send data between the BASIC Stamp and the SB72 boards. This is accomplished by writing a very simple program that takes input from mtty and sends it to the BASIC Stamp debug screen. We also need to send data from the BASIC Stamp to the SB72, so we will implement sending data via the BASIC Stamp debug command back to the SB72 and to the NetBurner debugger. This will validate that our baud rates, stop bits, parity, and handshake work the way we expect them to.

Once that is working we will wrap these functions in the uC/OS task manager so they run as tasks and will allow for Ethernet data to be sent and received at the same time. Finally, we will add the ability to send and receive data to the Ethernet interface while also handling serial port data. Figure 8-28 shows a diagram of the first task: sending data between the BASIC Stamp and SB72 boards.

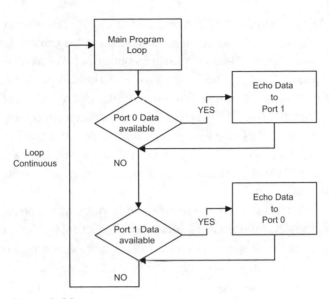

Figure 8-28

That's a pretty simple task and doesn't even require we use the operating system in the SB72. To get started let's walk through developing a NetBurner application together. If you've installed the NetBurner NNDK into the default directory, it will be located in C:\Nburn and a NetBurner NNDK program group will be created. To develop a NetBurner application we will create a template using the NBAppWizard. When started, the NBAppWizard displays the following screen.

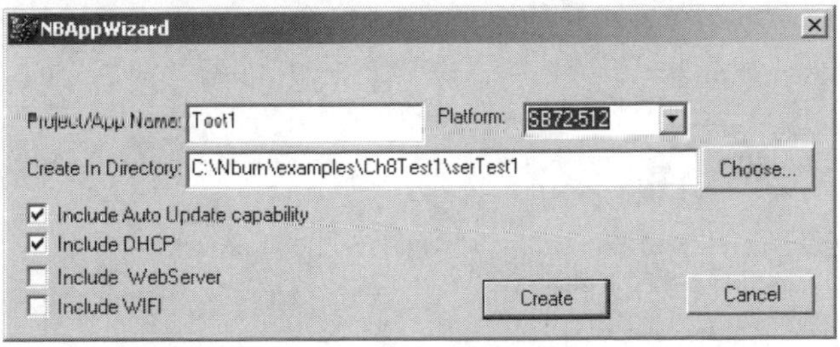

Figure 8-29

We've created a subdirectory named Ch8Test1\serTest1 to hold the project and source files. We've named the project Test1 and chosen the SB72-512 platform as our target. We have also checked the auto update and DHCP options. Auto update allows the program to be downloaded to the device automatically after compilation, and DHCP permits an IP address to be acquired automatically. Once we set the options we press the Create key; the project will be created and the window will disappear. Next, we load the project into the editor so we can finish writing the test program.

Start the Dev-C++ editor and load the main.cpp file located in the Nburn\examples\Ch8Test1\serTest1 folder. Below is the skeleton code generated from the application wizard. I entered the comments on the right side of the listing.

Listing 8-2

```
#include "predef.h"                    // Version Information
#include <stdio.h>                     // Standard I/O Definitions for C
#include <ctype.h>                     // C Type Definitions
#include <startnet.h>                  // Network Startup Include File List
#include <autoupdate.h>                // Autoupdate Definitions
#include <dhcpclient.h>                // DHCP Client Definitions

extern "C" {                          // Declare UserMain function as external C function
void UserMain(void * pd);
}

const char * AppName="Test1";          // User Application Name

void UserMain(void * pd)               // UserMain is where the work is done!
{
  InitializeStack();                   // Initialize TCP/IP Stack
  if (EthernetIP == 0) GetDHCPAddress();
  // If No IP address has been then assigned,
  // get one from DHCP Server
  OSChangePrio(MAIN_PRIO);             // Escalate Program Priority to Highest (5)
  EnableAutoUpdate();                  // Enable AutoUpdate facilities

  iprintf("Application started\n");    // Send Start Message to Terminal
```

```
while (1)                          // Loop infinitely
{
  OSTimeDly(20);                   // Delay every 20 ms to service background tasks
}                                  // End of Loop
}                                  // End of Program
```

If you're familiar with the C language you know that main() is where a program starts. In this case, however, main() initializes the uC/OS and our application is wrapped as a task in the function UserMain(* pd). *pd is a pointer to the process descriptor assigned by the task manager in main().

When our prototype is completed we will no longer use the SB72 I/O board because our connections will go directly to the SB72 processor. For now, however, we need to connect both boards together for debugging purposes. Since we have chosen TTL serial between the Stamp and SB72, we will need to take one of those ports from either mtty or the SDB debugger. To eliminate the need for a third serial port, we will implement the RS-232 send and receive routines for test purposes to the mtty program. Once we have those routines working we will disconnect mtty and connect serial port 0 via TTL to the BASIC Stamp. This will give us the chance to debug our serial I/O using a PC Terminal program and narrow any problems in the interface to the BASIC Stamp code. Using the same template program created earlier, we will add the six lines of code shown in bold in Listing 8-3.

Listing 8-3

```
#include "predef.h"               // Version Information
#include <stdio.h>                // Standard I/O Definitions for C
#include <ctype.h>                // C Type Definitions
#include <startnet.h>             // Network Startup Include File List
#include <autoupdate.h>           // Autoupdate Definitions
#include <dhcpclient.h>           // DHCP Client Definitions
#include <gdbstub.h>              // Debugger Stub
#include <serial.h>               // Used for serial I/O to Stamp
#include <taskmon.h>              // Used to monitor uC/OS tasks

extern "C" {                      // Declare UserMain function as external C function
```

```
void UserMain(void * pd);
}


const char * AppName="Test1";          // User Application Name

void UserMain(void * pd)               // UserMain is where the work is done!
{
  InitializeStack();                   // Initialize TCP/IP Stack
  OSChangePrio(MAIN_PRIO);             // Escalate Program Priority to Highest
  EnableAutoUpdate();                  // Enable AutoUpdate facilities
  InitGDBStubNoBreak(1, 57600);        // initialize Debugger to Port 1
  iprintf("Application started\n");    // Send Start Message to Terminal
  EnableTaskMonitor();                 // Start Task Monitor
  while (1)                            // Loop infinitely
  {
    OSTimeDly(20);                     // Delay every 20 ms to service background tasks
    iprintf("Hello from Embedded Systems!\r\n", Secs);
  }                                    // End of Loop
}                                      // End of Program
```

These additional six lines of code load and initialize the debugger
stub in the program, load the task monitor interface, and print a
message to the second serial port (connected to the mtty terminal window). If you read the documentation on how to build and
debug a program, you may find you can't get the debugger to
work properly. Before we continue with running the debugger
let's go through the proper steps to compile, load, and debug the
source code.

1. Compile a debug version of the code by selecting Build |
    Make Debug Version. This will place a binary file in the
    Nburn\bin folder with the prefix DB.

2. Run the AutoUpdate utility and download the file in step 1 to
    the SB72.

3. Run the Insight Debugger by selecting Tools | GDB
    INSIGHT.

4. After Insight has loaded, select File | Open and load the debug file with the same filename in step 1 but with the elf extension. This file will be located in your project folder and not in the bin folder.

5. Unplug the power connector to the SB72 for 30 seconds, then plug it in again.

6. Select Run | Connect from the Insight menu bar.

You should see a message box pop up with a success message. If you don't see the success popup box, follow the troubleshooting instructions found in the online help of NNDK. This is accessible from the Help button in DevCpp. Look for the topic "Using the GDB/Insight on the NetBurner Platform." Read the topic and check the debug connection to see if data is being exchanged properly.

Connecting the SB72 to the BASIC Stamp

Now that we've tested the SB72 and its functions, it's time to connect it to the BASIC Stamp. First, disconnect the power to the SB72, then disconnect the SB72 serial adaptor board by disconnecting the ribbon cable attaching it to connector J5 on the SB72. The last program we loaded to the SB72 is in flash memory so it will be retained even without power. According to Table 8-2 the following connections are for port 0: 1 = Gnd, 6 = RTS0, 7 = CTS0, 8 = TX0, 10 = RX0. For power and ground connections, we have 1 = Gnd and 9 = +5 volts (Vcc). We will use port 0 since port 1 is attached to the debugger. If we connect the BS2 to connector J5 we can leave the mtty program attached to port 0. All data to and from the Stamp will go through the RS-232 transceiver on the I/O board and be displayed in the mtty screen. To use mtty this way we need to turn off handshaking since the SERIN and SEROUT commands will provide this at the TTL level. Before we continue let's update our schematic to reflect the four I/O lines needed for our TTL serial interface.

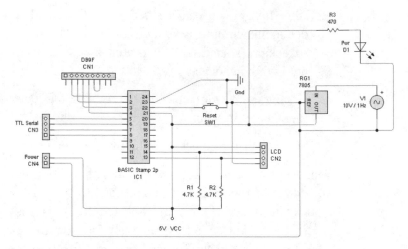

Figure 8-30

In Figure 8-30 we have allocated the BS2 pins 0-3 to the 4-Wire TTL serial interface. Our pin assignments are: P0 = TX, P1 = RX, P2 = CTS, and P3 = RTS. We will also connect the VSS from the BS2 to Gnd on the SB72. In Chapter 7 we covered how the RS-232 interface works. The following listing will echo any inbound data to the debug terminal screen.

Listing 8-4

```
// {$STAMP BS2p}
// {$PBASIC 2.5}
//
// Test Program for RS-232 TTL I/O using RTS Handshaking
// for Embedded Systems Desktop Integration Chapter 8
// Copyright 2004 - Oliver H. Bailey
//
// Pins are assigned in the following order:
// Pin 0 - Transmit Data   (TX or TD) =>
// Pin 1 - Receive Data    (RX or RD) <=
// Pin 2 - Clear To Send   (CTS)      =>
// Pin 3 - Request To Send (RTS)      <=
//
TX CON 0
RX CON 1
CTS CON 2
```

```
RTS CON 3

InData VAR Byte
OutData VAR Byte

LOW RX                              // Set RD Low
LOW RTS                             // Set RTS Low

Main:.
  SERIN RX\CTS, 110, [InData]       // 1=RD, 2=CTS, 110=9600, N, 8, 1
  IF InData = 13 THEN               // If InData = CRLF
    DEBUG CR, LF                    // Send to Terminal
  ELSE                              // ELSE
    DEBUG InData                   // Send the Data
  ENDIF                             // End of IF Statement
GOTO Main:                          // Start Again
```

Before we can test this program we need to change the baud rate
on SB72 port 0 to 9600 baud. The BS2 cannot operate at speeds
over 19200 so this change is required. To make this change we
need to close serial port 0 on the SB72 and reopen it with a new
baud rate. Listing 8-5 shows the changes needed to connect to
the BS2.

Listing 8-5

```c
#include "predef.h"
#include <stdio.h>
#include <ctype.h>
#include <startnet.h>
#include <autoupdate.h>
#include <serial.h>
#include <iosys.h>
#include <utils.h>
#include <taskmon.h>
#include <gdbstub.h>


#define DATAPORT 0                  // Port 0 for the BS2
#define DEBUGPORT 1                 // Port 1 for the Debugger
```

```
extern "C" {
void UserMain(void * pd);
}

const char * AppName="serialtest";
void UserMain(void * pd)
{
  InitializeStack();                          // Initialize TCP/IP
  OSChangePrio(MAIN_PRIO);                     // Change to priority 50
  EnableAutoUpdate();                          // Allow program updates
  SerialClose(DATAPORT);                       // Close current Data Port
  SerialClose(DEBUGPORT);                      // Close current Debug Port

  InitGDBStubNoBreak(DEBUGPORT, 57600);        // Initialize Debugger
  int fddata = OpenSerial(DATAPORT, 9600, 1, 8, eParityNone);
  writestring(fddata, "Application started\r\n");
  EnableTaskMonitor();
  while (1)
  {
    OSTimeDly(20);
    writestring(fddata, "Hello from Embedded Systems!\r\n");
  }
}
```

Notice how we close both data and debug serial ports and then reopen them. You'll also notice that we are using the writestring C function instead of printf or iprintf. This is because we have not redirected where the stdin and stdout go. Instead, writestring uses the file descriptor from the OpenSerial function call. We could check fddata to see it is valid, but the purpose is to demonstrate the process. If you have mtty attached you will see the message "Hello from Embedded Systems!" displayed every 20 clock ticks. The same data is being sent to the BS2 via the TTL level RS-232.

Now that we've tested receiving data from the BS2 it's time to test sending data from the BS2. Since we don't need the debugger right now, we can disconnect the power from the SB72 I/O card and disconnect the card from the main SB72 board. Our first task is to connect the power and ground wires to the SB72 from our BS2 board. The center pin of the J8 connector on the SB72 is ground. Either of the outside pins on J8 are +5. Make sure the power to the BS2 is off before connecting these pins. Remember that port 0 on the SB72 is our data port and port 1 is our debug port.

Now it's time to add support for TCP/IP to our program. We are already initializing the IP stack since we are using Auto-Update to transfer programs to the SB72 board. Now we will add support for testing our BS2 data I/O to a host computer. To do this we will use the telnet program to connect to the SB72, send data to the BS2, and display data from the BS2 in the telnet terminal window. Now things get a little tricky because we need to write software for the SB72 and the BS2. Since we've already got our BS2 receiving data, we need to only add the send data routine. This time, however, instead of our mtty program we will substitute the telnet program, which in effect is an Ethernet terminal program. Since we will be developing our host software later, using telnet will allow us to not only test but also provide us with a working code foundation. Let's start with the software for the SB72 in Listing 8-6.

Listing 8-6

```c
#include "predef.h"
#include <stdio.h>
#include <ctype.h>
#include <startnet.h>
#include <autoupdate.h>
#include <serial.h>
#include <iosys.h>
#include <utils.h>
#include <ip.h>
#include <tcp.h>
#include <taskmon.h>

#define TIMEOUT (60)                        // Timeout between packets
#define OVERRIDE_DLY (20)

#define MSG_WAITING "Waiting to Connect\r\n"  // IP waiting
#define MSG_CONNECT "Connection Opened\r\n"   // IP open
#define MSG_CLOSED  "Connection Closed\r\n"   // IP closed
#define MSG_TO      "Connection Timeout\r\n"  // IP timeout
```

```
#define MSG_TO_CLOSED "Connection Timeout, Connection will be closed\r\n"

#define DATAPORT 0                              // Data com port
#define DEBUGPORT 1                             // Data debug port
#define BAUDRATE 9600                           // Serial baud rate
#define STOPBITS 1                              // Stop bits
#define DATABITS 8                              // Data bits

#define TCPIP_PORT 23                           // Telnet port

extern "C" {
void UserMain(void * pd);
}

const char * AppName="TestTCP";                 // Set Application Name
void UserMain(void * pd)
{
  InitializeStack();                            // Initialize TCP/IP Stack
  OSChangePrio(MAIN_PRIO);                       // Move priority up to 50
  EnableAutoUpdate();                           // Allow Ethernet based updates
  EnableTaskMonitor();                          // Enable Task Monitor
  SerialClose(DATAPORT);                        // Close and reopen data port with
                                                // new parameters
  int fdserial = OpenSerial(DATAPORT, BAUDRATE, STOPBITS, DATABITS, eParityNone);
  writestring(fdserial, "Application Starting\r\n");      // Display start message
  int fdlisten = listen(INADDR_ANY, TCPIP_PORT, 5);      // listen for any remote request
  if (fdlisten > 0 )                            // Connection request = fdlisten > 0
  {
    IPADDR host_addr;                           // address of connecting client
    WORD port;                                  // port request came in on
    writestring(fdserial, MSG_WAITING);         // display wait message

    while (1)                                   // Do forever
    {
      int fdnet = accept(fdlisten, &host_addr, &port, 0);  // accept connection request
      writestring(fdserial, MSG_CONNECT);       // Display connect message
      writestring(fdnet, MSG_CONNECT);          // Display message to telnet
      int ip_timeout = 0;                       // Set timeout to zero
      while (fdnet > 0)                         // While active socket connection
      {
        fd_set read_file;                       // create read file descriptor
        fd_set error_file;                      // create error file descriptor
```

```
FD_ZERO(&read_file);                // zero read_file descriptor contents
FD_SET(fdnet, &read_file);          // set fdnet with read_file descriptor info
FD_SET(fdserial, &read_file);       // set fdserial also with read_file descriptor info
if (ip_timeout >= OVERRIDE_DLY)     // If timeout > delay
{
  FD_SET(fdlisten, &read_file);     // set fdlisten with read_file descriptor info
}


FD_ZERO(&error_file);               // Zero error file descriptor
FD_SET(fdnet, &error_file);         // set fdnet with error_file info

// Wait for descriptor events - IO Event
if (select(FD_SETSIZE, &read_file, (fd_set *) 0, &error_file, TIMEOUT))
{
  // Check for event descriptors
  if (FD_ISSET(fdnet, &read_file))          // fdnet read_file
  {
    char buf[40];                           // allocate buffer
    int n = read(fdnet, buf, 40);           // read up to 40 characters
    write(fdserial, buf, n);                // echo to serial port
    ip_timeout = 0;                         // reset timeout value to zero
  }


  if (FD_ISSET(fdserial, &read_file))       // fdserial read_file - Input from BS2
  {
    char buf[40];                           // allocate 40-character buffer
    int n = read(fdserial, buf, 40);        // read up to 40 characters
    write(fdnet, buf, n);                   // write to telnet device
  }


  if (FD_ISSET(fdnet, &error_file))         // fdnet error_file
  {
    writestring(fdserial, MSG_CLOSED);
    // send close message to serial port - Error to BS2
    close(fdnet);                           // close IP port
    fdnet = 0;                              // Set file descriptor to zero
    writestring(fdserial, MSG_WAITING);     // Send waiting message to BS2
  }


  if (FD_ISSET(fdlisten, &read_file))       // No data timeout
  {
    writestring(fdserial, MSG_TO);          // Send message to BS2
    writestring(fdnet, MSG_TO);             // Send message to telnet
```

```
        close(fdnet);                      // close telnet port after message
        fdnet = 0;                         // Zero file descriptor for socket
      }
    }
    else                                   // Else we have no pending events so
    {
      ip_timeout++;                        // increment ip_timout counter
      if(ip_timeout > TIMEOUT)             // timeout period exceeded
      {
        writestring(fdserial, MSG_TO);     // Send Stamp timeout message
        writestring(fdnet, MSG_TO);    // send connected socket device timeout message
        close(fdnet);                      // close socket
        writestring(fdserial, MSG_TO_CLOSED); // send close message to BS2
        fdnet = 0;                         // Set file descriptor for socket to zero
      }
    }                                      // End of else statement
   }                                       // End of open socket handler
  }                                        // End of While (1) loop
 }                                         // End of Connection Request Loop
}                                          // End of main program
```

Every connected device has an associated file descriptor once opened. In Listing 8-6 the BS2 is the fdserial device and the telnet program is the fdnet device. The fdlisten descriptor is the socket waiting for a connection request, whereas the fdnet descriptor is the opened socket device. The call to select is looking for an event change so further processing can take place. If an fdnet device is opened and receiving data, a timeout counter is kept. If no data is received before the counter expires, the opened socket is closed.

For the sake of clarity I used text messages for status, but since we are communicating between machines, we can replace those messages with single-byte numeric values in the finished prototype. If you compile and download this program, you need to connect the mtty program to port 0, at 9600 baud, 8 data bits, 1 stop bit, and no parity. On the Windows OS, open a command box and execute the telnet program as shown in Figure 8-31.

Figure 8-31

From a Windows XP command prompt type **telnet** and press
Enter. You will get the telnet> prompt. Type **open** and press
Enter and you will see a <to> prompt displayed on the next line.
Enter the IP address of the SB72 board, which in this case is
192.168.0.252. If you typed the correct address, you will get a
connect message. The escape character for telnet is Ctrl+] (right

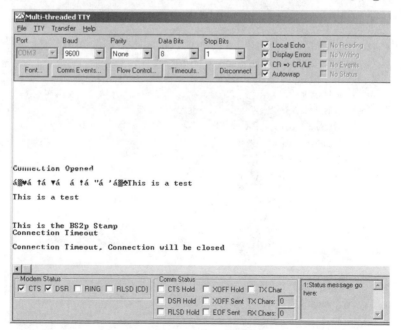

Figure 8-32

bracket). Pressing these control keys will allow you to enter telnet command sequences that are not echoed to the SB72. Remember, the telnet program is a simple Ethernet-based terminal program. It will display characters sent from the Stamp and the Stamp will echo characters received from telnet. I kept the mtty program attached to monitor data traffic. Figure 8-32 shows the data that was seen by the BASIC Stamp.

When the telnet program opened a socket to the SB72 a "Connection Opened" message was sent to the BS2. I typed "This is a test" two times and the BS2 responded with "This is the BS2p Stamp" message. Nothing further was sent from the telnet program, so after a couple of minutes the SB72 closed the connection. The first message was a "Connection Timeout" message, which was followed by a close message. Once closed, the SB72 goes back into listen mode. The final code listing for the BS2 is in Listing 8-7.

Listing 8-7

```
// {$STAMP BS2p}
// {$PBASIC 2.5}
//
// Test Program for RS-232 TTL I/O using RTS/CTS Handshaking
// for Embedded Systems Desktop Integration Chapter 8
// Copyright 2004 - Oliver H. Bailey
//
// Pins are assigned in the following order:
// Pin 0 - Transmit Data    (TX or TD)    =>
// Pin 1 - Receive Data     (RX or RD)    <=
// Pin 2 - Clear To Send    (CTS)         =>
// Pin 3 - Request To Send  (RTS)         <=
//
TX   CON 0
RX   CON 1
CTS  CON 2
RTS  CON 3

InData VAR Byte
OutData VAR Byte
```

```
LOW 14                                        // Set RD Low
LOW 15                                        // Set RTS Low

Main:
  SERIN RX\CTS, 110, [InData]                 // 1=RD,2=CTS,110=9600,N,8,1
  IF InData = 13 THEN                         // If InData = CRLF
    DEBUG CR,LF                               // Send to Terminal
    GOSUB SendMsg                             // Send Response Message
  ELSE                                        // ELSE
    DEBUG InData                              // Send the Data
  ENDIF                                       // End of IF Statement
GOTO Main:                                    // Start Again

SendMsg:
  SEROUT TX/RTS, 110, ["This is the BS2p Stamp"]
Return
```

You now have a pretty fair idea of the capabilities of the SB72 and the amount of work and code needed to provide Ethernet communications to the BS2. Now it's time to move on to our USB interface. Remember the code for the complete listings are available at www.wordware.com/files/embsys or at www.time-lines.com.

The USB Interface

The USB interface is a very complex topic. Rather than cover the entire topic here, we will instead cover only the necessary items to get our prototype working. If you want to become a USB wizard, go to www.usb.org and download the documentation. The USB 2.0 specification file is over 200 pages in PDF format.

Having said that, we will take the ten-cent tour on how USB works. Electrically USB is a pretty neat interface. It has only four wires, a 5-volt supply line, a positive data line, a negative data line, and a ground wire. Data is transmitted and received by differential signaling, which means that data bytes are sent by inverting signals on the data lines. The host is also known as the root hub and initiates all data transactions. Actual communications occur within frames and a very formal protocol. A client termination point is known as an endpoint; a client may have multiple endpoints. A collection of endpoints is known as an interface, and a collection of interfaces is known as a connection. A good example would be a multi-function printer. The cable receptacle on the printer would be the "connection," and each of the following would be controlled by separate software functions: printer, fax, and scanner. Each of these would be a separate endpoint, and as a group would be the printer interface. So the printer would be endpoint 0, the scanner endpoint 1, and the fax endpoint 2. When connected to a PC host the device driver would be broken into three separate functional areas. The complete driver would encapsulate the printer connection, with a device interface that would support separate functions for printing, scanning, and faxing. In short, USB is a layered protocol.

Implementing the USB Circuits

We are going to implement two different versions of the FTDI 232BM chip interface. The first one we will implement is from DLP Designs, a company that builds some real neat USB devices around the FTDI chip. The second interface we will implement is from Parallax and is a little different in the way it was implemented.

The FTDI USB Chips

FTDI is one of the more popular USB chips with companies that want to move from RS-232 to USB with minimal investment in time and resources. The FTDI chips have been around for several years and are easy to use and interface to, and inexpensive. They provide the ability to convert TTL RS-232 data to USB without much effort. Not only do they act as a direct replacement for RS-232, but they offer complete RS-232 handshaking as well and in fact look just like a COM port to Windows, all the way down to using the Windows serial communications drivers.

From a developer's view, FTDI provides what is termed "virtual COM port drivers" for Windows, Linux/UNIX, and Mac OS X (and higher) based systems. This approach means that these chips can replace an RS-232 port with virtually no software changes to the user application. Cost savings don't get much better than that. There is also the ability to access the chip via a direct access software kit. If you need higher speeds, accessing the chip in this manner not only allows a higher data rate but also provides some features that would be unavailable with the RS-232 drivers. It should be noted that the FTDI chips come in several flavors to replace not only RS-232-based devices but parallel devices as well. Following is a list of the features available to us using this chip:

- Full RS-232 handshaking

- TTL interface

- Data rate up to 1M baud

- 384-byte receive buffer

- 128-byte transmit buffer

- Programmable receive buffer timeout

- USB suspend/resume functions

- Sleep and awake functions

- Orderly power up through PWREN pin

- 5- and 3.3-volt support

- Power-on reset circuit

- Bulk or isochronous data transfer support

- Preprogrammed vendor ID, product ID, serial number, and product strings

- Description strings in external EEPROM

- Virtual COM port drivers

We have chosen two different vendor versions for our BS2 to USB interface for several reasons. The FTDI part has onboard transmit and receive buffers, which frees us from having to allocate space for these buffers, but we still must service the existing buffers in a timely fashion or risk losing data. We also chose this because it can be a direct replacement for a TTL level

RS-232 interface, complete with CTS/RTS handshaking. I've chosen to cover two different product versions to illustrate how there can be some differences in how vendors implement the FTDI interface.

The DLP-232BM Product

DLP Designs makes several different products that use the FTDI chips. These products range from a simple no-frills RS-232 USB converter to microcontroller based products. For our purposes we will be using the DLP-232BM product, which is inexpensive and provides all the features needed to simply replace the 4-Wire TTL RS-232 interface we just used for Ethernet. The advantage here is obvious — we can reuse all of the software we developed for the Ethernet interface with no change in the BS2 code. That's right — we will use the code on the BS2 developed for communicating to the SB72 unchanged.

Note:

You may be asking yourself how this can be accomplished since the SB72 provides a many-to-many relationship while USB provides a many-to-one relationship. The answer to that question lies in how and where the many-to-many relationship is handled. If we examine how we are implementing the host interface, we quickly see that the BS2 does not see more than one device from its host communications interface. In other words, all of the code managing the host relationship is in the SB72. So from the BS2 perspective it is only communicating with one host device.

The DLP Designs interface provides legacy support for RTS and CTS, and uses them exactly as RS-232 would. Our TX and RX data lines are also identical, so the 4-Wire TTL interface we used for the SB72 will work unchanged for the DLP-232BM device. To the BS2 both are simple serial I/O devices that communicate at 9600 baud, 1 stop bit, 8 data bits, and no parity.

USB is designed to be either self powered or externally powered. Remember that a power and ground is part of the USB hardware specifications. In fact, USB can provide power to a device providing it does not use too much current. This can be a little tricky because if a device that is plugged in exceeds the maximum current, the USB host controller will shut the device down. In fact, any USB device that exceeds maximum current usage at any time will be removed and shut down.

USB Power Choices

Let's cover this topic here because the next USB interface doesn't provide us with a power choice. During the prototype stage I would not use the USB bus to power your board. This not only eliminates the problem of exceeding USB allotted current, but since USB is hot plug-and-play, it also lets you know how well the system and your board will adjust if started and shut down from a running system. Remember that USB devices can be added, started, and removed while the system is running. A ground does need to be shared to provide a common ground for signal levels. For our purposes we will power the DLP-232BM from our +5 supply, just as we have the SB72. In Figure 8-33 we see a close-up view of the DLP-USB232BM part.

Figure 8-33

For our purposes we will be using just a handful of these pins even though this is a standard 24-pin package. Figure 8-34 illustrates how the DLP-USB232BM is wired for power and communications.

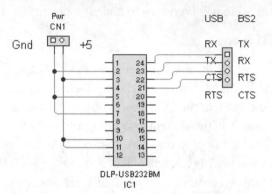

Figure 8-34

As you can see, pins 2, 5, and 7 get connected to Gnd. Since we are powering the DLP-USB232BM from the BASIC Stamp, pins 3, 10, and 11 get connected to VCC (+5) on the BASIC Stamp. This circuit assumes we are using the power supply we built at the beginning of this chapter. Note how the handshake and data lines are swapped between the USB232BM and the BS2. The four-pin header in Figure 8-34 has pins 0 and 1 crossed for connecting to header CN3 in Figure 8-30.

Testing this is a fairly simple process since no code changes are actually required. To test our handshake, however, let's enter and run the following program on the BS2 to see how well things really do work.

Listing 8-8

```
// {$STAMP BS2p}
// {$PBASIC 2.5}
//
// Test Program for RS-232 TTL I/O using RTS/CTS Handshaking and USB
// for Embedded Systems Desktop Integration Chapter 8
// Copyright 2004 - Oliver H. Bailey
//
// Pins are assigned in the following order:
// Pin 1 - Transmit Data   (TX or TD) =>
// Pin 0 - Receive Data    (RX or RD) <=
// Pin 2 - Clear To Send   (CTS)      =>
// Pin 3 - Request To Send (RTS)      <=
//
TX  CON 1
RX  CON 0
CTS CON 2
RTS CON 3

LOW RX                                     // Set RD Low
LOW RTS                                    // Set RTS Low

Main:
  GOSUB SendMsg                            // Send Message via USB
  PAUSE 1000                               // Wait 1 Second
GOTO Main:                                 // Start Again

SendMsg:
  // Output Data to TX, use CTS, if no CTS by count of 2000 goto NoData
  SEROUT TX\CTS, 240, 2000, NoData, ["BS2p Stamp", CR, LF]
  DEBUG "BS2p Stamp", CR                   // Send Message to Debug screen
  RETURN                                   // Return
  NoData:                                  // If No CTS
  DEBUG "Waiting..", CR                    // Send Waiting Message
RETURN                                     // Return
```

Running this program attached to any terminal program will produce the following output at the terminal program side.

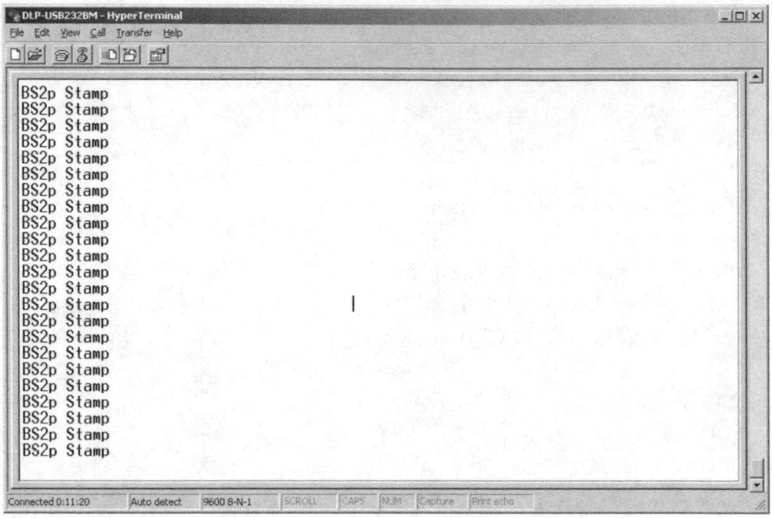

Figure 8-35

To see if our handshake works correctly, select File | Properties | Configure and set Flow Control to Hardware. Now, connect to the USB port; you will see the same message displayed to the BASIC Stamp Debug screen when connected.

Select Disconnect from the terminal program. The debug screen for the BS2 will begin showing "Waiting.." as shown in Figure 8-36.

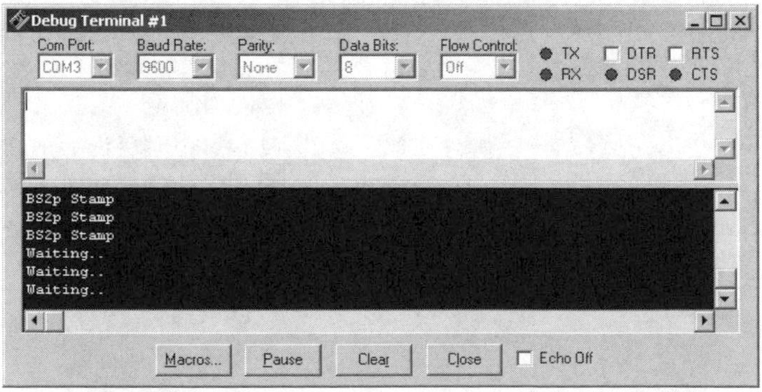

Figure 8-36

We have now replaced our Ethernet interface with a USB interface by simply swapping one connection for another. Let's look at a different type of USB interface.

The Parallax USB2SER Device

Parallax has recently introduced the USB2SER board. This board also uses the FTDI 232BM chip. Even though it uses the same serial to USB chip, the interface design is completely different. Figure 8-37 shows the USB2SER board from the back with the pins clearly defined.

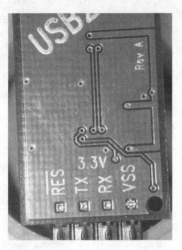

Figure 8-37

In order to use the USB2SER we must build a converter to get the signals that are available to the proper pins. Figure 8-38 illustrates how the crossover should be done.

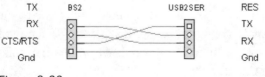

Figure 8-38

With those details taken care of you will notice the complete absence of CTS/RTS signals. These have been replaced with ATN, which is connected to the FTDI reset pin. The documentation states this pin is connected to the DTR signal in the virtual COM port drivers. You are probably asking why someone would prefer to use DTR instead of CTS/RTS. There are several possibilities. First, DTR is set manually from most applications that use RS-232 ports. Few standard terminal programs enable the use of DTR and those that do claim its use may or may not correctly set the pin based on the application toggling the pin. That isn't a problem for us because we are writing our own device handlers, but if you simply wanted to connect using a terminal program, signaling the BS2 to turn data on and off may become a problem.

This device, however, is very useful if you want to use a high-speed data link between the BS2 and a host system. In a case where the host has control of the DTR pin, the serial communications interface on the BS2 can use the ATN pin as a regular RTS/CTS pin, providing the host has software to properly handle turning this pin on and off. Before we run software to test this interface it should be noted there is no reason not to use split speed communications using the BS2 and FTDI interfaces. Data being sent from the host is for control and monitoring commands where data coming from the BS2 contains packets of information regarding temperature status and alarms. Experiment with higher baud rates to see where performance is best. Keep in mind the limitations of the variable storage area of the BS2p and see how fast you can send and receive data. You can also experiment using the direct access drivers, which removes the baud rate limitation completely. I caution you in attempting to send data to the BS2p at high speeds simply due to the same variable space constraints. The BS2p series can operate very nicely at speeds up to 19200 baud. We will look at this more closely in Chapter 11.

The following listing will send data from the BS2 through the USB-Comport interface to a terminal program.

Listing 8-9

```
// {$STAMP BS2p}
// {$PBASIC 2.5}
//
// Test Program for RS-232 TTL I/O using the Parallax USB2SER
// for Embedded Systems Desktop Integration Chapter 8
// Copyright 2004 - Oliver H. Bailey
//
// Pins are assigned in the following order:
// Pin 0 - Transmit Data   (TX or TD)   =>
// Pin 1 - Receive Data    (RX or RD)   <=
// Pin 2 - Clear To Send   (CTS)        =>
// Pin 3 - Request To Send (RTS)        <=
//
TX  CON 0
RX  CON 2
CTS CON 4
RTS CON 4

LOW RX                                  // Set RD Low
LOW RTS                                 // Set RTS Low

Main:
  GOSUB SendMsg                         // Send Response Message
  PAUSE 1000                            // Wait 1 Second
GOTO Main:                              // Start Again

SendMsg:
  // Output Data to TX, use CTS, if no CTS by count of 2000 goto NoData
  SEROUT TX\CTS, 240, 2000, NoData, ["BS2p Stamp", CR, LF]
  DEBUG "BS2p Stamp", CR                // Send Message to Debug
  RETURN                                // Return
  NoData:                               // No CTS
  DEBUG "Waiting..", CR                 // Send Waiting Message
RETURN                                  // Return
```

Note that we use the CTS pin even though it is attached to the host computer's terminal program. Using a terminal program set to the same baud rate, stop bits, data bits, and parity you will see the following display.

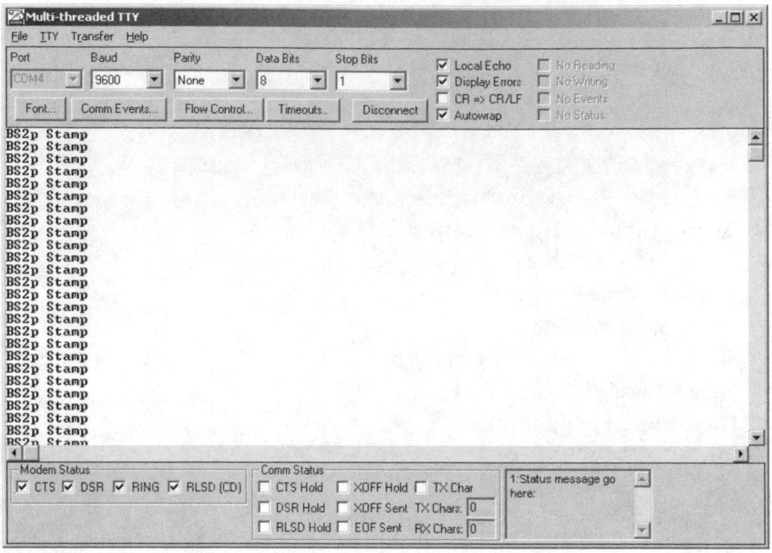

Figure 8-39

Try disconnecting the port. You will notice that unlike the earlier version that went into wait mode, the BS2 continues to send data. Once again, if you wish to shut the data off you will need to toggle the DTR line manually or use a terminal program that allows you to configure the state of the DTR line.

Before we leave the USB part of this chapter, remember that the two USB interfaces are powered differently. The DLP-USB232BM is powered by our power supply. The USB2SER board is powered by the host USB controller or hub. This means that disconnecting the USB2SER board will have no effect on the host plug-and-play system, whereas unplugging the DLP design board will remove the device because power has been lost.

The Maxim/Dallas Hardware Interfaces

The 1-Wire Interface Hardware

Now it's time to connect our 1-Wire interface. Since we covered testing the 1-Wire in Chapter 7, we will now attach it to the BS2p and modify the test program to test our connections. Remember that the 1-Wire uses a data line, power, and ground line as shown in Figure 8-40.

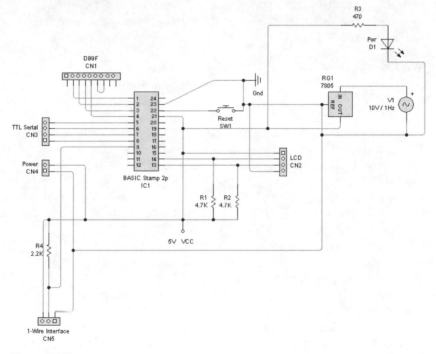

Figure 8-40

We added a three-pin connector and a 2.2 K resistor, and attached a 2.2 K between the data and +5 volt line. This circuit uses one additional BS2p pin, which is pin 4. Listing 8-10 is a modified version of the test program from Chapter 7 designed to work with this schematic.

Listing 8-10

```
// {$STAMP BS2p}
// {$PBASIC 2.5}

// Test Program for Dallas 1-Wire Thermometer
// for Embedded Systems Desktop Integration
// Copyright 2004 - Oliver H. Bailey
//
// This program uses Pin 4 for both Input and Output
// Pin 4 - Transmit/Receive 1-Wire Data      <=>
//
Temp VAR Word                               // Temperature Storage Variable
TempLo VAR Temp.LOWBYTE                      // Temperature Low Order Byte
TempHi VAR Temp.HIGHBYTE                     // Temperature High Order Byte
TempSign VAR temp.BIT11                      // Temperature Sign Bit
signBit VAR Bit
tempCel VAR Word                            // Centigrade
tempFar VAR Word                            // Fahrenheit
ChkLoop VAR Byte                            // Three attempts

// This is a very simple program for testing a DS1822 Temp sensor. Rather than using
// the traditional Read ROM command we simply make an attempt to read the temperature.
// If a device is present then the temperature is returned; otherwise it is assumed
// no DS1822 is attached.

ChkLoop = 0                                 // Set to Zero Tries

Main:
  GOSUB ChkDev                              // Check for DS1822
  // Reaching this line requires a response from the DS1822
  tmpLoop:                                  // Read temperature loop start
    GOSUB Read_Temp                         // Gosub read temperature
    DEBUG HOME, SDEC tempCel," C", CR       // Display Centigrade
    DEBUG SDEC tempFar," F", CR             // Display Fahrenheit
    PAUSE 500                               // Wait
  GOTO tmpLoop                              // Start again

  // If the code reaches here, it was by mistake.
  GOTO forever                              // Loop forever


// Check Device Subroutine
```

```
ChkDev:
  OWOUT 15, 1, [$CC, $44]                    // Check for temperature
NotDone:
  PAUSE 25                                   // Wait for response
  OWIN 15, 4, [Temp]                         // Check Status
  ChkLoop = ChkLoop+1                        // Increment Loop Counter
  IF ChkLoop = 100 THEN no_Dev               // Max Tries then Stop
  IF Temp = 0 THEN                           // No Response
    GOTO NotDone                             // Otherwise Try Again
  ENDIF
  RETURN                                     // Return if Found


// Read and Convert Temperature
Read_Temp:
  OWOUT 15, 1, [$CC, $44]                    // Check for temperature
notReady:                                    // Start completion loop
  PAUSE 25                                   // Wait for response
  OWIN 15, 4, [Temp]                         // Check results
  IF Temp = 0 THEN notReady                  // Not done, start again
  OWOUT 15, 1, [$CC, $BE]                    // Read Scratchpad Temp
  OWIN 15, 2, [TempLo, TempHi]               // Get Temp Bytes
  signBit = TempSign                         // Get sign bit (0 = +, 1 = -)
  tempCel = Temp                             // Store to variable
  tempCel = tempCel >> 4                     // Store Temp to variable
  IF (signBit = 0) THEN PosCel               // Shift to get actual temperature
    tempCel = tempCel | $FF00                // Check for sub-zero
                                             // Adjust if below zero

PosCel:
    tempFar = tempCel */ $01CD               // Positive Temperature
    IF signBit = 0 THEN PosFar               // Adjust for display
      tempFar = tempFar | $FF00              // Check for sub-zero
                                             // Adjust Fahrenheit scale

PosFar:
  tempFar = tempFar + 32                     // Not sub-zero
RETURN                                       // Add 32 for Fahrenheit display
                                             // All Done, return


no_Dev:
  DEBUG "No DS1822 Device Found", CR         // No response at startup so display
                                             // message

forever:                                     //
  GOTO forever                               // and loop forever
```

Since we used the BS2p in Chapter 7 to test our 1-Wire design, we have only modified the existing code to be certain it works with the BS2p I/O pin 4.

The 3-Wire Hardware Interface

The Dallas 3-Wire interface is all that remains to be implemented for directions from the BS2p. Again, we will add this to the existing circuit and make only the necessary changes required to test this part of the circuit. We covered this interface in Chapter 7 but did not provide a schematic since it is a common SPI interface that is made up of only three wires — reset, clock, and data. We will implement this interface on pins 6, 7, and 8 as shown in Figure 8-41.

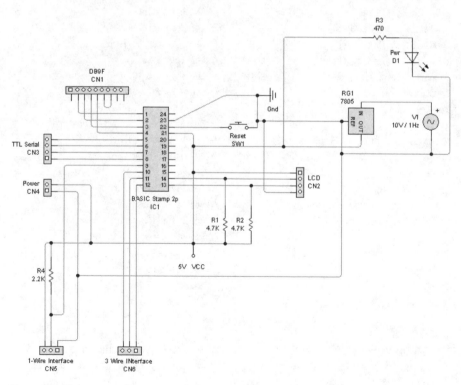

Figure 8-41

With both the 1- and 3-Wire interfaces implemented, we can access the DS2404 using either interface. Listing 8-11 has been modified from Chapter 7 to use the 1-Wire interface.

Listing 8-11

```
// {$STAMP BS2p}
// {$PBASIC 2.5}


// Test Program for Dallas 1-Wire Time/Date Chip DS2404
// for Embedded Systems Desktop Integration
// Copyright 2004 - Oliver H. Bailey
//
// This program uses Pin 5 for all I/O. It should be noted that all
// communications with
// the DS2404 memory functions on the 1-Wire bus are done using bit I/O
//
// This is a very simple program for testing a DS2404 Time chip.
// ChkDev Variables
ChkLoop VAR Byte                        // Loop Counter for Reset
TmpByte VAR Byte                        // Presence Pulse Indicator


                                        // Write_SP_Mem Variables

CTA CON $0077


TA VAR Word
TA1 VAR TA.LOWBYTE                      // Target Address 1
TA2 VAR TA.HIGHBYTE                     // Target Address 2
EADDR VAR Byte
tempVar VAR Byte(8)
index VAR Nib
TestByteOne VAR Byte                    // First Test RAM Location Byte
TestByteTwo VAR Byte                    // Second Test RAM Location Byte
TestByteOne = %01010101                // Byte One is 01010101
TestByteTwo = %10101010                // Byte Two is 10101010
TA1 = $26                              // Hex 26
TA2 = 0                                // Hex 00


// Read_SP_Mem Variables
SA1 VAR Byte                           // Storage Address 1
SA2 VAR Byte                           // Storage Address 2
LEN VAR Byte                           // Data or Offset Length
ByteOne VAR Byte                       // Test Byte 1
```

```
ByteTwo VAR Byte                          // Test Byte 2
SA1 = %00000000                           // SA1 = 0
SA2 = %00000000                           // SA2 = 0
Len = %00000000                           // Len = 0
ByteOne = %00000000                       // ByteOne = 0
ByteTwo = %00000000                       // ByteTwo = 0

// Misc. Variables                        // For Bit Bang Mode
// CurBit VAR Byte                        //
TA=$0000                                  // Target Address is Page 0, Byte 0

PAUSE 1000                                // Wait for Debug

Main:
  ChkLoop = 0                             // Set to zero again
  GOSUB ChkDev                            // Check for DS2404
// DEBUG DEC ChkLoop, CR                  // Debug Display
// Reaching this line requires a response from the DS2404
// DEBUG HOME, "DS2404 Device Found..",CR
// Write to RAM Locations 0026H and 0027H. Write binary 01010101 and 10101010 to
// check RAM locations
  GOSUB Write_SP_Mem                      // Write to scratchpad memory
  FOR index = 0 TO 3                      // Loop through variables and
    tempVar(index) = $95                  // write asterisks * to data area
  NEXT
  PAUSE 100                               // Wait for 3 ms.
  GOSUB Read_SP_Mem                       // Read scratchpad memory
// PAUSE 1000                             // Wait
// GOTO Main                              // Start all over
// If the code reaches here, it was by mistake.
  GOTO forever                            // Loop forever

// Check Device Subroutine - This subroutine looks for a presence pulse to determine
// if a 1-Wire device is available. There are a couple of things to be aware of here.
// First, the normal state of the line is high since a pull-up resistor is used. This
// means that with ChkLoop being 0 upon entry, at least one state transition is needed
// to determine a 1-Wire device is available. Without at least one state transition
// there is no way to determine if the line was pulled low after the inquiry was done.
  ChkDev:
    OWOUT 14, 1, [$CC]                    // Read Memory Page
  NotDone:
    OWIN 14, 0, [TmpByte]                 // Check Status
    ChkLoop = ChkLoop+1                   // Increment Loop Counter
```

```
  IF ChkLoop = 100 THEN no_Dev          // Max Tries then Stop
  IF TmpByte = 0 THEN                    // If no Response
    GOTO NotDone                         // Otherwise Try Again
  ENDIF
  IF (ChkLoop <> 1) THEN no_Dev          // State Change was detected
  RETURN                                 // Return if Found


// WRITE Scratchpad Memory
Write_SP_Mem:
  DEBUG CLS, "***** Sent Data Info *****", CR
  FOR index = 0 TO 3                     // Loop through 4 Bytes
    tempVar(index) = index + $30         // Write 0, 1, 2, and 3
  NEXT                                   // Write next number
  DEBUG "Data Sent: ", STR tempVar\4, CR // Send debug string to terminal

  DEBUG "TA: ", HEX2 TA2, HEX2 TA1, CR   // Print Settings to Debug Terminal
  OWOUT 14, 1, [$CC, $0F, TA1, TA2, STR tempVar\4] // Set up Address and Length
RETURN                                   // Return to Caller


PAUSE 5000


// Read Scratchpad Memory
Read_SP_Mem:
  OWOUT 14, 1, [$CC, $AA]                // Read Scratchpad Function
  // Read Address, Length, and Memory Contents
  OWIN 14, 2, [TA1, TA2, EADDR, STR tempVar\4]
  DEBUG "***** Received DATA Info *****", CR
  // Send Target Address to Debug Terminal
  DEBUG "Target Address  :", HEX2 TA2, HEX2 TA1, CR
  // Send End Address to Debug Terminal
  DEBUG "End Address     :", HEX2 EADDR, CR
  // Send Received Data Bytes to Debug Terminal
  DEBUG "DATA Received:", STR tempVar\4, CR
RETURN


  no_Dev:
    DEBUG "No DS2404 Device Found", CR // No response at startup so display message
  forever:                             //
GOTO forever                           // and loop forever
```

So how do we interface the DS2404 using the 3-Wire interface, you ask. Since we have already implemented the 1- and 3-Wire interfaces in hardware, let's write a short example program to access the DS2404 via the 3-Wire interface. Listing 8-12 contains a simple time and memory access routine using the 3-Wire interface. You will note that the amount of code needed is much less than the same functions using the 1-Wire protocol. This is simply due to the fact that we no longer have to look for a device type or serial number since this interface has a dedicated data line to the BS2.

Listing 8-12

```
// Test Program for DS2404 3-Wire Interface
// for Embedded Systems Desktop Integration Chapter 8
// Copyright 2004 - Oliver H. Bailey
//
// {$STAMP BS2p}
// {$PBASIC 2.5}

Reset CON 5                      // Reset/Chip Select Line
Dio   CON 6                      // Data IO Line
Clk   CON 7                      // Clock Line

Wrsp  CON $0F                    // Write Scratchpad command
Rscp  CON $AA                    // Read Scratchpad command
Cscp  CON $55                    // Copy Scratchpad command
Rmem  CON $F0                    // Read Memory command

TA1   VAR Byte                   // Target Address 1
TA2   VAR Byte                   // Target Address 2
EA    VAR Byte                   // Ending Address
DLen  VAR Byte                   // Length of Data Read/Written

SMem  VAR Byte                   // Start Memory Location in DS2404
EMem  VAR Byte                   // End Memory Location in DS2404
DByte VAR Byte                   // Data Byte from the DS2404


LoopCtr VAR Byte                 // Loop Counter for Reading Data
Ctr1  VAR Word                   // Start Counter
Ctr2  VAR Word                   // Current Counter

Initialize:
```

```
   LOW Reset                                // Pull Rest Line Low
   LOW Dio                                  // Set Data Line Low
   LOW Clk                                  // Set Clock Line Low


   PAUSE 1000                               // Wait for things to settle

Main:
   TA1 = $E0                                // Start Memory Location
   TA2 = $01                                // End Memory Location


   GOSUB WriteSP                            // Write to Scratchpad
   TA1=255                                  // Assign new values to TA1
   TA2=255                                  // and TA2
   GOSUB ReadSP                             // Read Scratchpad
// Print Start Address, End Address, Length
   DEBUG DEC3 SMem, " ", DEC3 EMem, " ", DEC3 DLen, CR
   GOSUB WriteMem                           // Write Scratchpad to Memory
   GOSUB ReadRAM                            // Read RAM Contents
END


// DS2404 3-Wire Subroutines - Copyright 2004, Oliver H. Bailey
// For the book Embedded Systems, Desktop Integration
//
WriteSP:                                    // Write Data to Scratchpad
   HIGH Reset                               // Bring Reset High
   SHIFTOUT Dio, Clk, LSBFIRST, [Wrsp]      // Output control byte
   SHIFTOUT Dio, Clk, LSBFIRST, [TA1, TA2]  // Output start and end address
   SHIFTOUT Dio, Clk, LSBFIRST, ["This is the DS2404"]    // Write message to scratchpad
   DLen = 18                                // Set Datalen to new number
   LOW Reset                                // Bring Reset line Low
RETURN

ReadSP:                                     // Read Data from Scratchpad
   HIGH Reset                               // Bring Reset High
   SHIFTOUT Dio, Clk, LSBFIRST, [Rscp]      // Output control Byte
   SHIFTIN Dio, Clk, LSBPRE, [SMem, EMem]   // Read Start & End memory Addresses
   Dlen = 0                                 // Set Data Length to 0
   SHIFTIN Dio, Clk, LSBPRE, [DLen]         // Read Data Length
   FOR LoopCtr = 0 TO Dlen                  // Loop and
      SHIFTIN Dio, Clk, LSBPRE, [Dbyte]     // Read scratchpad Data
//   WRITE DLen, DByte                      // Store to EEPROM
```

```
  DEBUG Dbyte                                  // Display to Debug Console
NEXT                                           // Until LoopCtr = DLen

  DEBUG CR                                     // Send CR to debug Console
  LOW Reset                                    // Bring Reset Low
RETURN

WriteMem:                                      // Write Scratchpad to RAM
  HIGH Reset                                   // Bring Reset High
  SHIFTOUT Dio, Clk, LSBFIRST, [Cscp]          // Output Control Byte
  SHIFTOUT Dio, Clk, LSBFIRST, [SMem, EMem, DLen] // Output RAM Start, End, and Length
  DEBUG DEC3 TA1, DEC3 TA2, DEC3 DLen, CR      // Check Values to debug Screen
  DO                                           // Do
    PAUSE 1                                    // Wait 1 ms
  LOOP UNTIL (Dio <> 0)                        // Until Data Line is Low
  LOW Reset                                    // Bring Reset Low
RETURN

ReadRAM:                                       // Read from DS2404 RAM
  HIGH Reset                                   // Bring Reset High
  SHIFTOUT Dio, Clk, LSBFIRST, [RMem]          // Output Control Byte
  SHIFTOUT Dio, Clk, LSBFIRST, [SMem, EMem]    // Output Start & End RAM Locations

  FOR LoopCtr = 0 TO Dlen                      // Loop from 0 to DLen
    SHIFTIN Dio, Clk, LSBPRE, [Dbyte]          // Read RAM Location Byte
  // WRITE DLen, DByte                          // Write to EEPROM
    DEBUG Dbyte                                // Send to Debug Terminal
NEXT                                           // Increment LoopCtr

  DEBUG CR                                     // Send CR to Debug Console
  LOW Reset                                    // Bring Reset Low
RETURN
```

Listing 8-12 is much smaller than Listing 8-11. Running this listing on either of the 3-Wire boards from Chapter 7 will produce the following output to the BS2 Debug terminal.

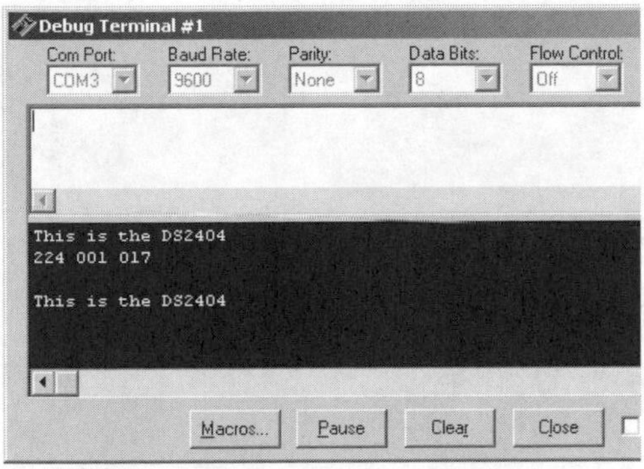

Figure 8-42

The first line of output is echoed from the read scratchpad sub-routine. The second line is the decimal display $E0 $01 $1F, which is the starting address, ending address, and data length. The last line is from the read RAM subroutine, which validates the data we wrote to the scratchpad was properly copied to RAM and read back.

Adding RS-232 Communications

I waited to add the RS-232 host interface to see how many I/O pins remain unused on the BS2. We have six unused pins so we will add the RS-232 interface on I/O pins 12 to 15, which are pins 17 to 20 in Figure 8-43.

Since the I/O pin assignment remains unchanged from Chapter 7, the following program listing (Listing 8-13) should work without modification. It contains the test program modified to reflect the pin assignments we are using for the BS2p.

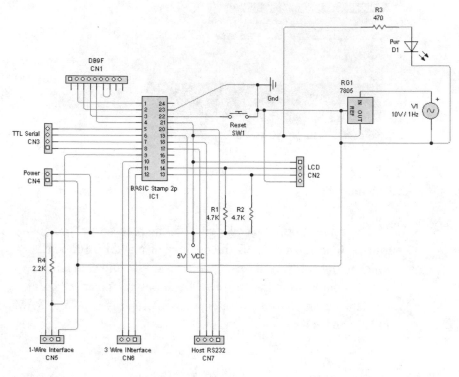

Figure 8-43

Listing 8-13

```
// Test Program for RS-232 output using MAX232 with RTS/CTS Handshaking
// for Embedded Systems Desktop Integration Chapter 8
// Copyright 2004 - Oliver H. Bailey
//
// Pins are assigned in the following order:
// Pin 12 - Transmit Data    (TX or TD) =>
// Pin 14 - Receive Data     (RX or RD) <=
// Pin 13 - Clear To Send    (CTS)      =>
// Pin 15 - Request To Send  (RTS)      <=
//
// This program uses the FPin variable on SerIn and SerOut commands. Example follows below
// Serout 12\15, 110, "Mary had a little lamb" CR, LF
InData VAR Byte
OutData VAR Byte
```

```
LOW 14                              // Set RD Low
LOW 15                              // Set RTS Low

Main:
  SFRIN 14\13, 110, [InData]        // 14=RD,13=CTS,110=9600,N,8,1
  OutData = InData                  // Assign to output variable
  IF OutData = 13 THEN              // Turn CR into CRLF
    SEROUT 12\15, 110, [CR, LF]     // Echo Back to Terminal
    DEBUG CR, LF                    // Echo to Debug port
  ENDIF

  SEROUT 12\15, 110, [OutData]      // Just print the RAW data
  DEBUG OutData                     // Echo to Debug Port
GOTO Main:                          // Start Again
```

Finishing Touches for Our BS2p Prototype

We have finally reached the end of the prototype development cycle for our embedded system using the Basic Stamp BS2p24. By sharing the same I/O pins for the Ethernet and USB interfaces we have two I/O pins left over for future use. Remember that this is a prototype so we will simply plug and unplug the USB and Ethernet interfaces for test purposes. I mounted the boards all together on a poster board backing that cost about $3. I used #6 screws and nuts to make the boards stand off the backer board for test purposes. Figure 8-44 shows the finished prototype using the boards we developed in Chapter 7.

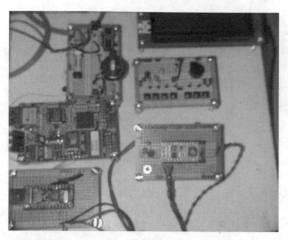

Figure 8-44

From the upper left going clockwise, are the Dallas tempera-
ture/clock/relay board, Matrix Orbital LK202-25 display,
keyboard/alarm board, BS2p board, DLP Designs USB232BM
board, and the NetBurner SB72 board. Not shown are the RS-232
host interface, the Parallax USB2SER board, and 7805 power
supply.

Chapter Summary

We covered a lot of ground in this chapter and implemented
several types of communications interfaces, two different
Maxim/Dallas interfaces, and an I²C interface for the LCD. All of
the remaining hardware chapters will use the same I/O boards
and we will focus on the differences in the processors we use.
The finished programs for the thermostat can be found at
www.wordware.com/files/embsys or at www.time-lines.com.

Chapter 9

The PIC Prototype

In the previous chapter we implemented our prototype using the BS2p. I like using the BASIC Stamp for several reasons but the two that come to my mind first are fast prototyping and ease of programming. In short, I can take an idea and quickly see if it works using the BASIC Stamp. At the core of the BS2p is a microcontroller processor.

The microcontroller takes us a level closer to how the hardware actually works and provides features not available in the BASIC Stamp. Just about anyone can use a BASIC Stamp, and the BASIC Stamp is used widely in schools to educate students in electronics, robotics, and other areas. Using a microcontroller, on the other hand, requires a higher degree of knowledge to use but offers more flexibility to the professional engineer. Both devices have their place in the market. Let's see first-hand how similar and dissimilar these devices really are.

Note:

Before continuing I want to say that I use both devices (and the others as well) all the time. All of these devices are unique and have their strengths in the commercial marketplace. We are not comparing these devices as acceptable or not acceptable but exploring which is best suited to this need based on cost, development effort, and functionality.

This chapter has fewer photos and diagrams than the previous chapters. This is not an accident. The MPLAB IDE that is used in this chapter has its own documentation. I could never do that product justice by attempting to cover its features here so I have chosen to provide the logic and code snippets behind the implementation. This eliminates distracting you, the reader, from the main objective, which is developing the embedded device using the PIC microcontroller. I provide just enough code for you to test each feature and leave the main listings for you to download. Each listing is fully annotated as to what happens when and why it happens. This allows me to present the complete thought and implementation logic without again distracting you from the main development objective. Since the code is fully annotated it also allows you to use the code to build upon the design without having to have the book open. There is nothing I hate worse than having to open multiple documents or books at the same time to understand a subject.

Similarities between the BASIC Stamp and the PIC

The BASIC Stamp and the PIC share a similar BASIC language. This allows a quick prototype to be developed using the BASIC Stamp and then compiling the source using a third-party compiler to achieve the same functionality in the PIC. There are some implementation differences between the BS2p and the PIC. One example of this is POLLIN and POLLOUT commands on the BS2. The PIC instead supports interrupts — hardware features handled by software functions — so there is no need for these commands. An interrupt does not wait to be serviced as the POLL commands on the BASIC Stamp do. There is also no extra code needed between each BASIC command.

Differences between the BASIC Stamp and the PIC

The PIC does not contain an interpreter but rather executes actual machine language. This increases the speed of program execution and provides the ability to support interrupts and other functions that may require faster processing. The most important difference is the availability of multiple langauges to develop with.

The BASIC Stamp has a built-in interpreter in EEPROM. This EPROM may be internal or external. Typically a language interpreter like PBASIC resides within the device for spced and security purposes. While both devices provide for variable storage and static data storage, the big difference is the amount of storage available to the developer. This brings us directly to the biggest difference — the sheer number of available parts and configurations. At publication time there were hundreds of different PIC parts and several product families to choose from. There are low-range, mid-range, and high-range parts defined as such by instruction length, which also determines the amount of addressable memory and execution speed. In just the DIP (dual inline package) parts range from six I/O pins to over 40 I/O pins. Clocks range from an internal 4 mHz clock to external clocks of 20 mHz and above. The PIC line also has a wide variety of built-in peripherals suce as USB and power management.

Types of PIC Microcontrollers and Development Languages

There are literally hundreds of different PIC microcontroller configurations, but they can be broken down into different groups. They are:

- 8 bit
- 16 bit
- Digital signal processing
- Peripheral processing
- Memory management
- Power management

All of the PIC microcontrollers utilize the Harvard memory architecture, which uses a banked memory scheme instead of linear addressing.

Now let's take a look at available compilers for the PIC processor line. The products range from free to about $1,000 depending on the source and type of compiler. Let's take a look at the available languages for the PIC processor lines:

- Assembler — Available free from Microchip and included with other products as well. Comes complete with an IDE.

- The C language — Available from several vendors both in the U.S. and abroad. Prices range from free to about $1,000.

- The C++ language — Available from at least one vendor, this product is priced below $100.

- Pascal — Available from at least one vendor and also priced below $100.

- BASIC — Available from several vendors and priced from $50 to $250 depending on compiler type and features.

There are many compiler vendors. Following is a short list that was used to develop this book:

- microEngineering Labs — PicBasic and PicBasic Pro
- HI-TECH — ANSI C
- Custom Computer Services — C compiler
- SourceBoost — C, C++, and Pascal compilers
- Microchip — Assembler and several C compilers
- GNUPIC — Free C compiler

The Microchip Assembler (MPASM) provides an integrated workbench that all of the other compilers can be integrated into. All of the other compilers also provide a development interface of their own. If you want to have a consistent development interface, use the Microchip IDE. Each of the other IDEs have unique features, so you can experiment to see which suits your needs best.

The PIC Development Cycle

The PIC development cycle is different from BASIC Stamp development. Using the Stamp we wrote the code, downloaded it to the port, and used debug statements to output run-time information. We did all this from within the BASIC Stamp IDE. The PIC development cycle is much different, as shown in Figure 9-1.

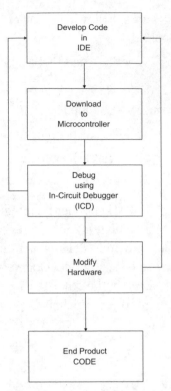

Figure 9-1

Figure 9-1 assumes the passive component placement is completed and you are ready to add the intelligence that makes the circuit work. This iterative process begins with writing your source code, downloading to the target processor that is attached to the circuit, stepping through your source code, making changes to source and hardware (if necessary), and starting the process over again.

Development Strategy

Unlike the BASIC Stamp, we will be using several languages and components to demonstrate the PIC implementation. We will develop two solutions using PIC processors; here's why: The PIC processor line has an older part that supports low-speed USB. This part comes in a 28- and 40-pin version (16C747/16C765). These parts are "one-time" programmable, which means they can't be reprogrammed. These chips are used in two different demo kits: the PICKit 1 and the PICDEM USB. The PICKit 1 is a very inexpensive (under $40) tool that uses the 16C745 part as a USB programmer for other Microchip parts. The board has a flash-based 12F675 part that can be programmed via the USB port on a Windows PC. There are LEDs for simulating output on the target part, a push button switch, and pot for input. There is also another program that expands the variety of parts that the board can program. All of the source code to the USB part, the Windows portion, and sample target programs are included along with data books in PDF format. The board has a "break-away" prototype board that can be used to interface the sample 12F675 to the world.

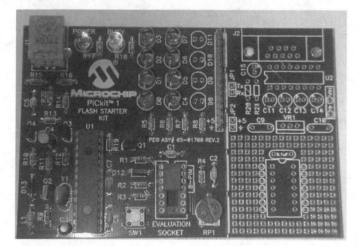

Figure 9-2

The PICDEM USB board is larger in size and has the 16C765 40-pin part installed with a second socket for the 16C745 part. The kit also includes several 16C745 and 16C765 parts that are EEPROM based. These parts can be purchased and have the postfix of /JW when ordering. In addition, the PICDEM board has eight status LEDs, a DB9 RS-232 interface, a DB15 game adapter interface, a PS/2 connector/interface, keypad, and LCD connector.

Figure 9-3

The PICDEM USB also comes with all the source to the USB interface and several Windows programs that can be used for testing the different interfaces on the board.

What Is HIDmaker?

HIDmaker is a unique product that assists embedded developers who use the 16C745 chips to develop their data flow and Windows HID interface. To understand the usefulness of this product you need to first understand what HID is. In the Windows operating system Microsoft implemented a tiered device driver scheme so developers of human interface devices (HID) like trackballs, mice, and keyboards could quickly bring their products to market. If this sounds unique to Microsoft, it isn't. The USB specification includes the HID driver interface. The idea is that all human interface devices share some common properties, so the USB implementer forum decided to include a higher level interface just for such devices. The device type determines how the low-level driver that is part of the operating system will handle data to and from these devices and use one of the built-in handlers or a vendor-installed handler.

HIDmaker wraps code around the PIC USB firmware to bring the embedded systems into the HID data handling specification. So code is generated for the embedded processor, and a Windows HID driver interface with the data handling layout and scheme are also generated. When completed, the wrapper code for the PIC is embedded into the chip along with the USB firmware and a listing in the language of your choice is created for the Windows driver. So what about Linux and UNIX? This is a book about cross-platform development. The truth is that Linux allows the developer to handle this without a tiered driver interface. We will cover this topic in Chapter 11.

The following flowchart illustrates the development process using HIDmaker.

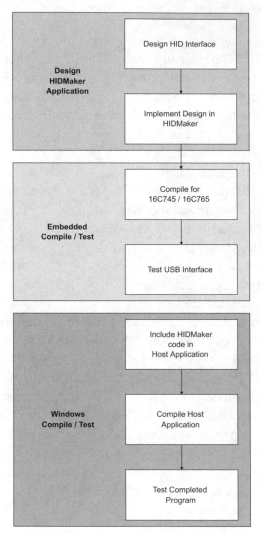

Figure 9-4

Using HIDmaker we could define our communications protocol, but we will instead use USB as a method of sending and receiving data. We will add only the TTL serial communications to the 16C745 to support serial I/O from the dsPIC. This is the identical method we used in Chapter 7 to build an interchangeable RS-232/USB/Ethernet interface. The difference here (aside from using different components) is that we are building both the USB interface and embedded controller. Once we have completed the dsPIC thermostat interface, the only remaining task is to be certain we can use either the low-speed 16C745 or full-speed 18F2455 devices. So let's begin by writing the necessary software to interface our dsPIC to the thermostat boards.

For this example will use the Microchip C30 compiler and ICD 2. These combined with MPLAB will afford us the ability to not only develop but also debug our code at the source level as well. To develop our prototype we will use a modified version of the dsPICDEM 28 board, which provides us with a dsPIC 2010 28-pin part, reset switch, power LED, program-accessible LED, power interface, RS-232 interface, and a prototype area.

Figure 9-5

To develop our code and provide a debugging interface we will need the ICD 2 debugger. This unit is USB driven and attaches to a six pin telco jack next to UART1 on the dsPICDEM 28 board. This arrangement will provide a development environment similar to the one used in Chapter 8.

The dsPIC30F2010 Processor

We begin with the dsPIC30F2010 development. We need an I²C interface for our LCD, an SPI (3-Wire) for our DS2404 memory, a 1-Wire interface for the DS1822, and at least one TTL-RS-232 interface to communicate with our host interface. Actually, we should have two TTL-RS-232 interfaces. Figure 9-6 illustrates the communications interfaces we need.

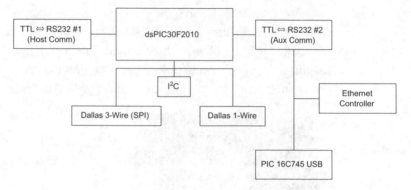

Figure 9-6

This is indentical to the interface in Chapter 7 except the first RS-232 port was connected to a transceiver for programming and debugging. In this case we are using an in-circuit debugger (ICD) as shown in the following photo.

Figure 9-7

There are two ways to debug embedded systems using the PIC processor line. The first tool is the ICD that we've been discussing. The ICD is very versatile in that it also allows you to reprogram the chip in circuit on the finished board in the field. For debugging purposes it is an excellent tool; however, it does use the target processor pins so if you are are debugging, the I/O pins used for the debugger are unavailable for I/O. Second, your target board has to be working and powered. The alternative to the ICD is the in-circuit emulator, or ICE as it's commonly called. The ICE is a small device that looks like a black box with a ribbon cable coming out of it. The ICE unit actually emulates the processor so you can download and run code without using any processor pins at all. The ICE also has its own power supply so it doesn't need to be connected to anything other than the development system to work. The difference in price is considerable as the ICD is around $150 and the ICE is around $4,000. If you're doing time-sensitive or real-time development, the ICE is the way to go. For our purposes, the ICD will work fine so we will develop using it.

The Ethernet Interface

Once again we will use the NetBurner SB72 single board Ethernet interface. In the last chapter we used TCP/IP to connect to a single host. This time we will use UDP (the User Datagram Protocol) to send and receive messages from the host.

Figure 9-8

The dsPIC Code Development Environments

Before we continue let's get familiar with the dsPIC and the PIC development IDE MPLAB. MPLAB is a free IDE provided by Microchip, the same people who make the PIC and dsPIC products. MPLAB contains support for a simulator, debugger, programmer, and third-party tools. All of the code we develop will be written in C. The first compiler we will use is the C30 product from Microchip. This compiler is an enhanced GNU compiler that provides support for the dsPIC family of processors. We will also be using the language tools library that is included with the C30 product but can also be freely downloaded. This library provides C language wrappers around the silicon impementation of the communications and I/O functions we will need for this proto- type. We will also use the HI-TECH dsPICC compiler, which is ANSI compliant, for one of our sample programs. HI-TECH also provides C compilers for all of the PIC products. We will also use the C18 and PIC18 products for developing software for the 18F4550 USB chip and PicBasic Pro for developing and testing code for the older 16C745 low-speed USB chip.

The MPLAB IDE

To provide a consistent development interface, we will use MPLAB 7 from Microchip. MPLAB is free and available for download from www.microchip.com; look for it under develop- ment tools. MPLAB includes a built-in simulator, programmer support, debugger support, and support for most third-party tools. We will be using C30 and C18 from Microchip, PICC Enterprise from HI-TECH software, and PicBasic Pro from microEngineering Labs. This combination of tools will give us varied experience along with the quickest path to completion. Once you've installed MPLAB an icon on your desktop is used to start the program. We have plenty of I/O pins on the dsPIC30F-2010 but we need to be careful how we implement our I²C and SPI communications interfaces. Both of these interfaces are implemented in the chip and have software wrappers that provide easy software access. The problem is that both of these hardware implementations use the same pins. To overcome this challenge we will implement and test each of these functions using the built-in simulator. We will then implement and test each function using the dsPICDEM 28 board. Once completed we will design our own board for implementing this version of the prototype.

The RS-232 Interface

The dsPIC has two RS-232 TTL interfaces built in. These interfaces do not have flow control but adding this feature is really pretty simple. In keeping with our original design, we will use one RS-232 TTL interface and add CTS/RTS handshake signals. This single interface will connect to the communication host via RS-232 (with the use of our transceiver from Chapter 7), Ethernet, and USB (using the 16C745). Rather than modify the dsPICDEM 28 board, we will simply test the serial, SPI, and I²C I/O and then make final design changes to our board.

To show the differences between the Microchip GNU-based compiler and the HI-TECH dsPICC compiler we will write a short test program using each for our serial I/O. Let's begin by starting the MPLAB workbench by double-clicking the desktop icon. Once the program has started, select Project | Project Wizard, select the dsPIC30F2010 device, and press Next. The next screen allows you to select the toolset. We will start by selecting the MPLAB C30 compiler.

Note:

If you haven't already done so, please download and install the trial version of the C30 compiler before continuing.

Press the Next button and type RSTest as the project name. Select an existing folder to store the project files in. I created a folder named dsPIC\Examples\Chapter9, but you can choose a different directory if you wish.

The dsPIC Peripheral Libraries

Microchip provides a peripheral library that provides "wrapper" functions around dsPIC hardware functions. This library is included with the C30 compiler but can also be downloaded from the Microchip web site. The functions can be called from C or Assembler. We will use the UART, RTC, and SPI libraries. We will implement I²C and the Dallas 1-Wire in software using general-purpose I/O pins.

MPLAB requires we add the source files for the peripherals to our project. If we don't, we will get compiler errors since the workbench won't know where to look for the functions we are using from the UART libraries. In addition, we need to create a source file for testing the serial functions.

The Project Manager window has the project name and a list of file types that can be associated with our project. With the mouse, highlight Source Files, right-click, and select Add Files from the menu. Browse to the pic30_tools\src\peripheral\src\pmc\uart folder and add OpenUART1.c, CloseUART1.c, and putsUART1.c to the source files. Next, create a new file and name it uart.c, save it to our project directory, and then add it to the source file list. Highlight Linker Scripts in the project view and add pic30_tools\support\gld\p30f2010.gld to the linker script list. This is the default linker script for the dsPIC30F2010 device. Now we are ready to write a short test program. All of our code will be in the uart.c program. Listing 9-1 illustrates how to implement RS-232 in code using the C30 compiler from Microchip.

Listing 9-1

```c
/******************************************************************************
uart_test - Test the alternate UART using the C30 "C" compiler toolsuite from
Microchip. Copyright 2004 Oliver H. Bailey

written: 06/13/2004 - Oliver H. Bailey
modified 12/16/2004 - Oliver H. Bailey
******************************************************************************/
#define __dsPIC30F2010__                        // Define Device Type
#include <p30fxxxx.h>                            // Include Generic Header
#include <uart.h>                                // Include UART Header

char recBuf[80];                                 // Receive Buffer
char * recData = recBuf;                         // Character Pointer to Receive Buffer

void __attribute__((__interrupt__)) _U1TXInterrupt(void)   // Uart 1 TX Interrupt Routine
{
  IFS0bits.U1TXIF = 0;                           // Clear Interrupt Flag
}

void __attribute__ ((__interrupt__)) _U1RXInterrupt(void)  // UART 1 RX Interrupt Function
{
  IFS0bits.U1RXIF = 0;                           // Clear Interrupt Flag
  while (DataRdyUART1())                          // While DataReady = True
  {
    (*(recData)++) = ReadUART1();                 // Next Buffer Position = Character
  }
}


int main(void)                                   // Main Program
{
  char tstData[] = {"Hello from Embedded System\r\n\0"};   // Test Character Data String
  unsigned int baud;                             // Baud Rate
  unsigned int mode, dbgmode;                    // UART Mode
  unsigned int intmode;                          // UART Interrupt Mode
  unsigned int loop;                             // Loop Counter if Needed

  CloseUART1();                                  // Close UART for Saftey
  baud = 5;                                      // 9.6K Baud @ 7.37 MHz
  ConfigIntUART1(UART_RX_INT_EN & UART_RX_INT_PR6 &  // Enable RX Interrupt, Priority 6
          UART_TX_INT_DIS & UART_TX_INT_PR2);    // Disable TX Interrupt, Priority 2
```

```
intmode = UART_INT_TX_BUF_EMPTY &      // Transmit Buffer Empty
          UART_TX_PIN_NORMAL &          // TX Pin Normal
          UART_TX_ENABLE &              // Enable Transmit Interrupt
          UART_INT_RX_3_4_FUL &         // RX Buffer 3/4 full
          UART_ADR_DETECT_DIS &         // Disable Address Detect
          UART_RX_OVERRUN_CLEAR;        // Receive Overrun Clear

mode = UART_EN &                        // Enable UART
       UART_IDLE_CON &                  // Idle
       UART_DIS_WAKE &                  // Wake State
       UART_EN_LOOPBACK &               // Loopback
       UART_EN_ABAUD &                  // Autobaud
       UART_NO_PAR_8BIT &               // No Parity 8 Bit Data
       UART_1STOPBIT;                   // 1 Stop Bit

dbgmode = mode & UART_EN_LOOPBACK;      // Add Loopback Mode

OpenUART1(dbgmode, intmode, baud);      // Open the UART

for (loop=0;loop < 255; loop++){        // Send Message
  putsUART1((unsigned int *) tstData);
}

while(BusyUART1());                     // Loop while busy

while(DataRdyUART1())                   // While there is data
{
  (*(recData)++) = ReadUART1();         // Read it
}

CloseUART1();                           // close UART
return 0;                               // Return No Error
}
```

Note:

To make this work with the dsPICDEM 28 board, pins 2 and 3 on the DB9 must be reversed. This will make the dsPICDEM 28 board the DCE.

Now let's see how this same program would be written in dsPICC from HI-TECH software. The following program is written in dsPICC and does the same task as above.

Listing 9-2

```
#include <dspic.h>                               // dsPIC definitions
#include <string.h>                              // Used for string functions

// Alternate method of setting configuration bits.
_CONFIG(FOSC, POSC & XTPLL4 & CLKSWDIS & FSCMDIS);
_CONFIG(FWDT, WDTDIS);
_CONFIG(FBORPOR, PWRT16 & MCLREN & BORDIS);
_CONFIG(FGS, GCPU & GWRU);
_CONFIG(FCOMM, PGEMU);


#define BAUD        9600                          // Baud Rate
#define OSC         7372800                       // Oscillator Speed
#define DIVIDER     (((OSC/BAUD)/16)-1)           // Calculation for bus speed
char stmsg[]={"Hello From Embedded Systems\n\r\0"};     // Test String

void main(void)                                   // Start of main program
{
  unsigned int slen;                              // Length of stmsg
  int loop;                                       // Array Element Number

  U1BRG = DIVIDER;                                // UART BIT RATE BYTE VALUE
  U1_UARTEN = 1;                                  // Enable UART 1
  U1_UTXEN = 1;                                   // Enable TX 1

  slen = strlen(stmsg);                           // Get String Length

  for(loop = 0; (loop < slen); loop++){           // Loop through string
    U1TXREG = stmsg[loop];                        // Put Array Element in Transmit Register
  };

  while(1){
    while(!U1_URXDA);                             // While there is no receive data
    while(!U1_TRMT);                              // and no transmit data
    U1TXREG = U1RXREG;                            // Echo received data to transmit
  };
};
```

There are a couple of differences. Using the C30 compiler we activate and set up both transmit and receive interrupts to clear the interrupt flags, whereas using the dsPICC version we stay in an endless loop echoing characters. Even so, the way dsPICC handles the hardware "wrappers" is slightly different from Microchip's method. Using dsPICC we directly manipulate the registers through the uppercase names defined in the dspic.h file, while the C30 compiler handles these functions through function calls.

Both methods have advantages and disadvantages. Using C30 the code will be larger, but if Microchip makes changes to the register addresses it will require only a recompile. Using dsPICC will result in smaller code and shorter programs. If you're an Assembly code person you will probably favor the dsPICC compiler, whereas a C programmer will favor the C30 compiler. Both compilers are excellent products.

The SPI Interface

With the UART interface done, let's move on to the SPI interface, which is how we will access the non-volatile memory of the DS2404 chip. Again using the Microchip C30 compiler, the code to output SPI data would look similar to Listing 9-3.

Listing 9-3

```
#define __dsPIC30F2010__              // Define dsPIC type

#include <p30fxxxx.h>                 // Include generic header
#include <spi.h>                      // Include SPI header
#include <string.h>                   // Include string conversion routines

char tstData[] = "Test SPI Routine\r\n\0";   // Test output string
int loop;                            // Loop counter for character output
int slen;                            // Length holder for test string
```

```
void attribute_((interrupt)) SPI1Interrupt(void)   // Interrupt declaration
{
  IFS0bits.SPI1IF = 0;                             // Clear interrupt flag
}


int main(void)
{
  unsigned int SPIConfig;                          // SPI configuration bits
  unsigned int SPIStat;                            // SPI status configuration

  SPIConfig = FRAME_ENABLE_ON &                    // Turn on framing for DS2404 3-Wire
              FRAME_SYNC_OUTPUT &                  // SYNC OUPUT TO CLOCK
              ENABLE_SDO_PIN &                     // ENABLE Serial Data Out
              SPI_MODE16_OFF &                     // 8 BIT MODE
              SPI_SMP_ON &                         // Input Sample OFF
              SPI_CKE_OFF &                        // Clock EDGE Select OFF
              SLAVE_ENABLE_OFF &                   // Slave Mode OFF
              CLK_POL_ACTIVE_HIGH &                // Clock Polarity Active HIGH
              MASTER_ENABLE_ON &                   // Enable MASTER
              SEC_PRESCAL_7_1 &                    // Secondary Prescaler
              PRI_PRESCAL_64_1;                    // Primary Prescaler

  SPIStat = SPI_ENABLE &                           // Enable SPI
            SPI_IDLE_CON &                         // Continue Operation when IDLE MODe
                                                   // is Active
            SPI_RX_OVFLOW_CLR;                     // Clear Receive Overflow Bit

  CloseSPI1();                                     // Close SPI1

  ConfigIntSPI1(SPI_INT_DIS & SPI_INT_PRI_7);      // Configure SPI 1 Interrupt
  OpenSPI1(SPIConfig, SPIStat);                    // Open SPI 1

  slen = strlen(tstData);                          // get length of tstData

  for(loop = 0; (loop < slen); loop++)             // Output a character at a time
  {
    putcSPI1((unsigned int) tstData[loop]);
  }

  putsSPI1(slen, (unsigned int *) &tstData[0]);    // Output Entire String
```

```
CloseSPI1();                                    // Close SPI 1
return 0;                                       // No Error Condition
}
```

Now, let's output that same data using the dsPICC compiler from HI-TECH. In the following listing we are sending the same string a character at a time out the SPI port.

Listing 9-4

```
/****************************************************************************
htspi - HI-TECH SPI interface for dsPIC. Copyright 2004, Oliver H. Bailey

This program implements the SPI interface using the HI-TECH dsPICC compiler.
To use the built-in SPI interface(s) there are two registers and a buffer.
The registers are:
        SPI1STAT  - The SPI Status Register
        SPI1CON   - The SPI Control Register
The buffer is defined as:
        SPI1BUF   - The SPI Buffer Area


****************************************************************************/
#include <dspic.h>                              // dsPIC definitions
#include <string.h>                             // Used for string functions

// Alternate method of setting configuration bits.
_CONFIG(FOSC, POSC & XTPLL4 & CLKSWDIS & FSCMDIS);
_CONFIG(FWDT, WDTDIS);
_CONFIG(FBORPOR, PWRT16 & MCLREN & BORDIS);
_CONFIG(FGS, GCPU & GWRU);
_CONFIG(FCOMM, PGEMU);

char stmsg[]={"Hello From Embedded Systems\n\r\0"};  // Test string

void main(void)                                 // Start of main program
{
  unsigned int slen;                            // Length of stmsg
  int loop;                                     // Array Element Number

  // Set up SPI control register
  S1_FRMEN = 1;                                 // Enable Framing
  S1_SPIFSD = 0;                                // Master Mode
  S1_DISSDO = 1;                                // SDO1 Pin is controlled by the module
```

```
S1_MODE16 = 0;                          // 8 Bit Mode
S1_SMP = 1;                             // Input sampled at end of clock cycle
S1_CKE = 0;          // Serial Output data changes on transition from idle to active clock
S1_SSEN = 1;         // Slave enable line will be handled automatically by module
S1_CKP = 0;                             // Idle Clock State is Low
S1_MSTEN = 1;                           // Enable Master Mode


// Using the following prescaler values the data rate with the processor clock at 30 MHz
// will be 59 KHz
// See the dsPIC family reference guide for information on calculating SPI data rates.
S1_SPRE0 = 0;                           // Secondary prescale = 8:1
S1_SPRE1 = 0;
S1_SPRE2 = 0;
S1_PPRE0 = 0;
// Primary Prescale = 64:1
S1_PPRE1 = 0;
// Enable SPI in master mode
S1_SPISIDL = 0;                         // Continue when Idle
S1_SPIEN = 1;                           // Enable SPI 1


slen = strlen(stmsg);                   // Get String Length

for(loop = 0; (loop < slen); loop++){   // Loop through string
  while(S1_SPITBF);                     // Wait for Transmit Buffer to Empty
  SPI1BUF = stmsg[loop];                // Put Array Element in Transmit Register
};
};
```

The I²C Interface

The next communications interface we need to implement is the
I²C interface. As you may recall this interface allows us to communicate with the LCD display. It's a very important interface
since the LCD handles all user I/O and alarm functions.

We've used the I/O pins allotted for I²C on the dsPIC for
other purposes. Even so, I've written a generic I²C handler that
can use any general-purpose pair of I/O pins. I've kept the naming conventions the same as the dsPIC peripheral library so the

generic routines can be used with the same function calls. The difference is that a separate header file is needed to set up the pins for I²C use. The generic I²C routines can be downloaded from www.wordware.com/files/embsys or www.time-lines.com. Keeping that in mind, the following I²C code will work with either library. The following is a C30 example of how the I²C communications work on the dsPIC.

Listing 9-5

```
/*****************************************************************************
I2C Test program for the Microchip C30 compiler.
Copyright 2004, Oliver H. Bailey


This program implements the I2C interface for the dsPICC using the Microchip
C30 Compiler.
*****************************************************************************/
#define __ dsPIC30F2010__                       // define dsPIC chip

#include <p30fxxxx.h>                            // Include dsPIC definition header
#include <i2c.h>                                 // Include I2C header


int main(void)                                   // Main program
{
  unsigned int baudrate;                         // Define transfer speed
  unsigned int setup;                            // Define setup bits

  unsigned char * msgPtr;                        // Character pointer to message string
  unsigned char tstMsg[] = "Hello I2C";          // Message string

  msgPtr = tstMsg;                               // Assign message address to pointer

  baudrate = 0x11;         // 1:8 prescale value for A, 1:2 prescale value for B

  setup = I2C_ON &                               // I2C ENABLE
          I2C_IDLE_CON &                         // Continue when processor IDLE
          I2C_CLK_HLD &                          // Hold Clock Line
          I2C_IPMI_DIS &       // Disable Intelligent Peripheral Management Interface
          I2C_7BIT_ADD &                         // Use 7 bit slave address mode
          I2C_SLW_DIS &                          // Disable Slew Rate
          I2C_SM_DIS &                           // Disable SMBus Input
```

Chapter 9

```
        I2C_GCALL_DIS &                    // Disable General Call
        I2C_STR_DIS &                      // Disable SCL Clock Stretch
        I2C_NACK &                         // Enable Acknowledge Bit
        I2C_ACK_DIS &                      // Disable ACK
        I2C_RCV_DIS &                      // Disable Receive
        I2C_STOP_DIS &                     // Disable Stop Condition Enable
        I2C_RESTART_DIS &                  // Disable Repeat Start Condition
        I2C_START_DIS;                     // Disable Start Condition Bit

StopI2C();                                 // Stop Interface just to be safe
CloseI2C();                                // Close if already open

OpenI2C(setup, baudrate);                  // Open with new configuration settings
IdleI2C();                                 // Wait until bus is idle
StartI2C();                                // Start I2C bus

while(I2CCONbits.SEN);                      // Loop until Start Sequence is complete
MasterWriteI2C(0x50);                      // Wait up the slave device

while(I2CSTATbits.TBF);                     // Wait until Transmit Buffer is Empty
while(I2CSTATbits.ACKSTAT);                 // Wait for slave acknowledgement

MasterputsI2C(msgPtr);                     // Send message string
StopI2C();                                 // Stop I2C Bus
while(I2CCONbits.PEN);                      // Wait for Stop condition to complete
CloseI2C();                                // Close device
};
```

As you can see there are a couple of vague similarities between RS-232 and I²C I/O. The first is baud rate. Just as we declare a baud rate in RS-232 we also declare a transfer speed in I²C, but it is not the same. We are declaring the bus speed or clock for which the data is sent. I know this may sound just like a baud rate generator but there is one major difference: The clock pulse is sent along with the data in I²C, whereas in RS-232 the clock is physically separate at each end. In the I²C definition we only need to worry about the maximum speed at which the slave can receive data, and make sure we stay within that speed range.

The second similarity is the number of data bits defined. Again, this is different from RS-232 in that the 7-bit definition applies only to the slave device ID length. Remember that the clock and data lines can be attached to many different devices. The slave ID defines which device is to be awakened to be given commands to or receive data from. If you are asking for the difference between the SPI and I²C communications, here is the answer: Both devices can be attached to multiple slaves. In SPI communications one line is allocated to keeping the attention of the device being addressed. So in SPI we can use a common data and clock line, but each device must have its own attention line. If you have many devices you will either need additional components to select the active device or use a processor pin for each device. In I²C we replace that additional attention line with a device ID, eliminating the need for the additional components or processor pins.

The following program is written in HI-TECH C and performs the same functions as Listing 9-5.

Listing 9-6

```
/*****************************************************************************
htI2C - HI-TECH I2C interface for dsPIC. Copyright 2004, Oliver H. Bailey

This program implements the I2C interface using the HI-TECH dsPICC compiler.
*****************************************************************************/
#include <dspic.h>                        // dsPIC definitions
#include <string.h>                       // Used for string functions

// Alternate method of setting configuration bits.
_CONFIG(FOSC, POSC & XTPLL4 & CLKSWDIS & FSCMDIS);
_CONFIG(FWDT, WDTDIS);
 CONFIG(FBORPOR, PWRT16 & MCLREN & BORDIS);
_CONFIG(FGS, GCPU & GWRU);
_CONFIG(FCOMM, PGEMU);

char stmsg[]={"Hello From Embedded Systems\n\r\0"};  // Test String

void main(void)                           // Start of main program
{
   unsigned int slen;                     // Length of stmsg
   int loop;                              // Array Element Number


   // Set up I2C control register
```

Chapter 9

```
I2C_SIDL = 0;                              // Continue in Idle Mode
I2C_SCLREL = 0;                            // Hold SCL Clock Low
I2C_IPMIEN = 0;                            // IPMI Mode Disabled
I2C_A10M = 0;                              // 7 Bit Slave Address
I2C_DISSLW = 1;                            // Disable Slew Rate
I2C_SMEN = 0;                              // Disable SMBus Input
I2C_GCEN = 0;                              // Disable General Call Address
I2C_STREN = 0;                             // Disable SCL Clock Stretch
I2C_ACKDT = 1;                             // Send NACK During Acknowledgement
I2C_ACKEN = 0;                             // Disable Acknowledge Sequence
I2C_RCEN = 0;                              // Disable Receive Sequence
I2C_PEN = 0;                               // Disable Stop Condition
I2C_RSEN = 0;                              // Disable Repeated Start Condition
I2C_SEN = 0;                               // Disable Start Condition

I2CBRG = 0x18F;                            // 100 KHZ clock @ 40 MHz CPU

I2C_EN = 1;                                // Enable I2C

slen = strlen(stmsg);                      // Get String Length

I2CADD = 0x50;                             // LCD Address
while(I2C_TBF);                            // Wait until Transmit Buffer Empty
while(I2C_ACKSTAT);                        // Wait for Acknowledgement Status

for(loop = 0; (loop < slen); loop++){      // Loop through string
  while(I2C_TBF);                          // Wait for Transmit Buffer to Empty
  I2CTRN = stmsg[loop];                    // Put Array Element in Transmit Register
};

I2C_EN=0;                                  // Disable I2C
};
```

Before we continue it should be noted that the dsPIC peripheral library is also compatible with the HI-TECH compiler. I chose to write different source code to illustrate the differences in how the same routines can be written. In the dsPIC.h file all the I/O declarations are defined. The naming conventions follow the names found in the dsPIC family reference manual under the proper topic (uart, SPI, I²C). If these same register names exist in the C30 header files, these snippets of code should be completely interchangeable.

The differences between how C30 and dsPICC implement the built-in dsPIC functions come down to the amount of "wrapper code" implemented by the vendor. The function calls we've written in C30 read or set the registers for us, whereas the dsPICC product gives us direct access, which allows us to write our own "wrapper" code. I like to use both techniques, depending on the amount of available program space available. These days I tend to use the direct access method when working with parts that have smaller program memeory areas.

The Dallas 1-Wire Interface

Our final communications method to implement on the dsPIC is the Dallas 1-Wire protocol. Now you may think that we have quite a chore ahead of us in writing the Dallas 1-Wire handlers for the PIC. Fortunately, that is not the case. There are several sources of 1-Wire interface routines written both in Assembler and C. If you want to understand how the 1-Wire and other communications interfaces work at the assembly level, then I would suggest reading *Serial Communications* by Square 1. That book provides an in-depth view of how many communications interfaces are implemented in Assembler for various PIC processors. Sadly, the dsPIC isn't covered since it is a new device.

If you already understand the 1-Wire protocol (if you've read Part I of this book, you should) and want to find a starting point for C code implementation, I would recommend the 1-Wire Public Domain Kit from Dallas Semiconductor at www.dalsemi.com. This kit comes with source code for various platforms and drivers for several types of interfaces as well. This is a very comprehensive kit and will take some time to completely understand.

If you just want a starting point without a lot of extra files and documentation, I suggest the 1-Wire interface available from www.microchipc.com. This site contains many useful C language routines including I²C and the Dallas 1-Wire. These routines are well documented and cost nothing to view and use for testing. Most are very simple to understand and use as a starting point for other projects. While none of these routines are written for the dsPIC, several can be easily converted. For this project download and review the Dallas ds1821 thermometer, found in the source code folder. It consists of three files: delay.c, delay.h, and 1wire00x.c. These three files are easy to understand and can easily be modified to work with the dsPIC and HI-TECH dsPICC compiler. If you not up to writing your own C files, then download the source files for this book at www.wordware.com/files/embsys or www.time-lines.com. You'll find the dsPIC 1-Wire source in the chapter 9\dsPIC\1-Wire folder.

Implementing USB and Ethernet Communications

This completes the implementation of the requirements for the dsPIC. Next, we will complete the USB communications controller. The TTL serial interface we developed earlier will handle all of our host hardware interfaces. The same four wires will allow the dsPIC to communicate with Ethernet, USB, or RS-232 communications interfaces. The same source code will also work on the dsPIC, so the communications hardware is actually transparent to the dsPIC.

Now you may be asking how this is possible since there are big differences in how RS-232, USB, and Ethernet interfaces work. The answer to that question lies in our design. We have designed in the ability to have one microcontroller that manages the environment by monitoring and controlling the temperature and air circulation for our thermostat. We have also chosen to implement a standard 4-Wire TTL interface to an external communications processor. As we've moved through this chapter we have kept in mind the fact that we will need to use a DIP switch or jumper for selecting the USB or Ethernet interface. Or do we?

We will be using the PIC 16C745 low-speed USB interface chip. In addition to being a USB interface, this microcontroller also has other I/O capabilities. So we're using the USB port on the chip and a 4-Wire TTL serial interface from the dsPIC. This is a 28-pin device with remaining capability. In this chapter we are using an inexpensive Ethernet controller chip with built-in TCP/IP capabilities. The Ethernet controller also has a 4-Wire TTL serial interface. The PIC 16C745 is a 28-pin device and the 765 is a 40-pin device. This means both devices have more than enough capacity to handle the Ethernet transceiver in addition to the dsPIC. Now you may be asking why we don't eliminate the dsPIC altogether; that is a reasonable question. The dsPIC is a faster processor with more memory and program space. If we limit the use of the 16C745 to being a communications processor, we will be able to avoid running out of program space and timing issues. Remember that only one communications interface is active at a time.

The PIC 16C745 USB Chip

This chip is a 28-pin EPROM- or ROM-based chip that contains a low-speed USB interface with two endpoints. Now this isn't the fastest chip in the world, but for our needs it will work just fine. Since we've decided to add the Ethernet interface to this chip we need to break down our development efforts because they will cover two separate areas. First, we need to develop our USB to host interface. This task will entail the development of our embedded protocol and associated host routines.

To simplify the Windows development effort, we'll make the 16C745 appear as an HID (human interface device) and use HIDmaker to develop the host application code for Windows and the USB communications piece for the PIC. Next, we will develop the serial I/O required for the 16C745 to communicate with the Ethernet controller. This will also require code to set up the IP address and other configurable items related to Ethernet

communications. Finally, we need to implement the serial interface to the dsPIC and find a way to let the commmunications
controller (16C745) know which communications interface (USB
or Ethernet) is being used. Since we have plenty of I/O pins
available on the dsPIC and 16C745, we can use an I/O pin to tell
which communications interface to use. If the I/O pin is low, the
USB interface will be used. If the pin is in a high state, then the
Ethernet controller will be used instead. The following implementation diagram shows how the finished unit will work.

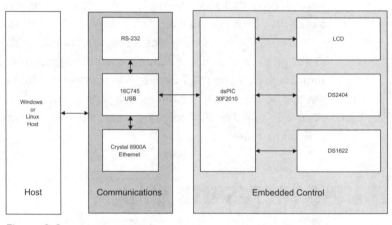

Figure 9-9

This implementation change will work very well. With this
change, the dsPIC is in total control of the embedded appliance
with the PIC 16C745 in complete control of all host communications. This makes diagnosing problems and development much
easier. We can now concentrate on developing and debugging our
embedded controller, then move on to our communications controller. If a communications problem arises it can immediately be
isolated from the embedded controller, making diagnostics easier
and development more clear. Having made this decision makes
the task of implementation somewhat easier as our task list for
the 16C745 device is clear and concise.

We need to take a look at the pinout of the 16C745 device to see which pins are best used for our needs. We need three TTL serial ports and one USB port. One of the TTL ports will be connected to the dsPIC and in use all the time. The remaining two ports will be our RS-232 and Ethernet host interfaces. The USB port will also be a host interface option.

The Microchip USB Developer Kits

Currently, Microchip has three development kits for USB. The first is a new product designed to support the full-speed devices. The second kit is an inexpensive PIC programmer with a break-away prototype area that uses the 16C745 as the host interface. The PICKit 1 uses the 16C745 to drive a charge circuit and program lower end chips. In the following photo the 16C745 is the long chip on the left.

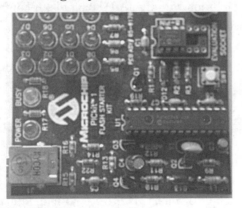

Figure 9-10

Microchip also has a low-speed development kit — the PICDEM USB product. This kit has a comprehensive users manual, CD, and quite a few on-board accessories as shown in Figure 9-11.

Figure 9-11

The PICDEM USB is driven by the 16C765, which is a larger chip with more memory and I/O. In Figure 9-11 the 16C765 is the large chip on the left. Note the empty socket that can be used for the 16C745 device.

The 16C745 has 8 K of program space, 256 bytes of RAM, and 8-bit A/D resolution with five A/D channels. It conforms to the USB 1.1 specification and has 64 bytes of dual-port RAM, 22 I/O pins, and eight available interrupts.

The Microchip USB Engine

The 16C7x5 USB series has a built-in USB engine that you can use or modify to your own needs. The software interface is available for Assembler, C, or Basic. There are both an interrupt and polled versions of the engines. There are five functions supported by the Microchip USB engine: InitUSB, PutEP1, GetEP1, PutEP2, and GetEP2. The Put functions send data to the host while the Get routines receive data from the host system. These are the application layer functions. Beneath these functions are the protocol layer functions where all the background work is done. At the protocol layer we have ServiceUSBInt, StallUSBEP, UnstallUSBEP, SoftDetachUSB, CheckSleep, ConfiguredUSB, and SetConfiguration functions.

The USB without doubt is the most complicated of the interfaces we need to implement. What makes the USB software more complex is the fact that the host implementation differs more than RS-232 or Ethernet. In addition, defining USB descriptors can be a time-consuming and tedious task. While there are no cross-platform tools to aid in this development effort, we can expedite our Windows development through the use of HIDmaker. Since Windows is the most complex of the USB driver models this will reduce the amount of time needed on the most time-consuming platform.

Note:

During the course of writing this book I made several attempts to reach the people at usb.org and never received any reply or answers to my inquiries. My questions were related to why the documentation for USB devices wasn't written to be more friendly to engineers who have had development experience with RS-232, RS-485, or Ethernet. I also questioned the expense for small developers in the purchase of a device ID. Neither question was answered nor did I receive a response to my emails. Being as usb.org is made up of very large companies, it has occurred to me that if the USB standard were easier to understand the companies who make the standards would not have the marketing edge for USB appliances they currently enjoy.

Defining a USB Device to the Host System

Developing a good working USB device can be tricky. Consider the fact that if the USB descriptors are wrong your device will simply be ignored by the host system. Even worse, you may need to purchase a USB analyzer, which will cost upward of $1,000. There are software tools available to make things easier. The PICDEM USB kit includes software to help get the USB descriptors correct. There is also a tool that will walk you through the process of developing an HID-based USB device and even generate the code for the PIC and Windows application.

While it's true we are developing for cross-platform use, using this tool leaves us with only the need to develop the Linux/UNIX USB application interface. Of more importance is the fact that this tool builds both ends of the USB code, which may seem to be a minor point but is a very important development fact. The tool I'm describing is HIDmaker from Trace Systems. Before we walk through a sample USB device definition, please review how the USB interface works. Having said

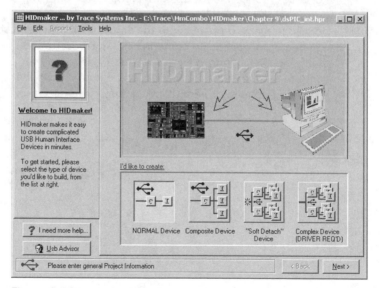

Figure 9-12

that, let's build a simple USB device with HIDmaker. After installation HIDmaker will reside in a program group under Trace. To
start HIDmaker, select Start | Programs | Trace | HIDmaker.

1. Since this is our first USB device, choose **NORMAL Device**
    and press **Next**. A project info screen will appear.

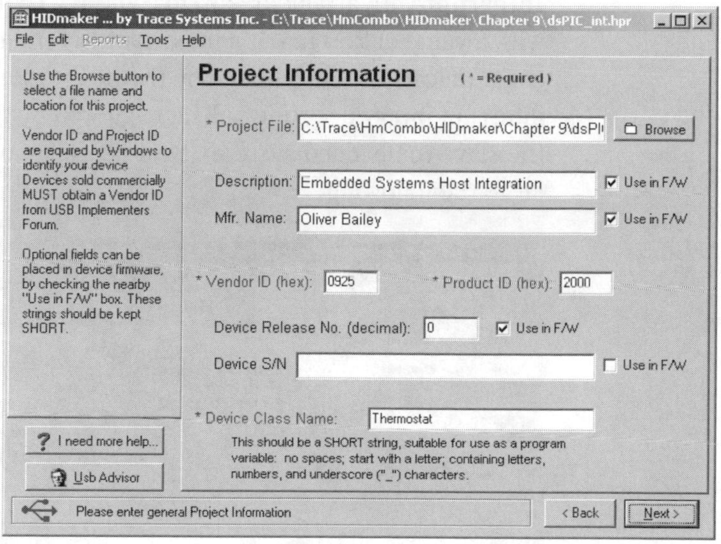

Figure 9-13

2. In this window we enter a path to our project and a project
    name. This is followed by a description string and manufac-
    turer string. The check boxes at the far right indicate these
    will be in the PIC firmware. The next two fields are vendor
    and product IDs. For development and test purposes you can
    use the default contents, but you must get your own IDs
    from usb.org before going to market. The next fields are the
    release number, which can also be inserted into the firm-
    ware, a device serial number, and a USB class name. Input
    your information into these fields and press the **Next** button.

3. The next window is where a lot of the work that HIDmaker
    performs is done. This is a very important window because it
    defines our descriptors and variables. For our example we

will use the default values for the Configuration and Interface descriptions. Our device has its own power supply so check the **Device has its own power supply** radio button.

4. We will not be using remote wakeup in our prototype so check **Not Used by Device**. Next, we will select **EP1 In: Interrupt** with a value of **250** ms, and **EP1 Out: Interrupt** with a value of **250** ms. It's important to remember that *all* communications are initiated by the host system, so these interrupt interval setting will be triggered by the host, not the slave (embedded system). Your screen should look similar to the following:

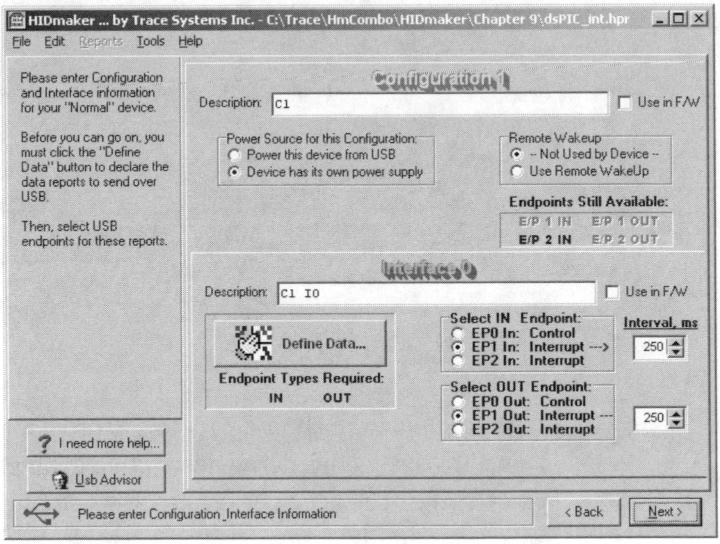

Figure 9-14

5. Now it's time to define our data, so press the **Define Data** button. Before we continue it's important to note that *all* data views are from the host. So input would be input to the host and output would be output from the host. With that in mind, let's define our data variables. When you press the Define Data button, you will be presented with a screen similar to the following:

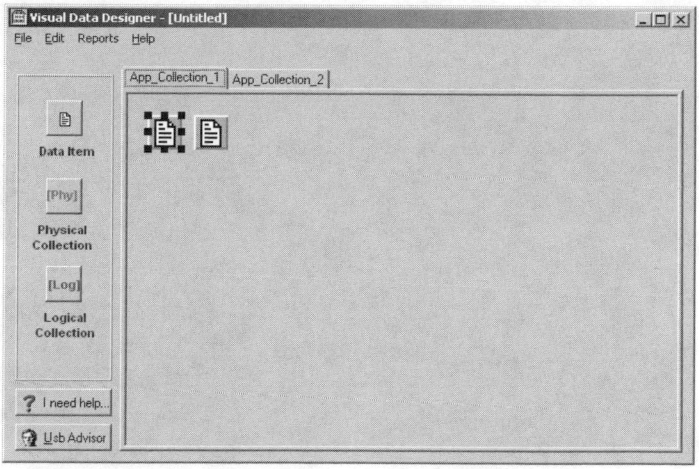

Figure 9-15

6. For our first sample we will define two data items. We can actually get much more complicated, but let's walk before we run. Click the **Data Item** button, then click inside the recessed open area. You should see a button appear. Repeat this process once more for our second data item; your screen should look like Figure 9-15. To set the parameters for each item, double-click on that item and a Data Item Properties dialog will appear.

7. Select **Input** from the Data Type drop-down dialog box and **Usage ID 1** from the Usage Info box. Check the **Data** radio button since this is not a constant and the **Variable** radio button since this is not a keyboard array of characters. Select the **Absolute, No Wrap, Linear, No Preferred State, No Null State**, and **Bit Field** radio buttons. The Report Size in bits should be **8**, or the size of a byte. The Report Count will be **12** and will contain the string "Hello World" and a null terminator. Go to the Name field and name this **HelloData**. When the host initiates an input interrupt to the PIC, the message sent will be "Hello World." Your screen should look similar to the following:

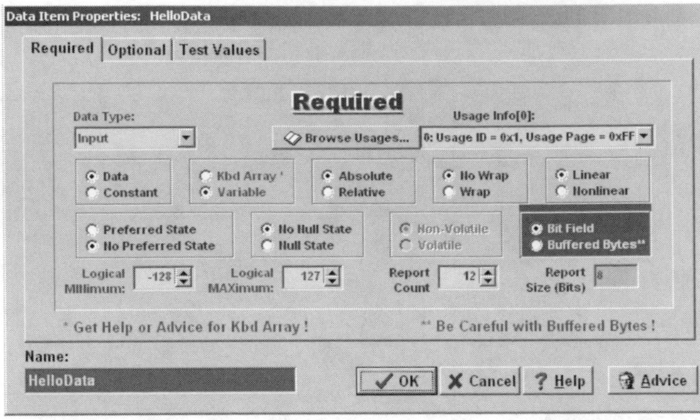

Figure 9-16

8. Click the **OK** button to return to the Visual Data Designer. Next, click the second data item and define it as **Output** with a Usage ID of **2**, and a Report Count of **14**. This will send a string "Goodbye World" and a terminating null character. Name this **GoodbyeData** and press **OK**. Upon returning to the Visual Data Designer this time, select **File | Save As** to save our data definitions. After the data definitions have been saved, close the Visual Data Designer and press the **Next** button.

9. Now we are ready to generate code for both the USB device and the Windows host. We have a nice selection of languages for the PIC. HIDmaker supports Assembler, PicBasic Pro from microEngineering Labs, HI-TECH C (which is also ANSI C), and CCS C. You can choose more than one; as you can see I've chosen all but Assembler. On the host side we have Visual Basic 6, Delphi, and C++ Builder for our choices. I've chosen C++ Builder and Delphi. Press the **Next** button to generate your code; a summary will be displayed along with the contents of each generated file. At this point you can press the **Finish** button to leave HIDmaker.

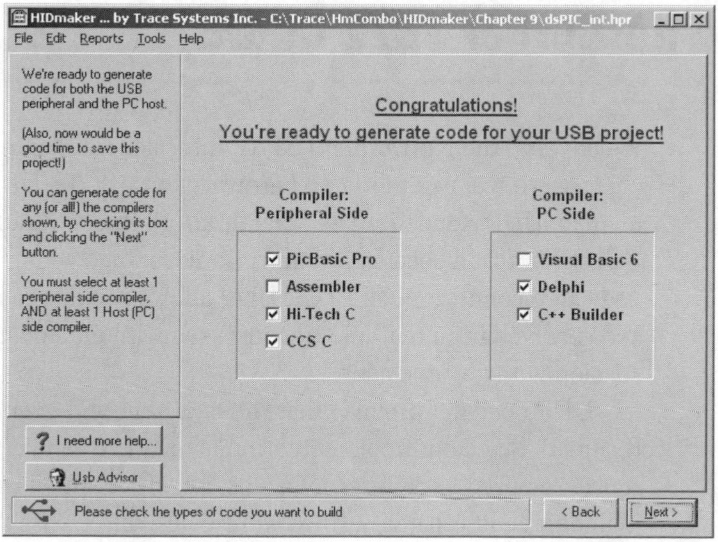

Figure 9-17

Finishing the Communications Tasks

With our USB communications handler finished, we need to move on to adding TTL serial I/O support for the remaining communications methods. Before we do that, however, I would suggest that you compile and test both the PIC and Windows projects to check for compiler errors.

The NetBurner SB72 Board

We covered the NetBurner TCP/IP interface in Chapter 8. In this chapter we will use the same hardware but use the UDP protocol instead. UDP stands for User Datagram Protocol. It differs from TCP/IP in that a session is connectionless. Instead of having a dedicated connection like TCP, UDP allows packets to be sent and received from multiple IP addresses without a dedicated session with any one address.

UDP does not promise that the data sent will ever be received. Since our implementation is on a LAN and is not currently required to be Internet accessible, UDP should provide a high degree of reliability. If we were using this across the Internet we probably would not select UDP, but this protocol has some advantages for working in a LAN environment. One example of this benefit is the ability to have temperature updates broadcast across the network to multiple workstations. If our thermostat were in use in a cold storage warehouse, this would allow anyone to "dial-in" to the thermostat and get real-time temperature and alarm data. Controlling the thermostat could become a nightmare unless we filter who or which terminals can access the control functions. This could be as simple as checking the origination IP address to see if it is an authorized control station. We could also add a password so that the user could be authenticated and allow access by only certain individuals from specific workstations. In short, there are several ways to provide controls prohibiting unauthorized use.

We could use the TCP/IP methods from Chapter 8 and they would work just fine. The TTL serial interface is identical in both situations. The following listing illustates one way of implementing UDP.

Listing 9-7

```
/*****************************************************************************
UDP Test Program — Copyright 2004, Oliver H. Bailey
This program is for Embedded Systems, Desktop Integration Book
*****************************************************************************/
#include "predef.h"
#include <stdio.h>
#include <ctype.h>
#include <startnet.h>
#include <ucos.h>
#include <udp.h>
#include <autoupdate.h>
#include <string.h>
#include <taskmon.h>

extern "C"
{
  void UserMain(void *pd);
}

// We have to use 4-byte alignment for the NetBurner
DWORD UdpTestStk[USER_TASK_STK_SIZE] attribute_((aligned(4)));

/*****************************************************************************
    The UDP Read Packet Function. - Waits for 100 clock ticks and then returns
    if no data arrived.
*****************************************************************************/
void UDPRead(void *pd)
{
  int UDP_port = (int) pd;                    // UDP Port Number assignment
  printf("Using port #%d\n", UDP_port);       // Print Port Number

  OS_FIFO Read_fifo;                          // Create Read fifo
  OSFifoInit(&Read_fifo);                     // and Initialize the fifo

  RegisterUDPFifo(UDP_port, &Read_fifo);      // Register the port number and buffer

  while (1)                                   // Do Forever
  {
    UDPPacket upkt(&Read_fifo, 100);          // Return on data or timeout
```

```
    if (upkt.Validate())                              // If we receive valid data, process
    {
      WORD Data_len = upkt.GetDataSize();             // Data length
      printf("Got %d UDP Bytes From :", (int) Data_len);
      ShowIP(upkt.GetSourceAddress());                // Data Source IP Address
      printf("\n");
      ShowData(upkt.GetDataBuffer(), Data_len);       // Display actual data
      printf("\n");
    }                                                 // End of Valid Packet Data Handler
  }                                                   // End of do forever loop
}                                                     // End of UDPRead


const char *AppName = "UDP Example";


void UserMain(void *pd)
{
  int UDP_portnum;                                    // PortNumber Variable
  IPADDR UDP_addr;                                    // UDP Address Variable
  char buffer[80];                                    // Buffer

  InitializeStack();                                  // Initialize the Program Stack
  EnableAutoUpdate();                                 // Enable Auto Update feature
  EnableTaskMonitor();                                // Enable Task Monitor

  printf("UDP Test \n");                              // Program Purpose
  printf("Input the port number?\n");                 // Get Port Number from User
  scanf("%d", &UDP_portnum);                          // Scan and Store
  printf("\nEnter the IP Address to send to?");       // Get Target IP address
  buffer[0] = 0;                                      // Buffer element = 0
  while (buffer[0] == 0)                              // No keyboard data, wait
  {
    gets(buffer);                                     // else, get Keyboard data
  }
  UDP_addr = AsciiToIp(buffer);                       // Convert to dot notation

  // Print Port Chosen
  printf("%d UDP Port in use ", UDP_portnum);
  ShowIP(UDP_addr);                                   // Print IP Address
  printf("\n");
```

```
OSChangePrio(MAIN_PRIO);                   // Bump up task priority
OSTaskCreate(UDPRead,                      // Let's create a blocking read task
         (void *) UDP_portnum,
         &UdpTestStk[USER_TASK_STK_SIZE],
         UdpTestStk,
         MAIN_PRIO - 1);                   // Make it lower priority


while (1)                                  // Another Endless Loop
{

  buffer = "Hello World\n";                // The infamous Hello World
  printf("Sending %s on UDP port %d to IP Address ", buffer, UDP_portnum);
  ShowIP(UDP_addr);                        // Display Target IP Address

  UDPPacket pkt;                           // Create a UDPPacket instance
  pkt.SetSourcePort(UDP_portnum);          // Select Source Port Number
  pkt.SetDestinationPort(UDP_portnum);     // Set Destination Port Number
  pkt.AddData(buffer);                     // Put buffer data in transfer buffer
  pkt.AddDataByte(0);                      // Add terminating NULL
  pkt.Send(UDP_addr);                      // Send it to the destination address

  printf("\n");
};
}
```

This program is made up of two main tasks, each contained in its own do...forever loop. The first task checks for valid incoming UDP data. If no data is received in 100 clock ticks, then it starts the wait cycle over again. The second task sends UDP data repeatedly.

This is a very simple demo for the NetBurner device. We could add multicasting, which allows support for broadcasting temperature data to multiple receivers. The purpose of this program is to get you familiar with the differences between TCP/IP and UDP. It also serves as a simple program that illustrates the process of setting up UDP data handlers in the NetBurner environment.

The TTL Serial Routine

The only remaining communications routine to implement is the TTL serial interface for the 16C745 device. I need to again stress that the compiler suite for this device is different from the dsPIC, so we will be using different tools. There are differences in the number of pins and functionality of the different PIC processors. This time we will show how to create two TTL serial ports on Port B and handle SUB I/O using PicBasic Pro. Listing 9-8, when used in conjunction with the HIDmaker files and the USB init and I/O files from Microchip, illustrates how to set up our two serial ports and send a USB message.

Listing 9-8

```
// Chapter 9 USB & Serial Port Test
// Embedded Systems, Desktop Integration
// Copyright 2004, Oliver H. Bailey
//
// This program illustrates how USB and serial
// code can co-exist.
//

// First we define the I/O pins to use on the 16C745
// For this example we will assign two TTL serial
// ports to the pins on port RB. The following code
// will send the hello world string to our first
// defined TTL port.
//
// This code works in conjunction with the HIDmaker code defined
// earlier and the endpoint descriptors created by HIDmaker.
// This program is also dependent on the USB initialization,
// and I/O assembler routines from Microchip


// Declare Byte Array for Message
Msg var byte[11]

// Assign String to Array
Msg[0] = "H"
Msg[1] = "e"
```

```
Msg[2] = "l"
Msg[3] = "l"
Msg[4] = "o"
Msg[5] = "W"
Msg[6] = "o"
Msg[7] = "r"
Msg[8] = "l"
Msg[9] = "d"
Msg[10] = 0

// Serial Output with flow control, 84 = 9600 Baud
// First TTL Serial Port
SEROUT2 PORTB.0\PORTB.2, 84, [Msg]

// Do it Again for Second Serial Port
Serout2 Portb.4\portb.6, 84, [Msg]

// Initialize USB
usbinit

// SendUSB is defined as send from PIC, not Host!
sendUSB:
// Send the Msg Array to EndPoint 0.
// If transmission can't be made jump to busy and wait 10 ms
// Then try again
usbout 1, Msg, 11, busy
// Once the message is sent, goto complete.
goto complete
busy:
pause 10
goto sendUSB


// End of program
complete:
end
```

The Finished Circuit

Unlike the BASIC Stamp, there are a few more components required for the PIC version. To start with, we have to supply a clock source. The dsPIC can be controlled through an external or internal clock source. For this circuit we will use an external clock because it provides a higher speed. Following is the parts list for the dsPIC interface board:

- One 24 mHz crystal oscillator
- One 2.2 K ¼-watt resistor
- Two 4.7 K ¼-watt resistors
- One red power LED
- One 7805 voltage regulator
- One normally open push button switch
- One 1N914 diode
- One 2-pole terminal strip
- Two 3-pole terminal strips
- Three 3-pole terminal strips
- One dsPIC 30F2010 microcontroller

Since the dsPIC is a relatively new product, please check the current data sheet at www.microchip.com for the latest information on recommended clock crystals. The dsPIC 30F2010 can be purchased from Microchip, DigiKey, or Jameco, as can the rest of these parts. The terminal strips are standard 0.1" center-to-center and are also available from the above sources. In earlier parts list I have listed Radio Shack as a source. While Radio Shack does carry the resistors, diodes, and LEDs, they don't have a wide selection of terminal strips, which is why they are not listed here. DigiKey is the best source and has all of the above components.

Because of the increased complexity of our circuit, this time we will need to make a two-sided circuit board. If you wish to purchase the board instead, please visit www.time-lines.com and follow the Embedded Systems 1 Component link. If you choose to make your own boards, the schematics follow.

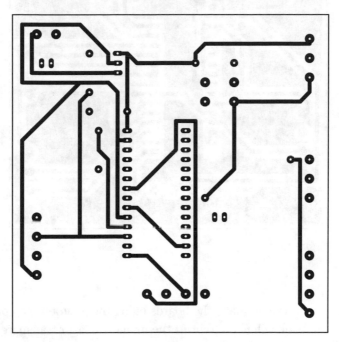

Figure 9-18

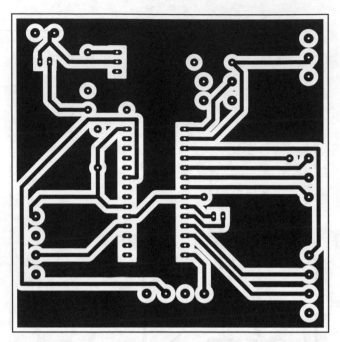

Figure 9-19

If you wish to make the boards using the photoetching process,
then you will need to print the images to laser transparency film
first. This differs from previous artwork, which can be transferred to transparency film using a copier.

Chapter Summary

We have covered a lot of ground in this chapter. Let's review the steps that we've taken to build our temperature control using the dsPIC and PIC 16C745 communications controller. We began by interfacing the dsPIC to a TTL serial port for interfacing to the host communications controller. We then added SPI support for communicating with the memory portion of the DS2404. We then implemented the I²C interface to our LCD display using a software implementation of the I²C protocol. Next, we developed the USB communications software for the PIC 16C745 communications processor and the Windows host software. We haven't worked with the application side yet because our product is cross platform. Then we implemented the UDP code for the NetBurner Ethernet controller. Finally, we implemented two TTL serial ports in the PIC 16C745, one for the Ethernet controller interface and the other for the RS-232 interface. Both interfaces will be used for host communications. A third serial interface will need to be implemented for communication with the embedded controller. I used RA0 to RA3 for the final TTL serial interface. Since we have a limited amount of storage RAM on the 16C745, we will use our protocol between the communications controller and the embedded system. This means we will be sending data in smaller chunks when necessary, so we will be using the handshake lines between the embedded controller and the communications controller to signal when data can be transmitted. All of the complete source code listings can be found at www.wordware.com/files/embsys or www.time-lines.com.

The next chapter is on using the Cypress EZ-USB and PSoC. Chapter 11 deals with cross-platform development.

Chapter 10

The PSoC Prototype

Well, we've finally made it to our last hardware chapter. Some of the information regarding Ethernet and RS-232 may seem redundant but covering the differences from prior hardware platforms is a very important topic. We will continue to use the NetBurner SB72 board and the same TTL-to-RS-232 interface we developed earlier, with a few code changes to each that are specific to the PSoC. I'll also introduce you to the EZ-USB from the same maker as the PSoC. This chapter will focus only on the differences in the hardware and software from prior hardware chapters. If you've made it this far, then read on because there are some very interesting things the PSoC and EZ-USB are capable of.

What Is the PSoC?

PSoC is an acronym for Programmable System on Chip. On the surface the PSoC appears to be just another microcontroller, but if we look a little closer there are some significant differences. We will begin by highlighting the unique features of the PSoC and then compare the PSoC to the PIC and finally to the BASIC Stamp. So let's begin with the PSoC highlights.

The short definition of the PSoC is software configurable silicon. When designing a PSoC system the hardware is defined through software using several different steps. The PSoC chip can actually be several different devices within the same chip that interact together or act as separate components. In addition the PSoC can be reprogrammed on the fly, allowing each device (or block) within the PSoC to have several personalities depending on event triggers or interrupts. This feature is what makes the PSoC different from the other microcontrollers we've worked with so far. This chapter will not cover on-the-fly programming because of the subject scope; instead we will implement functions comparable to the PIC and BASIC Stamp equivalents. For more information on the advanced features of the PsoC, visit the Cypress web site at www.cypress.com or my site at www.time-lines.com.

Developing PsoC-based hardware is heavily dependent on software, namely the PSoC Designer. Everything from designing PSoC hardware blocks and writing source code to debugging in-circuit emulation is handled by the PSoC Designer. The PSoC Designer provides a selection of "canned" hardware functions that can be plugged in by simply dragging and dropping the function onto the design screen. Using the Designer the engineer can define which pins provide associated functions. As different functions are added, how different hardware functions can interact through the use of registers and memory can be defined. Later in this chapter we will work through an actual design session for our thermostat.

Comparing the PIC and the PSoC

At first glance both of these microcontrollers seem identical. Both allow the engineer to design using a building block approach. Both allow analog and digital signals to be processed and both come with similar amounts of RAM and even similar packages. Even so, there are many differences between these devices.

The first major difference (and the most obvious) is the PSoC's ability to alter or load programs on the fly. In short, conditional events or interrupts can allow a program block to load alternate software for processing. While this is a useful feature, care must be taken to avoid problems that can arise from redefining I/O pins, their functions, and data direction. Unlike the dsPIC, which has all of its I/O pins predefined by function, the PSoC instead allows the engineer to develop in blocks and assign pins based on analog or digital functionality. There is more flexibility because the designer has more control over how the pins are defined and how the blocks interact and share data. For example, the dsPIC only provides two UARTs, whereas the PSoC can have as many UARTs as allowed by the number of pins and memory. It should be noted that there is a maximum number of analog and digital blocks available on every part, so there are limits to the design.

The last and most important difference is the ability to extend the PSoC Designer with custom devices. If a unique or custom block is developed, it can be added permanently to the Designer in one of the existing categories, allowing a starting point for a new hardware design. In fact, that is exactly how we implement the Dallas 1-Wire interface. The PSoC goes beyond the dsPIC in being able to define blocks of functionality, thereby allowing a custom processor to be built on the fly. The PSoC allows custom-defined microcontrollers to be developed while protecting the intellectual property within them. In short, a PSoC can be used to define a custom analog or digital chip that can be remarketed for a specific use while protecting the code and techniques used to create the part.

As we have already seen in Chapter 9, the differences between the BASIC Stamp and PIC are many. Those same differences apply here so we won't cover that topic again. If you've never used the PSoC before I strongly suggest going to the Cypress Semiconductor web site at www.cypress.com and taking a look at the documentation and samples. Learning how to use this chip takes some preplanning, and before changing functions on the fly, you must think about your end circuit so as not to program something that will damage components or hardware. Enough said! Let's take a look at this remarkable chip.

The PSoC Design Process

By technical definition the PSoC is a configurable mixed-signal array that integrates the microcontroller and related peripheral circuits typically found in an embedded design. This translates to two words — reduced components. The idea here is by defining the peripheral components into the PSoC, fewer parts will be needed for the finished circuit. From my experience I've found the PSoC can reduce support components by up to 30% depending on the circuit function. This will translate to smaller circuit boards and reduced manufacturing costs so the PSoC, if used wisely, will pay for itself. This information is very important since it affects the design process. This means a little extra care of the hardware design and a thorough review of the hardware should be done just before or after the first prototype is designed. To take advantage of the cost saving features of the PSoC means going through two or more iterations of the design to eliminate components and costs. This is the only way the PSoC can be utilized to its fullest capability.

The PSoC Designer

The PSoC Designer is very similar in appearance and functionality to the dsPIC designer. The difference is that the PSoC Designer is the only development tool required to develop, debug, and program the PSoC parts. Using the Designer the developer uses the following process to develop the hardware.

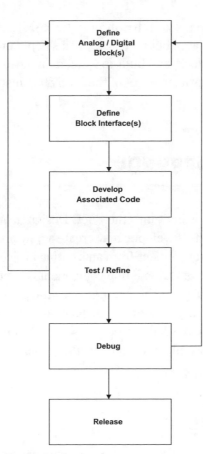

Figure 10-1

With this process the developer can make full use of the PSoC
and continue to reduce support components until the PSoC is
fully utilized. The PSoC Designer allows the developer to select
configurable, precharacterized library elements to provide analog
functions such as amplifiers, ADCs, DACs, filters, and compara-
tors, and digital functions such as timers, counters, PWMs, SPI,
and UARTs, and other digital communications processes. The
PSoC analog performance is instrumentation-quality (including
rail-to-rail inputs, programmable gain, 14-bit ADCs, and excep-
tionally low noise, input leakage, and voltage offset). In addition
to these features the PSoC is also an 8-bit microcontroller, with

up to 32 K of flash memory, up to 2 K of static RAM, an 8x8 multiplier, 32-bit accumulator, built-in power and sleep monitoring functions, real-time clock, and built-in I²C communications processor. The PSoC uses a superset of the Intel 8051 instruction set.

PSoC Assembly Language

The PSoC assembler is built into the PSoC Designer. When creating a new project, the developer may create a new project from a template, create a new project from an existing project, or create a new project from an existing component definition. If Assembly is the language of choice, then once the project is created, all the necessary header and include file stubs are available and ready to have block definitions inserted. If the developer chooses to use the assembler, then no further tools or investment is required.

The PSoC C Compiler

As an option the developer may choose to purchase the PSoC C compiler. The C compiler is actually provided by ImageCraft exclusively for the PSoC Designer. This is very inexpensive, at around $145, and is activated by simply typing a code into the PSoC Designer. If the C compiler is available, the developer has the choice of starting a project in assembler or C. Even if C is chosen as the primary language, inline assembler can be used and external assembler object files can be linked.

Available Hardware Development Tools

There are several hardware development tools available that range from an experimenter board to a complete in-circuit emulator system. The most expensive development kit is around $600, which includes a full in-circuit emulator. That is the PSoC Development kit, shown in Figure 10-2.

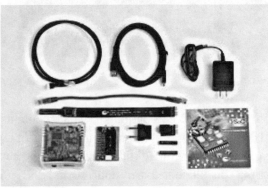

Figure 10-2

There is also the PSoC Basic Development kit, which sells for around $400. The PSoC Basic Development kit includes an in-circuit emulator, a variety of pods, the PSoC Designer software, and a small test board. It should be noted that this developer kit does not contain the C compiler, whereas the PSoC Development kit does.

Figure 10-3

Next, there is the PSoC Evaluation kit, which contains an evaluation board and MiniProg programming unit. This kit contains
everything needed to evaluate the PSoC, including a couple of
sample parts. This kit sells for around $70 and does not include
the C compiler.

Figure 10-4

And finally we have the PSoC Mini-Programmer kit, which includes a PSoC mounted on a DIP header, USB cable, and PSoC Designer software. This kit sells for about $40 and does not include the C compiler.

Figure 10-5

The PSoC Mini-Programmer is also known as the PSoC experimenter board. In this chapter we will use both the PSoC Basic Development kit and the PSoC Mini-Programmer board.

The EZ-USB Chip

To complement the PSoC we will also be introducing the EZ-USB chip, also from Cypress MicroSystems. In past chapters we used the FTDI-based DLP-Design USB interface, and the PICKit 1 and PICDEM USB from Microchip. So the first question we need to ask is how the EZ-USB differs from the prior devices. It differs in two ways. First, EZ-USB can be fully programmed on the fly, that is to say, upon USB initialization. So how does this compare to the other devices? Well, the FTDI-based products have limited ability to do custom programming since they are USB-to-RS-232 converters. Aside from a vendor and product ID there is little that can be added in the way of programmability. The PICKit and PICDEM USB are fully programmable devices; however, the PIC 16C745/16C765 series is EPROM based, which means the device cannot be electrically erased. The 18F4550 chips in the PICDEM USB 2 product are flash based, which makes them similar to the EZ-USB. Again, however, the boot code for the USB chips from Microchip must be present at boot or initialization time.

EZ-USB differs because upon EZ-USB initialization the device actually boots twice. The first boot is a generic USB device that then loads personality-specific code. This is actually a second boot process that when completed will have a fully functional USB device. This allows the secondary boot code to be updated while the device is running and then restarted with bug fixes or new features in place. The EZ-USB development kit contains everything needed to develop including a C compiler. This compiler, however, is from Keil Systems and not ImageCraft, so there are differences in both the compiler and development environment. Figure 10-6 shows the EZ-USB development board.

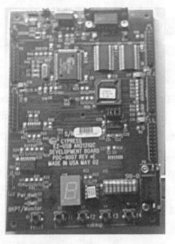

Figure 10-6

Development Strategy

Our development strategy for this chapter is a little different from prior chapters. We will first design the needed peripherals for the PSoC. We have options that will allow us to choose a hardware or software implementation of some of the functions. We will examine the pros and cons of hardware vs. software function implementation. Once we have the needed functions developed on the PSoC, we will write a short test program for testing I/O with each of the needed devices. This includes the 1-Wire interface, the 3-Wire (SPI) interface, TTL RS-232 interface, and the I^2C interface. We will also cover programming the PSoC and using the in-circuit emulator.

The next step will be to implement the interface to the EZ-USB chip, debugging and testing as we go, and finally test the Ethernet interface to the NetBurner board, making any changes necessary to support the PSoC.

Using the PSoC Designer

The PSoC Designer integrates visual development, code development, debugging, and programming into a single interface. The actual code listings for the finished thermostat are available at www.wordware.com/files/embsys and www.time-lines.com, but let's design the functionality of our part in this chapter. We will use the PSoC Mini-Programming kit for this exercise. This device is seen as a CY8C27443 PSoC. This device operates at 24 mHz (the same as the dsPIC) and has 16 K of program memory available.

Programming this device is a two-step process. First we develop the code within the PSoC Designer, and then download the code to the device. Later we will attach the in-circuit emulator (ICE) to our board and do real-time debugging. Let's start by designing our PSoC-based circuit.

1. From the Windows Start menu choose **Cypress Micro-Systems | PSoC Designer**. A screen that looks similar to the following will appear.

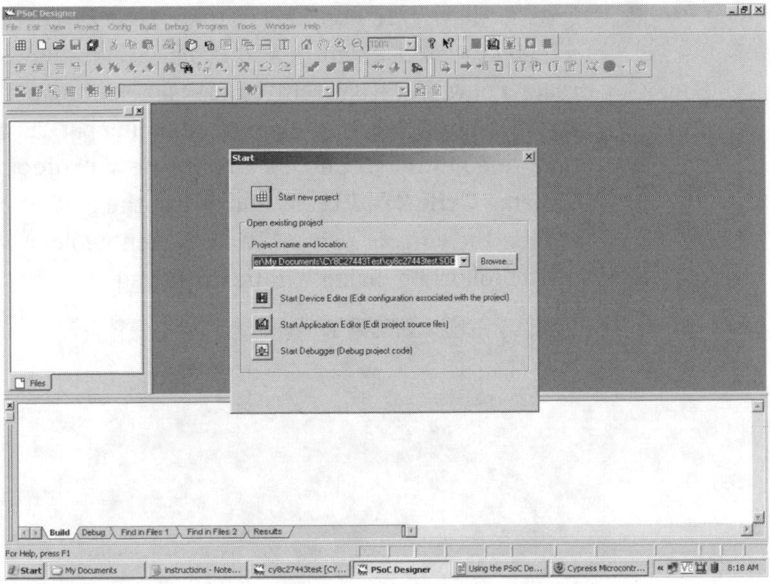

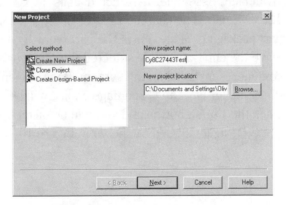

Figure 10-7

2. The options from this menu are: Start new project, Start the Device Editor, Start the Code Editor, and Start a debugging session. Press the **Start new project** button and the following screen will appear.

Figure 10-8

Chapter 10

3. Here, we have three options: Create New Project, Clone Project, and Create Design-Based Project. This allows us to create a new part from scratch, use an existing part as the start of a new project, or clone an existing part as a starting point for a new idea. Choose **Create new project** and give it the name **Cy8C27443Test** and select the default path, which is under the current users My Documents folder. Press **Next** and the following dialog will be displayed.

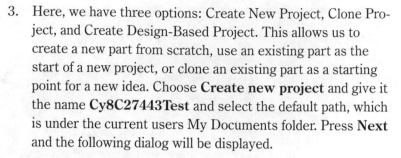

Figure 10-9

4. By default, Assembler is selected, as is the CY8C27443-12PVXE part. The characters after the hyphen indicate the part packaging. Since this is the part we will be using you can leave the entry as is. I've selected the C language since the compiler is installed on my system. If you haven't purchased the compiler key, the C language choice will be grayed out. Click the **Finish** button and you will be taken to the main PSoC Designer screen as shown in Figure 10-10.

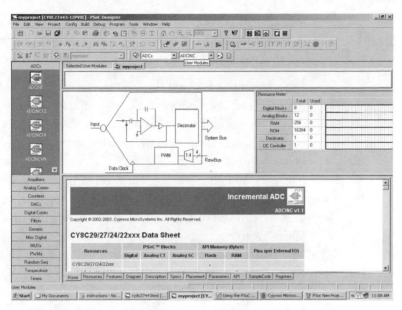

Figure 10-10

This is where most of our work will take place. Starting from the left side of the design window we have the available preconfigured features that can be added to the part by highlighting the component, right-clicking the mouse, and choosing Select, which will add the chosen feature to the white area directly above the function schematic. In the middle of the work area is a function schematic, and below that a data sheet showing the used resources by part number. The resource meter on the upper-right side of the screen shows us what part resources are used and available.

5. For our project we need a Dallas 1-Wire interface, a Dallas 3-Wire interface (SPI), an I²C master interface, and a TTL RS-232 interface. Move your cursor to the left side of the screen and select the **Digital Comm** button bar. Everything we will use is located under this heading. You can scroll by clicking the little down button inside the Digital Comm area. When you reach the bottom, an up button will appear. If you look closely you'll see there are different versions of the

same interface; some are hardware and others are software. The best part of using this design approach is that we can always remove a function and try something different.

6. Let's begin by choosing the I²C interface for interacting with our LCD display. There are two choices for this device. The first is the second choice from the top, I2CHW. This is a hardware implementation of the I²C controller. Directly below that option is the second I²C choice, I2Cm for I2C master. Highlighting and clicking on either of these will display their schematic in the middle of the design screen. If we look we can see that the major difference is the first choice allows us to communicate with I²C master and slave devices, whereas the second choice allows us to only communicate with I²C slave devices. Keeping this in mind, highlight the **I2Cm** component, right-click your mouse, and choose the **Select** menu item. This will duplicate the function icon in the white area above the function schematic. It will also update the resource meter to show how much RAM and other chip resources have been used. As you can see in Figure 10-11, our resource usage is minimal.

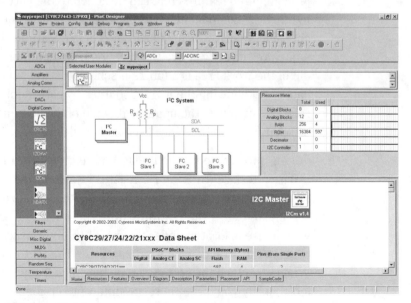

Figure 10-11

The tabs along the bottom of the design screen present the developer with different types of design information. For example, clicking the SampleCode tab shows an assembler listing on how to interface to a Dallas 1307 clock chip using the I²C interface.

To continue our design we need to allocate pins to our I²C interface. The five colored icons at the right of the topmost toolbar control which design view we are in. The view we are currently in is the User Module view. Let's change views to the Interconnect view, which is the rightmost icon. Our entire design area has changed to resemble the following.

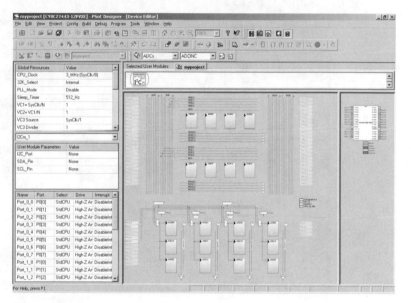

Figure 10-12

As you can see, the entire design screen has changed. On the far right side of the screen is an image of the chip. Different colors indicate pin usage. A legend below the image explains what each color of pin represents. In the center we have two different views of the part. The upper view shows how the internal interconnects are configured and to which pins they are connected. The graphic below shows the interconnects in a block view. There is a maximum of 12 blocks combined for analog and digital (fewer depending on the memory and pin count). On the far left side of the screen from top to bottom are global resource parameters, user module parameters, and the pin parameter list.

1. First, let's assign a port to our I²C interface. On the left side of the design screen, select **User Module Parameters** and choose **Port_0** for the I²C port. Next, select **Port_0_0** for the SDA pin and **Port_0_1** for the SCL pin. Now enlarge the view of the chip on the right side of the screen, and you will notice P0 and P1 reflect the new pin definitions, as shown in Figure 10-13.

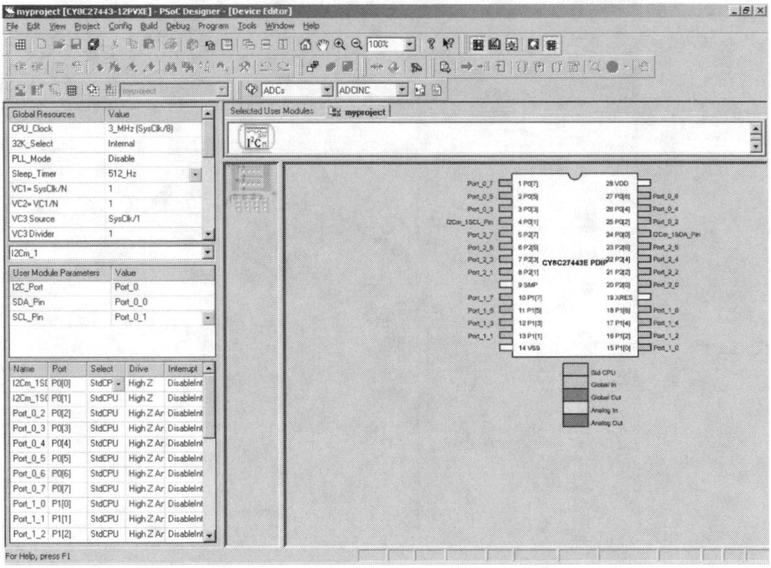

Figure 10-13

2. We will add in the remaining user modules we need before finishing our part configuration. Let's switch back to the User Module Selection view and add the following modules: a **1-Wire** SW module, a **UART** module, and an **SPIM** module. The SPIM is a 3-Wire master module. If you try adding a second UART, a message will be displayed, telling you that there aren't enough digital blocks available. Each UART uses

two digital blocks and this part only allows a total of four digital blocks.

If we look at our resources we can see we've used 3 digital blocks, 0 analog blocks, 18 bytes of RAM, and about 1600 bytes of ROM. We have plenty of memory and resources available to work with. When you've finished adding the remaining user modules, your screen should look similar to the following.

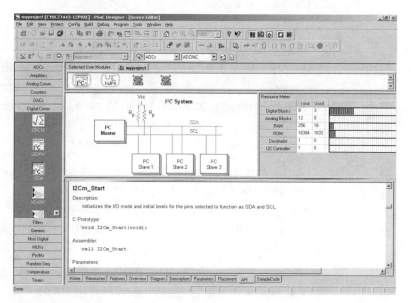

Figure 10-14

3. Now we will switch to the Interconnect view by pressing the rightmost icon on the top toolbar. We will need to place the UART and SPIM user modules in PSoC blocks. To do this, select the UART, right-click the mouse, and select the **Place** option. You will notice two PSoC blocks contain portions of the UART. Now repeat the same process for the SPIM by selecting the module, right-clicking the mouse, and again choosing the **Place** option.

4. Now that we have placed the user modules in PSoC blocks, we need to connect them to global I/O lines, which are called rows. This can be done by selecting the user module parameters and selecting the global line to attach each function to. As you connect the device to the internal PSoC I/O you will see lines drawn from the block device to the associated global I/O line. Once this step is completed each global I/O line needs to be attached to a pin so it can communicate with the outside world.

This may seem like a lot of work and it is. But earlier I stated how flexible the PSoC is, and the reason for so many steps in the process is because of the large amount of flexibility. For example, if you had several blocks that collected data and then converted it to a number to be sent out through the serial bus, you would connect many of your blocks together internally but only have one or two pins for output.

I know this has been hard to follow, so let me suggest that you visit the Cypress MicroSystems web site at www.cypress.com and choose the PSoC product. There are many tutorials and online videos that can quickly bring you up to speed.

When we've finished adding the required user modules our design screen will look similar to Figure 10-15.

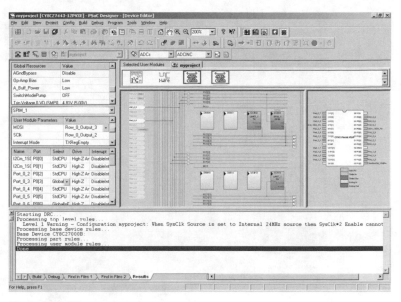

Figure 10-15

Before leaving the PSoC block designer, run a Design Rule Check from the Tools menu. If there are any major problems, they will be reported when this check is done.

5. The next step to competing the implementation is to switch to the application editor. This the second icon from the left in the group at the right of the uppermost toolbar. Here is where we will add the code specific to our embedded system. Once you've switched to the application editor, press **F7** or select **Build | Build All** from the menu. This step will generate all the files associated with the user modules we've selected and update the header files and libraries as well. When completed, your screen should look similar to Figure 10-16.

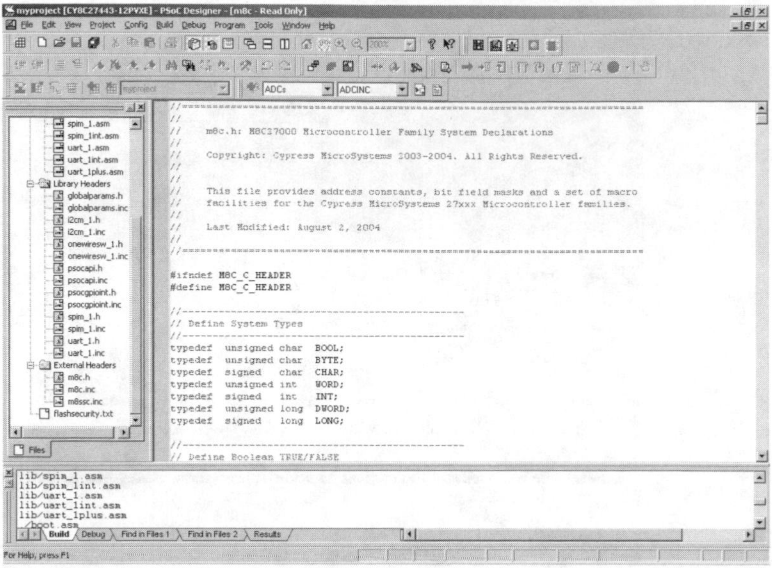

Figure 10-16

During the build process 30 files were created as was a hex file for download to the PSoC. The files are listed in the box at the left side of the screen. To edit a file simply select the filename and double-click it with your mouse. You'll also notice there are several different source file types associated with the project. Some are .c files, and others are .asm files. These files contain the source code for the associated user modules. User modules can be written in assembler or C.

The function calls associated with each type of user module can be accessed from the device editor screen (the first icon) by choosing the API tab at the bottom of the screen. Code examples can also be viewed by selecting the SampleCode tab next to the API tab. For this example we will output "Hello World" to the Matrix Orbital LCD display.

Even though there are 30 files associated with the project we will be modifying only one of these files, main.c. Since we communicate via the I²C interface, let's examine the requirements for setting up and using I²C.

The PSoC I²C Function Library

Since we've opted to implement I²C in software the following API function calls are available to us:

- I2Cm_Start — This function initializes the I²C interface and PSoC pins.

- I2Cm_Stop — Performs no function currently

- I2Cm_fReadBytes — Reads one or more bytes from a slave device and writes to a data array

- I2Cm_bWriteCBytes — Writes one or more bytes to a slave from a data array

- I2Cm_fSendStart — Generates an I²C-bus start condition

- I2Cm_fSendRepeatStart — Generates an I²C-bus repeat start condition

- I2Cm_SendStop — Sends I²C-bus stop condition

- I2Cm_fWrite — Sends a 1-byte bus write and ACK

- I2Cm_bRead — Initiates a 1-byte bus write and ACK

For our purposes we will start the I²C interface, send the string "Hello World" to I²C slave address 80 (hex 50), wait for a return ACK from the slave, and stop the I²C interface (in theory). The following listing illustrates how few lines of code are needed to accomplish this task.

Chapter 10

Listing 10-1

```
#include <m8c.h>                    // part specific constants and macros
#include "PSoCAPI.h"                // PSoC API definitions for all user modules

BYTE txBuf[12] = "Hello World";     // Create Storage for String

void main()
{
  /*****************************************************************************
          Send "Hello World" to the LK202-25
```

```
************************************************************************/

I2Cm_1_Start();                      // Start I2C Processing

// Output sizeof(txBuf) characters to I2C SlaveID 0x50 in a complete
// Data Transfer
I2Cm_1_bWriteCBytes(0x50, txBuf, sizeof(txBuf), I2Cm_1_CompleteXfer);
}
```

Two function calls are all that is required to send data via I²C. Next we will examine the 1-Wire interface used for collecting the temperature. Before we do, be aware that the 1-Wire user module is a third-party module. It can be downloaded from www.psocdeveloper.com and is included with the source files for this book, available at www.wordware.com/files/embsys and www.time-lines.com.

Adding User Modules to the PSoC Designer

To add the 1-Wire module simply copy the entire data directory to the C:\Program Files\Cypress MicroSystems\PSoC Designer\ Data folder. If you have the PSoC Designer open, close it and restart it; you should now see the 1-Wire user modules under the Digital Comm button.

The PSoC 1-Wire Interface

Next we have the 1-Wire interface to implement. Much of the work in implementation has been done in the Designer, so we need to add the code to address the 1-Wire devices. There are more functions available for the 1-Wire, so instead of going through them all we will only list those that are needed for our device. They are:

- OW_Start — Initializes the 1-Wire I/O pin

- OW_Reset — Resets any 1-Wire devices on bus and detects presence

- OW_WriteByte — Writes a byte to the 1-Wire bus

- OW_ReadByte — Reads a byte from the 1-Wire bus

- OW_Delay10mTimes — Provides number of 10 millisecond loops to delay

Reading and converting a temperature requires the following code:

Listing 10-2

```
/****************************************************************************
Do Temperature conversion for Dallas 1820 Chip
****************************************************************************/

OneWireSW_1_Start();                    // Initialize 1-Wire Bus
OneWireSW_1_Reset();                    // Reset Bus, Check for Devices
OneWireSW_1_WriteByte(0xCC);            // Skip ROM Command
OneWireSW_1_WriteByte(0x44);            // Convert Temperature Command
OneWireSW_1_Delay10mTimes(75);          // Wait 750 milliseconds for completion
OneWireSW_1_Reset();                    // Reset the bus again
OneWireSW_1_WriteByte(0xCC);            // Skip ROM Command
OneWireSW_1_WriteByte(0xBE);            // Read Scratchpad Command
OWTemp = OneWireSW_1_ReadByte();        // Read Converted Temperature
```

The PSoC SPI User Module

This brings us to the SPI user module definitions. In past chapters when we have implemented the SPI interface we have not designated it as a "master." There are two reasons for this. First, we have not connected multiple slaves to the SPI interface; it has been a one-to-one relationship with a single slave. The second reason is because we have not had a need to explore using multiple slaves simply because this is not a part of the specification for our prototype for the design. Having said that we will now explore the SPI master user module as it relates to our needs.

There are just a few API calls available in the SPIM user module. They are:

- SPIM_Start — Configures the SPI mode and sets the proper bits in the control registers

- SPIM_Start — Disables the SPI interface by clearing the enable bit in the control register

- SPIM_EnableInt — Enables the SP interrupt on an SPI done condition

- SPIM_DisableInt — Disables the SPI interrupt on an SPI done condition

- SPIM_SendTxData — Transmits a byte to slave device

- SPIM_bReadRxData — Returns a received byte from a slave device

- SPIM_bReadStatus — Returns the contents of the control/status register

As always, the slave's device signal must be asserted to a low state just before sending data. The RX Buffer full flag should be checked prior to a call to SPIM_bReadRxData to verify data has been received. The following listing sends the message "Hello from PSoC" to an SPI slave device.

Listing 10-3

```
/********************************************************************************
Send "Hello from PSoC" to SPI Device
********************************************************************************/
// Start the SPI interface with control mode 0 ans MSB First
SPIM_1_Start(SPIM_1_SPIM_MODE_0 || SPIM_1_SPIM_MSB_FIRST);
// While there are still valid characters, loop
while (*ptrSPI_MSG !=0) {
// Check RX Buffer and TX Data Buffer
        while(! (SPIM_1_bReadStatus() & SPIM_1_SPIM_TX_BUFFER_EMPTY)){;}
                // Send next byte
```

```
SPIM_1_SendTxData(*ptrSPI_MSG);
// Increment Message Pointer
ptrSPI_MSG++;
}
```

The PSoC RS-232 Interface

We've reached the fourth and final interface to the outside world, the RS-232 interface. The PSoC UART is very flexible, which also means there is a level of complexity associated with it. You won't see any API calls available to set baud rates. Instead, the clock source is used with a divider to set the baud rate. Having said this, the UART user module conforms to RS-232 data transmit and receive standards without handshaking. As we did with the dsPIC, we will support handshaking though the use of general I/O pins on the PSoC. Because RS-232 communications are more complex than the other communications methods used, the user module has two APIs available — a high-level and low-level API.

The low-level API allows fine control over interrupt configurations and buffer status controls, whereas the high-level API provides more control over transmit and receive functionality. For the purpose of explaining how to handle data I/O we will forego the discussion on interrupts; however, the associated project and source does both explain and use interrupts. Let's take a look at the high-level UART user module API. The routines are:

■ UART_IntCntl — Selects RX/TX interrupt control

■ UART_PutString — Transmits NULL-terminated string

■ UART_CPutString — Transmits NULL-terminated constants

■ UART_PutChar — Transmits single character when TX register is empty

- UART_cGetChar — Receives character from RX data register when available

- UART_Write — Transmits multiple characters to TX port

- UART_CWrite — Transmits multiple constant characters to TX port

- UART_cReadChar — Does immediate receive from RX port; returns either valid ASCII character or zero if no character is available

- UART_iReadChar — Same as above but returns 2 bytes, one with ASCII character and other with any error code or zero if no error detected

- UART_PutCRLF — Sends carriage return and line feed to TX port

There are several other high-level commands that deal with command buffer status and the transmission of hex data we will not be using. In addition, there are several low-level API functions we will be using. They are:

- UART_Start — Enables UART user module

- UART_Stop — Disables UART user module

Again, there are several other commands that deal with interrupts and register status that we will not be discussing at this time. Let's take a look at what is required to send the infamous "Hello from PSoC" message via the UART.

The UART divides the clock source by 8, which means we need a clock that is eight times the desired baud rate. The simplest method of implementing a clock is to use a Counter8 user module as a source. This, however, is not the only way to attain a clock source, but for the purpose of our listing we will assume a Counter8 clock is being used for our UART with a device clock speed of 24 mHz. The Counter8 parameters would be set as follows:

- Clock — 24 mHz
- Enable — High
- Output — None
- Period — 155
- CompareValue — 78
- CompareType — Less than or equal
- InterruptType — Terminal count

Using the above parameters we would calculate the UART baud rate as:

```
BaudRate = 24,000,000/((155 + 1) * 8) = 19.2K baud
```

Pay close attention to variables in the preceding equation. If you change the clock speed you will also change the baud rate, so keep this in mind when determining the PSoC main clock rate.

Using the above calculations we would set the UART user module parameters as follows:

- Clock — Counter8 Broadcast
- RX Input — UART Assigned Global Input
- TX Output — UART Assigned Global Output
- TX InterruptMode — TXComplete
- RxCmdBuffer — Enable
- RxBufferSize — 16 bytes
- Command Terminator — CR (Carriage Return)
- Param_Delimiter — 32 (Space)
- IgnoreCharsBelow — 32 (Ignore all control characters below a space)

We are using the broadcast line from the Counter8 user module as the clock source for the UART user module. The RX in is attached to the UART global input and the TX out is attached to the UART global output line. We are using an interrupt triggered on a transmit or receive complete. In order to use this mode the

RxCmdBuffer must be enabled. We have assigned a 16-byte buffer to the RxBufferSize. Since this is for sending text messages a carriage return signals the end of a transmission as the message terminator. The ASCII space is the delimiter between parameters and we ignore characters below decimal 32, which is the space. It is worthy to note that software handshaking will be masked out from the remote system because those characters fall below decimal 32. The following code will send the string "Hello from PSoC" to the TX port.

Listing 10-4

```
/*****************************************************************************
Send "Hello from PSoC" from the UART
*****************************************************************************/
UART_1_CmdReset();                       // Initialize UART 1 command/receive buffer.


UART_1_IntCntl(UART_1_ENABLE_RX_INT);  // Enable Receive Interrupt


// The following is a method of configuring the Counter8 user module in code.
/*****************************************************************************
Counter8_1_WritePeriod(155);             // Set Write Period
Counter8_1_WriteCompareValue(77);        // Set Compare Value
Counter8_1_Start();                      // Start Counter
*****************************************************************************/

UART_1_Start(UART_1_PARITY_NONE);        // Start UART 1 with No Parity bit

M8C_EnableGInt;                          // Enable PSoC Interrupts

// Send string
UART_1_CPutString("\r\nHello from PSoCb\r\n");
```

The completed listing for the PSoC follows:

Listing 10-5

```
#include <m8c.h>                       // part-specific constants and macros
#include "PSoCAPI.h"                   // PSoC API definitions for all user modules

BYTE txBuf[] = "Hello World";          // Create Storage for String
```

```
BYTE OWTemp;                            // Create storage byte for Temperature
CHAR SPI_MSG[]= "Hello from PSoC";      // Static SPI Message
CHAR *ptrSPI_MSG;                       // Pointer to SPI Message
CHAR * uartMsg;

void main()
{
   /***************************************************************************
        Send "Hello World" to the LK202-25
   ***************************************************************************/


   I2Cm_1_Start();                      // Start I2C Processing

   // Output sizeof(txBuf) characters to I2C SlaveID 0x50 in a complete
   // Data Transfer
   I2Cm_1_bWriteCBytes(0x50, txBuf, sizeof(txBuf), I2Cm_1_CompleteXfer);


   /***************************************************************************
   Do Temperature conversion for Dallas 1820 Chip
   ***************************************************************************/


   OneWireSW_1_Start();                 // Initialize 1-Wire Bus
   OneWireSW_1_Reset();                 // Reset Bus, Check for Devices
   OneWireSW_1_WriteByte(0xCC);         // Skip ROM Command
   OneWireSW_1_WriteByte(0x44);         // Convert Temperature Command
   OneWireSW_1_Delay10mTimes(75);       // Wait 750 milliseconds for completion
   OneWireSW_1_Reset();                 // Reset the bus again
   OneWireSW_1_WriteByte(0xCC);         // Skip ROM Command
   OneWireSW_1_WriteByte(0xBE);         // Read Scratchpad Command
   OWTemp = OneWireSW_1_ReadByte();     // Read Converted Temperature


   /***************************************************************************
   Send "Hello from PSoC" to SPI Device
   ***************************************************************************/
   // Start the SPI interface with control mode 0 and MSB First
   SPIM_1_Start(SPIM_1_SPIM_MODE_0 || SPIM_1_SPIM_MSB_FIRST);
   // While there are still valid characters, loop
   while (*ptrSPI_MSG !=0) {
    // Check RX Buffer and TX Data Buffer
        while(! (SPIM_1_bReadStatus() & SPIM_1_SPIM_TX_BUFFER_EMPTY)){;}
                // Send next byte
                SPIM_1_SendTxData(*ptrSPI_MSG);
                // Increment Message Pointer
```

```
                ptrSPI_MSG++;
        }
/*******************************************************************************
Send "Hello from PSoC" from the UART
*******************************************************************************/
UART_1_CmdReset();                      // Initialize UART 1 command/receive buffer.


UART_1_IntCntl(UART_1_ENABLE_RX_INT);        // Enable Receive Interrupt


// The following is a method of configuring the Counter8 user module in code.
/*******************************************************************************
Counter8_1_WritePeriod(155);                 // Set Write Period
Counter8_1_WriteCompareValue(77);            // Set Compare Value
Counter8_1_Start();                          // Start Counter
*******************************************************************************/


UART_1_Start(UART_1_PARITY_NONE);            // Start UART 1 with No Parity bit


M8C_EnableGInt;                              // Enable PSoC Interrupts


// Send string
UART_1_CPutString("\r\nHello from PSoCb\r\n");
}
```

Before we conclude with the PSoC device, please spend some
time getting familiar with how this device works and the proce-
dures to configure and program it. The PSoC really represents a
convergence of software and hardware in developing a hardware
component. There is no way possible to cover the capabilities of
this product in the space of this book. The idea is to provide you
with the information needed to understand and start using the
device in an intelligent fashion. If you're new to electronics I do
not recommend using this device until you've built several circuits using the BASIC Stamp or PIC components.

The Cypress EZ-USB Chip

Earlier we briefly discussed some of the advantages of the EZ-USB chip. Now it's time to take a serious look at this interesting and useful device. As mentioned earlier the EZ-USB boots twice, once as a generic device and a second time as a specific device type. The EZ-USB is not just a USB chip but a full microcontroller as well. The PSoC differs from the PIC 16C745/16C765 through the use of flash memory and a different instruction set. It is also a full speed device, whereas the PIC counterparts are slow speed devices.

The EZ-USB development kit contains a development board as shown in Figure 10-17 and a snap-on prototype board for custom development. The prototype board snaps onto the development board via five headers as shown in Figure 10-18.

Figure 10-17

Chapter 10

Figure 10-18

The EZ-USB development kit also includes a book on the USB bus, a technical reference manual for the kit, a getting started guide, USB cable, RS-232 cable, and a CD that contains all the information, data sheets, application notes, and Keil C compiler. The compiler uses a small memory model, so if you have a bigger project you may want to invest in the full version of the compiler. Unlike the PSoC, the EZ-USB development software is installed by default to the \Cypress\USB\ folder. There are several example projects in the \Examples\EzUsb folder.

There is a lot to learn to use EZ-USB to its fullest potential so we will work through a short project that illustrates how to use the developers kit. All of the project related files can be downloaded from www.wordware.com/files/embsys or www.time-lines.com. Let's get started.

1. The first step is to install the software from the EZ-USB CD. You can insert the CD or download the zip file from the Cypress web site. The most recent version supports several EZ-USB boards. During the software installation process the compiler and device driver will be installed for Windows. Some versions of Linux have built-in support for the EZ-USB chip, while others require a separate device driver file. The latest information is available in the downloaded companion files. This allows me to keep these projects current while at the same time keeping the book current.

2. Once the software is installed, reboot the system if prompted. Usually Windows versions prior to 2000 will require a reboot. Next, plug in the USB cable and connect the EZ-USB development board. A red light in the lower-left corner of the board will come on while the device driver is being located. Eventually you should be prompted to press the Finish button to complete the installation. Once the driver is installed correctly, a green light on the development board will become lit.

    If the installation went properly you can hold down the Reset button on the EZ-USB development board for a few seconds. This will disconnect the board and unload the driver. Releasing the Reset button will reload the driver and re-attach the board. The intelligence of this board lies in the chip directly below the USB connector at the top of the board. The board has four additional buttons, several dip switches and jumpers, two serial ports, and a seven-segment LED display. The headers along both sides extend the I/O pins to the prototype board. To debug a program we need to also install an RS-232 cable between a COM port on the PC and SIO-1 on the EZ-USB board. SIO-1 is the nine-pin connector at the top-right side of the board next to the USB connector.

3. If you have the EZ-USB board connected via the USB cable, disconnect it now. Next, go to **Start | Cypress | USB | EZ-USB Control Panel**. The following screen should be displayed.

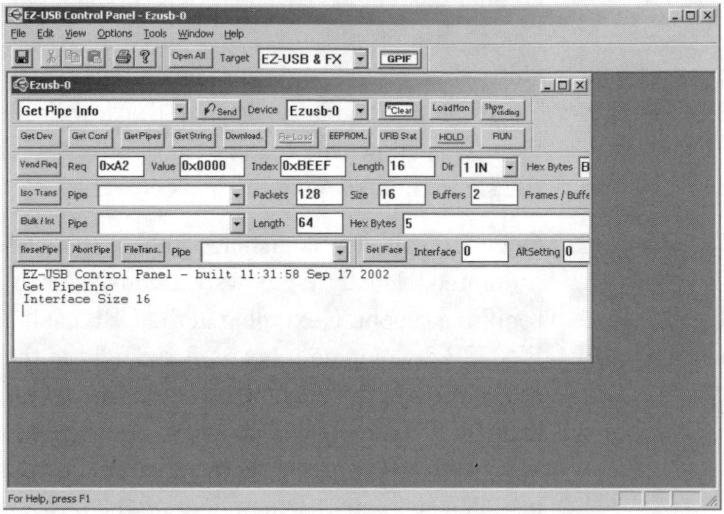

Figure 10-19

4. This program allows the developer to interrogate, control, and even download new software to the EZ-USB. Click the **Open All** button. For each EZ-USB device detected and working, a child window will appear. The window title will be the EZ-USB device number. In Figure 10-19, we have one EZ-USB device attached, titled Ezusb-0. Within the child window a GetPipeInfo command was executed and the results appear in the open area of the child window. The interface size will be displayed as the last line of information for each child window. In this case the interface size is 16.

The Clear button clears the message display of the associated EZ-USB device. To make sure the device is working properly, locate the LoadMon button and click on it with the mouse. You will see a large number of columns of hex data scroll through the message display; at the very end will be Toggle 8051 Reset, which is the final message that means the EZ-USB processor has been reset and is waiting for the next command. If you press the Reset button on the EZ-USB board, nothing happens because the EZ-USB is still in a reset condition. Press the Send button next to the current command (GetPipeInfo) and the interface size will again be returned. Now if you press the Reset button on the EZ-USB board the green light will go out until it is released. This means the EZ-USB is again running.

The second row of buttons in the control windows for Ezusb-0 request specific information about the device. Pressing one of these buttons will return the current contents of the request. The buttons along the left side also request specific types of device information. Some of these buttons will cause the EZ-USB to suspend operations until another request is sent or the Run button is pressed. For example, if you press the Vend Req button, nothing happens until the Reset button on the EZ-USB board is pressed; then the button on the display pops back up.

5. The EZ-USB Control Panel can also be used to download a new program to the board. As an example of this, press the **Download** button and select the **\Cypress\USB\Examples\EzUsb\dev_io\dev_io.hex** file. The following figure shows the screen that is displayed.

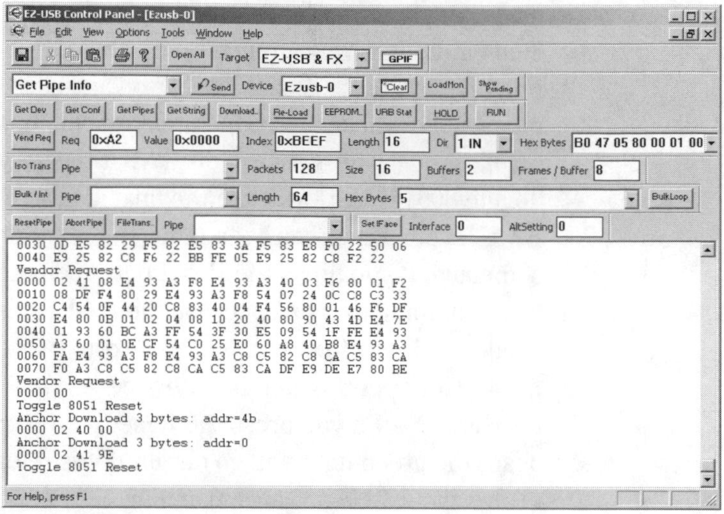

Figure 10-20

During the download each message from both the host and client is displayed in order. In Figure 10-20, after each block of data a Vendor Request message is sent. After the download is completed the EZ-USB is reset and the seven-segment display displays a zero. The four buttons below the display will take the following actions from left to right: Zero set, decrement, increment, and set to Hex F. You will notice the green light on the EZ-USB board is off. Pressing it once will stop the program that manages the buttons and display and will turn the green LED back on. Now pressing the buttons has no effect.

The seven-segment display will remain lit until the power is removed and reapplied to the EZ-USB board. Unplug the USB cable, wait 10 seconds, and plug it back in to turn the seven-segment display off again. As you can see, the Control Panel provides the developer with some access to EZ-USB development functions from within the Windows operating system.

1. Now it's time to start the compiler and test the debug connection. The first step in this process is to start the Keil
   uVision2 development IDE. There is a desktop shortcut
   installed along with the EZ-USB development software, so
   let's double-click it now. In a few seconds you will see the
   main IDE screen that looks similar to the following figure.

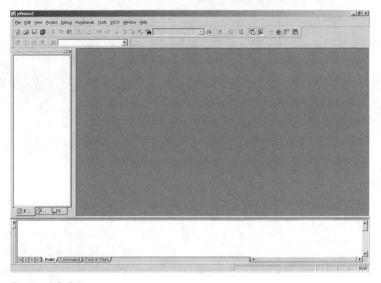

Figure 10-21

2. We need to load the dev_io project file located in the same
   directory as the hex file loaded before. Select **Project |
   Open Project** and choose **dev_io** project file. When the project has loaded, you will see a screen similar to the following.

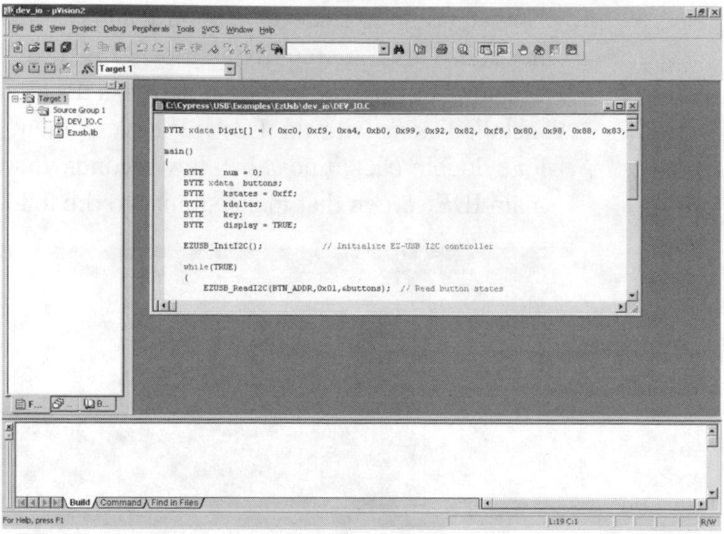

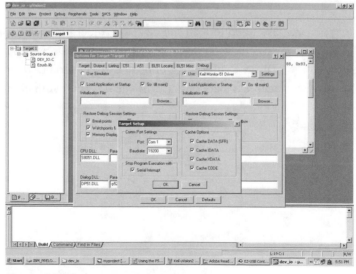

Figure 10-22

3. Before we can debug we need to make certain the PC Comm Port Settings and Baud rate options are correctly set. To check these, select **Project | Options** for [target 1] menu. The Options window will be displayed. Press the **Debug** tab and then choose settings as shown in Figure 10-23.

Figure 10-23

The default COM port is 2 and the baud rate defaults to 38400. If you're using the EZ-USB full speed board, the baud rate needs to be changed to 19200. If your system has only one COM port, set the port to COM 1. If these settings are incorrect, the debugger will not work and it will be unclear exactly what is wrong.

4. The next step is to initialize the debugger. This is done by selecting the **Debug | Start/Stop Debugger** menu item. This will initialize the debugger and connect to the EZ-USB debugging monitor. When fully initialized your screen will look similar to Figure 10-24.

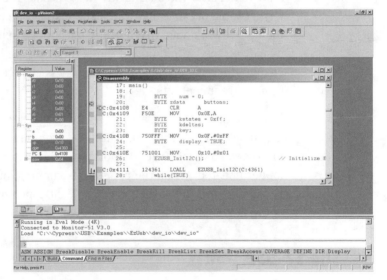

Figure 10-24

5. Before we begin our debug session let's make the debug commands available from the main display. To do this, select **View | Debug Toolbar** and make sure there is a check next to it. If it isn't checked, select the Debug toolbar; otherwise just exit this menu.

We are now ready to start a debug session. We can use the mouse and click the debug commands, which are on the

second toolbar on the far left side of the screen or the following function keys map to debug commands. They are:

- F5 — Run from current instruction
- F11 — Step into next subroutine
- F10 — Step over next subroutine

Pressing the F11 key will make the yellow arrow increment
to the next line. Pressing the F10 key will increment to the
next line or, if the next line is a subroutine the subroutine
will be executed and the debug cursor will stop at the next
instruction after the subroutine has exited. Press the F10
key a couple of times and watch the instruction pointer increment. You will notice that a green bar moves in the Register
display on the far left side of the screen. As the instructions
change the register values, the display is changed to reflect
their current contents.

6. Let's execute the program full speed. To do so, press **F5**.
   The display doesn't update when the program is running at
   full speed so the instruction pointer and register display is no
   longer updated. When the program is running, pressing the
   Escape key will reset the program. That concludes our tour
   of the development IDE and debugger.

The EZ-USB UARTs

Thus far we haven't mentioned the TTL serial ports on the
EZ-USB chip. The EZ-USB has two built-in TTL UARTs for
communicating with the outside world. The serial ports on the
EZ-USB are very similar to the PSoC with a few exceptions.
Either a timer or system clock with a divisor can be used as the
baud rate generator. There are four modes of configuring the
UARTs with respect to data size, start bit, stop bit, and parity. We
will also need to handle handshaking manually just as we did with
the PSoC. This is a simple task of changing a line or pin state to
indicate we are ready to receive data and checking the state of

the handshake line before sending data to a desktop system. In the listing files you will find both listings for using the system clock and a timer. Both methods have their advantages and disadvantages.

The Ethernet Interface

This is the final topic of discussion for the hardware chapters. For development purposes, we will use the SIO-0 port on the EZ-USB and connect that to the serial board on the NetBurner board. All that is needed is a standard RS-232 cable between the two. Once testing is complete we can use the TTL version of the RS-232 interface at both the NetBurner and EZ-USB sides.

The NetBurner SB72 Board

The NetBurner hardware and the TCP/IP interface are covered in detail in Chapter 8. In this chapter we will use the same hardware, but instead of using TCP/IP we will use the User Datagram Protocol, or UDP. Unlike TCP/IP, this protocol is connectionless. There is no dedicated connection between the PSoC and the desktop machine. UDP does not guarantee that the data sent will ever be received by anyone. If we were broadcasting across the Internet we would have reason for concern when using the UDP protocol; however, using that protocol on a LAN is pretty reliable. In fact, using UDP in a LAN environment has some distinct advantages. For example, using UDP we can broadcast the temperature to many computers at once much the same way a radio station broadcasts music. So if our thermostat is used in a cold storage facility, this would allow anyone with network access to "dial-in" to the thermostat and get real-time temperature and temperature alarm data. When it comes to controlling thermostat functions we need to limit that ability to a chosen few. This greatly reduces the possibility of tampering by unauthorized

people. There are several ways to limit access. One method is
to check the origination IP address against a list of accepted
addresses to see if it is an authorized control station. We could
also add a password so that the user could be authenticated,
limiting access to specific individuals working from specific
workstations. In short, there are many ways to provide controls
prohibiting unauthorized use. The following listing illustrates one
way of implementing UDP to connect to the PSoC.

Listing 10-6

```
/******************************************************************************
UDP Test Program for PSoC — Copyright 2004, Oliver H. Bailey
This program is for Embedded Systems, Desktop Integration Book
******************************************************************************/
#include "predef.h"
#include <stdio.h>
#include <ctype.h>
#include <startnet.h>
#include <ucos.h>
#include <udp.h>
#include <autoupdate.h>
#include <string.h>
#include <taskmon.h>

extern "C"
{
   void UserMain( void *pd );
}

// We have to use 4 byte alignment for the NetBurner
DWORD   UdpTestStk[USER_TASK_STK_SIZE] __attribute__( ( aligned( 4 ) ) );

/******************************************************************************
   The UDP Read Packet Function. - Waits for 100 clock ticks and then returns
   if no data arrived.
******************************************************************************/
void UDPRead( void *pd )
{
   int UDP_port = ( int ) pd;                 // UDP Port Number assignment
   printf( "Using port #%d\n", UDP_port );    // Print Port Number
```

```
   OS_FIFO Read_fifo;                                      // Create Read fifo
   OSFifoInit( &Read_fifo );                               // and Initialize the fifo

   RegisterUDPFifo( UDP_port, &Read_fifo );                // Register the port number and buffer

   while ( 1 )                                             // Do Forever
   {
     UDPPacket upkt( &Read_fifo, 100);                     // Return on data or timeout

     if ( upkt.Validate() )                                // If we receive valid data, process
     {
        WORD Data_len = upkt.GetDataSize();                // Data length
        printf( "Got %d UDP Bytes From :", ( int ) Data_len );
        ShowIP( upkt.GetSourceAddress() );                 // Data Source IP Address
        printf( "\n" );
        ShowData( upkt.GetDataBuffer(), Data_len ); // Display actual data
        printf( "\n" );
     }                                                     // End of Valid Packet Data Handler
   }                                                       // End of do forever loop
}                                                          // End of UDPRead



const char *AppName = "PSoC UDP Example";


void UserMain( void *pd )
{
   int UDP_portnum;                                        // PortNumber Variable
   IPADDR UDP_addr;                                        // UDP Address Variable
   char buffer[80];                                        // Buffer

   InitializeStack();                                      // Initialize the Program Stack
   EnableAutoUpdate();                                     // Enable Auto Update feature
   EnableTaskMonitor();                                    // Enable Task Monitor

   printf( "PSoC UDP BroadcastTest \n" );                  // Program Purpose
   printf( "Input the port number?\n" );                  // Get Port Number from User
   scanf( "%d", &UDP_portnum );                            // Scan and Store
   printf( "\nEnter the IP Address to send to?" );        // Get Target IP address
   buffer[0] = 0;                                          // Buffer element = 0
   while ( buffer[0] == 0 )                                // No keyboard data, wait
   {
```

```
   gets( buffer );                              // else, get Keyboard data
}
UDP_addr = AsciiToIp( buffer );                 // Convert to dot notation

// Print Port Chosen
printf( "%d UDP Port in use ", UDP_portnum );
ShowIP( UDP_addr );                             // Print IP Address
printf( "\n" );

OSChangePrio( MAIN_PRIO );                       // Bump up task priority
OSTaskCreate( UDPRead,                           // Let's create a blocking read task
              ( void * ) UDP_portnum,
              &UdpTestStk[USER_TASK_STK_SIZE],
              UdpTestStk,
              MAIN_PRIO - 1 );                   // Make it lower priority


while ( 1 )                                      // Another Endless Loop
{

    buffer = "Hello World\n";                    // The infamous Hello World
    printf( "Sending %s on UDP port %d to IP Address ", buffer, UDP_portnum );
    ShowIP( UDP_addr );                          // Display Target IP Address

    UDPPacket pkt;                               // Create a UDPPacket instance
    pkt.SetSourcePort( UDP_portnum );            // Select Source Port Number
    pkt.SetDestinationPort( UDP_portnum );       // Set Destination Port Number
    pkt.AddData( buffer );                       // Put buffer data in transfer buffer
    pkt.AddDataByte( 0 );                        // Add terminating NULL
    pkt.Send( UDP_addr );                        // Send it to the destination address

    printf( "\n" );
};
}
```

This program has two tasks, each contained in a do forever loop.
The first task checks for valid incoming UDP data. If no data is
received in 100 clock ticks, then it starts the wait cycle over
again. The second task sends UDP data repeatedly.

This is a very simple demo for the NetBurner device. We could add multicasting, which allows support for broadcasting temperature data to multiple receivers. The purpose of this program is to get you familiar with the differences between TCP/IP and UDP. It also serves as a simple program that illustrates the process of setting up UDP data handlers in the NetBurner environment.

PSoC Schematics

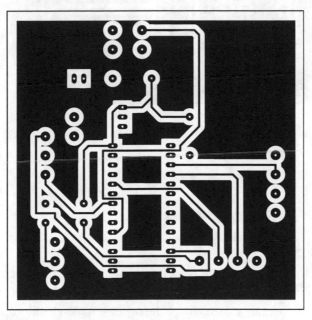

Figure 10-25: PSoC schematic

Chapter 10

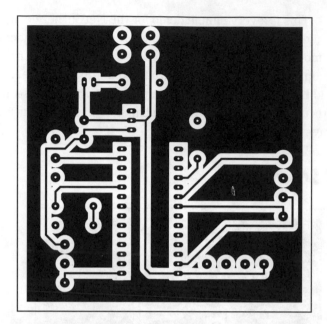

Figure 10-26: PSoC schematic

Chapter Summary

In this chapter we've seen how to implement the thermostat using the Cypress PSoC and EZ-USB. While the PSoC brings more flexibility than any of the other microcontrollers, it comes at the expense of much higher complexity and a deeper understanding of how the microcontroller internals work. The PSoC is a convergence of software and hardware technologies.

Hardware Summary

We have now implemented three different microcontrollers and three different USB interfaces. We have also used several different languages and methods of connecting each different type of interface to the desktop and embedded processor — from the simple to the complex. We could spend thousands of pages on these subjects and still not cover all the available information. The intention is to provide you, the reader, with the information to make a good decision in selecting components. In the course of developing each prototype we have published small code snippets to give you the experience of using different types of software tools and interfaces. For in-depth descriptions, please review the project source files as they contain very detailed information on how the software was implemented and interfaced to system clocks and other microprocessor-specific hardware. In the next and final chapter we look at the tools used to develop cross-platform software.

Chapter 11

Cross-Platform Application Development

We've finally reached the last chapter and desktop software development is our last remaining topic. We've planned all along to have our embedded system accessible from different platforms, so now we are ready to see how well our design works or even if it will work. Before we begin, let's review the three different types of hardware interfaces and how well supported they are on different platforms.

Even though we are developing prototypes using different brands of hardware tools, the rules for developing single-source cross-platform software remains the same. In this chapter we will focus on the development strategies and steps necessary to develop cross-platform device interfaces and cross-platform user applications. These will be covered as separate topics for clarity. Let's begin by looking once again at the three types of host interfaces we have implemented.

Ethernet, TCP/IP, and UDP

Ethernet is both well defined and well supported across all computers built today. As a wired interface it has become inexpensive and fast, making it the favored way to introduce DSL and cable into a building. Additionally, it is very well documented and supported on all computers as a means for creating and accessing a network. Today's Ethernet standards have evolved from several different technologies into a solid, well-defined and supported network standard.

The software that makes the Ethernet interface so widely available is TCP/IP. From the desktop integration point of view TCP/IP is supported on every major computing platform available today. Windows, Linux, UNIX, FreeBSD, Macintosh, and even IBM mainframes all support the TCP/IP protocol suite. Of even greater importance is the fact that all of the above mentioned systems are running either Windows, Linux, or a version of BSD as the core operating system, at least at the kernel level. Also of importance is the fact that TCP/IP is supported at the operating system level of all the above mentioned systems and using a common, well-defined and portable interface, the socket library.

With the exception of Microsoft Windows, the Berkeley sockets are the standard interface when using UNIX-, Linux-, or BSD-based systems. This includes the Mac OS X, which is based on the BSD kernel. Microsoft chose to implement a slightly different version known as Winsock. The differences can be distinguished by using the define statements in the program source code, allowing us to have a single source interface to the Ethernet layer of the operating system.

RS-232 Support

Also supported at the operating system level, and as well as Ethernet, is the old RS-232 interface. This interface is supported identically on Linux-, UNIX-, and BSD-based systems with the exception of naming. Different operating systems sometimes name these ports slightly differentlym but for the most part they are accessed as stty devices in the /dev directories. This is true for Linux, UNIX, BSD, and the Mac OS X systems.

Again Microsoft Windows developed RS-232 support differently, choosing instead to use the old DOS naming and interface conventions. While all the operating systems treat the COM port as a file type device, device control is the major difference between Windows and the other systems. Even so, by developing an intermediate library we can use the same high-level calls from our application on Windows- and UNIX-based systems.

USB Support

Of the three host interface types USB has the biggest number of differences in its device driver layer. This is mostly due to differences in how kernel mode drivers are implemented in Windows and the fact that Windows has a unique way of implementing human interface devices (HID). Adding the USB support layer will be the most challenging of all the device interfaces.

The User Application Layer

The user application layer can be implemented using a number of methods, languages, and tools. Now you may be asking exactly how we can write applications that execute unchanged on several different platforms. Let's start by looking at our choices for application development.

Commercial Compilers

We have an assortment of commercial products to aid in our cross-platform efforts. For our purpose we will examine two commercial products: C++ Builder and Delphi, both from Borland International. There are actually three flavors of these two languages.

Delphi/Kylix

Delphi evolved from the old Turbo Pascal from the DOS days. Several years ago Borland introduced Kylix, which is Delphi for Linux. Both products support extended controls for their native platforms, but a cross-platform library called CLX is also included. Developing a program on one platform using the CLX controls allows the project to be ported to the other platform and compiled with little or no changes (if the proper development steps have been taken).

C++Builder

This product is the C++ equivalent of Delphi/Kylix. Unlike the Pascal products, C++Builder is named the same for both Windows and Linux. Also, like the Pascal version, native control libraries are available to take advantage of platform-specific controls, or the CLX library can be used. Again, using the CLX library provides easy cross-platform porting and compiling.

C++BuilderX

This product differs from C++Builder in that the IDE is functionally identical on all implemented platforms, which are Windows, Linux, and Solaris. Even the debugger functions identically across all platforms. This product supports a number of compilers including Borland, Microsoft, GNU, and Solaris. New platforms can also be added. I cross-compiled the 64-bit GNU x86 compilers and added it to the tools list. Doing this allowed me to compile for a 64-bit target on a 32-bit machine, but debugging still needs to be done on the target processor.

GNU Compilers

Someone recently told me they weren't sure if they wanted to support the GNU compiler because they were hesitant to support new technology. The GNU compilers have been around for many years and have been the compiler of choice for UNIX for almost 20 years. If you ever used the old AT&T UNIX or DEC Ultrix and developed a C program, then chances are good you have already used the GNU compilers.

In fact, the GNU compilers are available for many embedded platforms as well. All our NetBurner code is developed in the GNU C compiler for the Motorola Coldfire processor. The GNU compilers are even used to test against ANSI compliance since they are strictly ANSI. The GNU compilers offer a wide variety of languages such as C, C++, Java, COBOL, and FORTRAN, just to name a few. In short, there isn't another compiler on the planet that supports as many languages as the GNU series.

Application Frameworks

What is an application framework, you ask? For the purpose of this book an application framework is a tool that allows us to develop a user interface that can be compiled and used unchanged on multiple platforms. We will examine wxWidgets, which is an application framework that allows a user interface to be developed on one platform and then compiled on other platforms while providing the same look and feel on all of them. What's more, some of these platforms can be integrated into cross-platform compilers, allowing development and compiling from within the same development environment on multiple platforms.

Common Application Layers

This differs from the application framework because the execution layer has been separated from the compile and link layers. In short, the same program image runs on multiple platforms without change. This is the newest of the technologies and this design is prevalent in the .NET framework. Now .NET doesn't run on Linux but the open source equivalent Mono does. I have been able to compile a program on Mono for Windows and run the executable on the Linux Mono runtime. By the time this book hits the market there should be tools and languages that allow you to develop a program on .NET and run it on .NET or Mono on any platform. Stay tuned to www.time-lines.com for this.

The Device Interface Layer

OK, so we have several options in writing cross-platform applications: What about USB, RS-232, and Ethernet?

Well, the answer to this lies in the design and implementation of our shared libraries or DLLs. None of the host communications methods is functionally the same on Windows and UNIX/Linux. In order to accomplish a single-source solution, we will have to write a middle layer that provides a consistent functional interface between the application and device layers. In this layer we will hide the platform-dependent code and distribute the shared objects in executable form only. This will allow us to take advantage of single-source application coding practices while providing a black box approach to the hardware interface layer. Best of all, once we have the middle layer coded and working, we will never again have to develop a platform-dependent user application unless we choose to do so. So where do we start? We will begin with the Ethernet wrapper, move on to USB, and finish the middle layer with the RS-232 implementation. Then we will move on to develop our application layer.

The Ethernet Software Interface

This may come as a shock but Ethernet was implemented and working on UNIX years before Windows existed. Remember, the Internet was developed on UNIX. As the software implementations of the Internet protocol was being built, it was documented and put up for public access. All documents that describe how the Ethernet transport protocols are implemented can be found in RFC documents (look for resources at www.wordware.com/files/embsys or the www.time-lines.com web site). When Microsoft implemented Windows, they did so using the RFC documents to be compliant with the existing protocols.

Welcome to the World of Sockets

The method of implementation for Ethernet at the software level is called a socket. This term comes from the days when telephone operators inserted a plug into a socket to complete a connection. There are several ways of communicating using the Ethernet transport, but for our purposes only two will be used: TCP/IP and UDP. As I've mentioned earlier, TCP/IP is a dedicated connection between two systems and UDP is connectionless.

The UNIX and Linux versions of Ethernet sockets are called Berkeley Sockets. The Microsoft implementation is called

Windows Sockets, or WinSock for short. While the resulting protocols are identical, there are some fundamental differences in
how Windows implemented TCP/IP sockets. This is mostly due
to differences in the Windows and UNIX architectures.

The similarities between Berkeley Sockets and WinSock
make developing a middleware interface layer a fairly straightforward task. With that in mind, we have three options for how to
develop our Ethernet interface layer. The first is to use #ifdef
statements in a single source file that can be compiled on either
platform. If we take this approach, we may find that over time as
the file gets bigger, maintaining the ifdef structure may become
cumbersome. Our second alternative is to build two separate
source files that are native to each platform and compile each of
them on their native platform. If we take this approach, our initial
development efforts would be for the UNIX version, using that as
a launch pad for the Windows version. Using this approach would
make the Windows product a modified version of the Berkeley
version (or UNIX/Linux) version. Out third option is to find an
existing product or library that will work on both platforms. This
would allow us to develop and concentrate on the implementation
of our prototype and leave the issues that rely on platform
dependency to someone else.

The Standard Function Library

The standard function library is an open source library that has
been around for almost 20 years. This library is downloaded and
compiled for each platform with the resulting routines linked to
the user application on the native platform. It works on over 20
different platforms including Windows, Linux, and BSD versions.
It will also compile with the GNU compilers. Choosing this
library provides us with a single-source interface in addition to
the source code. All of this will cost us only the time to add the
include files and compile and link for each platform. As it turns
out, the standard function library supports TCP/IP and UDP protocols. This makes our development effort much easier. The fact
that this library is available on all the supported platforms we will

be using does not preclude the fact we must compile it for each native platform. The complete cross-platform scripts and make files are available at www.wordware.com/files/embsys and www.time-lines.com.

Alternative Cross-Platform Choices

The Delphi/Kylix platforms include several TCP/IP implementations that work on all their supported platforms. If we browse to the Internet tab in the IDE we find three components that can serve our needs. These three components, which are to the left of the XML icon, are UDPSocket, TCPServer, and TCPClient. These components are highlighted by a box in Figure 11-1.

Figure 11-1

Delphi and Kylix also contain a second set of TCP controls included with the products. These are known as the Internet Direct, or INDY, components. TCP and UDP are just a few of the supported protocols. Figure 11-2 shows the Indy Servers components tab.

Figure 11-2

Both of these offer visual solutions for the development environment, where the standard function library offers a code-only solution.

Chapter 11

Visual vs. Code Solutions

As we've just seen there are two different solutions available on the Delphi/Kylix platforms. These same solutions are also available on the C++ Builder/Kylix C++ platforms as visual controls.

But what about the standard function library being used in a cross-platform environment? Well, as it turns out the standard function library is an excellent choice for use with C++BuilderX. The following is a C++BuilderX DLL project on Windows. The standard function library only requires we use an ANSI C compiler, and all of the C++BuilderX supported compilers meet that criteria. Figure 11-3 shows the DLL project being edited on the Windows platform.

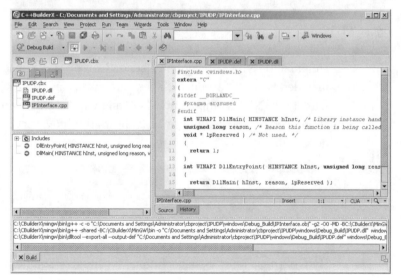

Figure 11-3

With C++BuilderX we can create a project that can be accessed on each platform. In this particular case we will create a separate project for Linux because the structure of a shared library is slightly different from a DLL on Windows.

Figure 11-4 shows the same project being developed on C++BuilderX running on a slackware 9.1 machine with the KDE Desktop.

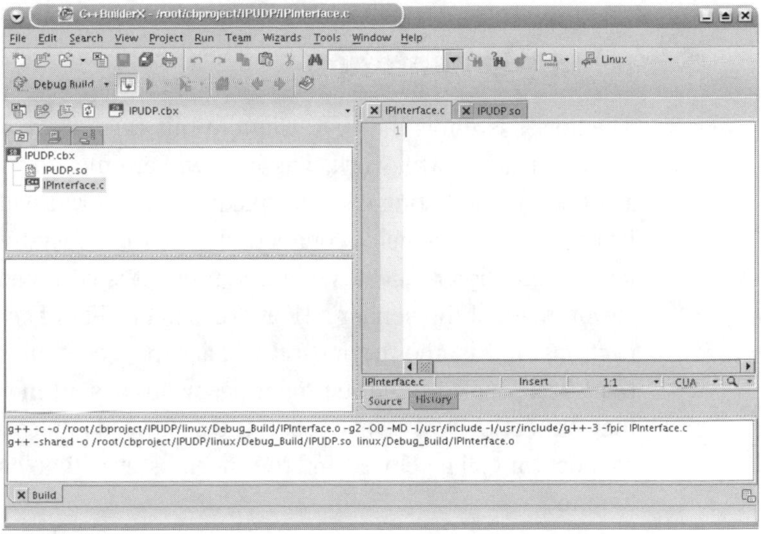

Figure 11-4

In case you didn't notice, both projects were compiled with the GNU C compiler. The GNU compiler is ANSI compliant so we now have a completely new working alternative to Delphi/Kylix that uses ANSI C and is a "code-only" solution.

If we choose C++BuilderX and develop a DLL/shared library, the level portability will be higher than when developing using GUI components. For this prototype we will build our middle layer of device interfaces using C++BuilderX. On Windows the end result will be a DLL named IPInterface.dll. The end result on Linux/FreeBSD will be IPInterface.so.

Keep in mind that using C++BuilderX allows us to generate executables and shared libraries for any platform we have a cross-compiler installed for. For example, we can build and install a GNU compiler for the AMD Athlon 64 system, then add that cross-compiler to the list of tools. We can set up C++BuilderX to allow the generation of the 64-bit target on a 32-bit machine.

Note:

For more information on cross-compiling on C++BuilderX, please visit www.time-lines.com.

Socket Implementation

The host system is the UDP client in this case. Here's how the communications will work. The host will attempt to connect to any thermostat listing on a specific port number. It will broadcast its request to establish a connection. The thermostat will "listen" for a connection request. When the request is received, it will check to see if the sender's IP address is in a list of accepted connections. If it is, the thermostat will accept the connection and request a password. If the proper password is sent in response, the connection will be opened. If the password is incorrect, the connection will be closed and the thermostat will go back into listen mode.

It's a little difficult to show how the code for this works in print. The best way to explain this further is to have you download the code for Chapter 11. In the Chapter 11 folder there will be two other folders — UDPSvr and UDBCli. Within each of these folders are Windows, Linux, and Embedded folders. You can set up a working UDB client and server using Windows or Linux. The Embedded folder only contains the UDP server since it is not initiating the client side of UDP.

Platform-Independent USB Development

Achieving the same success with developing a middle-tier USB interface requires the same strategy used for Ethernet. To employ that strategy we will use another open source library, libusb, which is available for Windows, Linux, and UNIX from the SourceForge.net web site. This product provides a consistent developer interface to USB devices. I would strongly recommend downloading one of the snapshots as they are frequently updated and have many features the previous release didn't have.

The libusb libraries work very similar to the standard function template by providing a consistent developer interface to the USB driver layer for Linux, UNIX, and Windows.

There are a couple of items that need to be mentioned at this time. First, the Windows version of libusb includes a device driver. This driver implements the native methods of the UNIX and Linux device drivers. In short, it makes the Windows USB driver layer look exactly like the UNIX/Linux version. Not all of the functionality is fully implemented, but enough is available to provide a consistent development interface under Windows, Linux, and UNIX to the HID drivers. Now you may be asking if the thermostat qualifies as an HID device. The answer to that is definitely a yes. Almost all of the UPS systems sold for the PC that have a USB interface are in fact seen as HID devices to Windows. Any device that interacts with a human being can be considered an HID device. Once again we will implement this middle tier in a code-only fashion and once again we will use C++BuilderX as our development IDE of choice. The function calls to the libusb library are identical across the Linux, BSD, and Windows platforms. The difference again is in the link process.

To fully understand how to access a USB device please review the code listings in the Chapter 11\USB folder available from the download sites. Each listing is very detailed and the C++Builder project files are included so you can get a feel for how to implement true cross-platform libraries in code.

Comparing Delphi/Kylix to C++BuilderX

This topic both concludes developing our middle-tier interface software and serves to lead into developing the user application layer. The products that we've used up to this point are all excellent products in their own right. Choosing code development over using a visual editor is not an easy decision to make. Several factors weighed heavily in using C++BuilderX over Delphi/Kylix for the middleware device interface.

The first item was the fact that Kylix does not generate native machine code that can be executed at the device driver level. Kylix has quite a few support libraries that make it an excellent user application development tool. Those same libraries, however, can wreak havoc when attempting to develop kernel or device driver level code.

The second compelling reason for selecting C++BuilderX for the device layer was the ability to add additional compilers along with the numbers of native compilers supported out of the box. The Borland code generators produce code that is of excellent quality. In my years of experience I've found Borland's code quality and execution speed is second to none. But the ability to add other third-party compilers like GNU and even Microsoft Visual C and Intel make it a very versatile product. The flexibility in the C++BuilderX IDE in adding cross-compilers and scripts make it very attractive for the developer who is doing exactly what we are — developing cross-platform libraries from a single-source code base.

The End User Application Layer

Well, we've reached the final topic for this book. Our choices for application layer development are somewhat greater than for developing the device interface layer. We can use an integrated IDE like Delphi/C++Builder/Kylix, or an application framework such as wxWindows. C++BuilderX has a preview feature for wxWindows but is far from a full implementation. So let's examine the pros and cons of each of these development methods.

Delphi/C++Builder/Kylix

These are proven products that are known to work on Linux and Windows and a single-source code base is attainable using the CLX controls. When we venture away from Linux to FreeBSD the certainty of the program executing becomes a bigger question mark. This issue can easily be eliminated by using a product named InstallMade, which rolls up all the required libraries and shared objects to be installed along with the application. As long as the BSD operating system is running in Linux compatibility mode, our program will run.

C++BuilderX

This product is an excellent choice for code-based cross-platform development. Since we are developing a user interface we would need to use an external tool to develop our user interface. C++Builder allows outside tool integration, so we could integrate a third-party GUI builder. This would allow us to develop the user interface on any platform and simply port it to the other platforms for cross-compilation.

Chapter 11

Mono and the .NET Framework

This is a brand new approach to development. Mono 1.1 is currently available, and I have successfully compiled C# code ported from the .NET framework without modifications. A lot of care has to be taken, however, in the use of the available .NET framework features available under Linux. This is a good approach but the framework isn't quite ready for us.

wxWidgets and DialogBlocks

The wxWindows cross-platform development library for application development was recently renamed wxWidgets. DialogBlocks is a GUI application designer. The output from DialogBlocks can be compiled on any platform that supports the wxWidgets libraries. wxWidgets are strictly C++ so if you're uncomfortable with C++, don't use wxWidgets or DialogBlocks.

As you build the user interface with DialogBlocks the header and C++ source files are updated to reflect your changes. An application class is created (sound familiar?) and once your design is finished all that is left is to fill in your event handler code. DialogBlocks is a very powerful designer and is much improved over many commercial products. DialogBlocks runs on the same platforms that wxWidgets supports, including the IBM S390 mainframes.

It's Time to Develop the User Application

Well, we're down to the final task of creating the user application. Here is where the payoff of separating the device interface layer from the user application really shows. We are going to take two approaches to the user interface application. One will use the Kylix/Delphi/C++ Builder approach and the other will use the DialogBlocks/wxWidgets/C++BuilderX approach. With the Delphi/Kylix approach we will write a small application using the CLX component libraries. We will demonstrate how to build and distribute an application using this method for both Windows and

Linux/UNIX. The second approach will use DialogBlocks to develop a simple application and C++BuilderX to maintain the finished result.

The Delphi Development Effort

There are several versions of Delphi currently on the market. For cross-platform development between Linux and Windows, we will employ Delphi 7 on Windows and Kylix 3 on Linux. Once the applications are developed we will deploy the Windows version using an open source product called the Nullsoft Install System. On Linux we will use a product called InstallMade to package and distribute our program.

1. On Windows, start Delphi 7 and close the current default application. Since it's empty, don't save it.

2. Next, choose **File | New | CLX Application**.

3. Add a file menu, edit box, memo box, push button, and status bar to the application.

4. Double-click the status bar and add two status panels. Next, double-click the menu bar icon and add a new item to the drop-down. Name the main menu item **File** and the drop-down item **Exit**.

5. With Exit item selected, choose **Events** and double-click the OnClick event handler. A new procedure will be generated. At the cursor add the following line:

```
Application.Terminate;
```

This will exit the application.

6. Now select the button component and change the text to **Add**. Again select **Events**, and double-click on the OnClick event handler and add the following lines:

```
Memo1.Lines.Add(Edit1.Text);
StatusBar1.Panels.Items[0].Text:= IntToStr(memo1.Lines.Count);
```

This will add the text in the edit box to the memo box and update the count of lines on the status bar.

7. Now it's time to run the application. Add some text to the edit box and press **Add**. You should see the text added to the memo box and the line count incremented in the status bar. Figure 11-5 shows the Windows version.

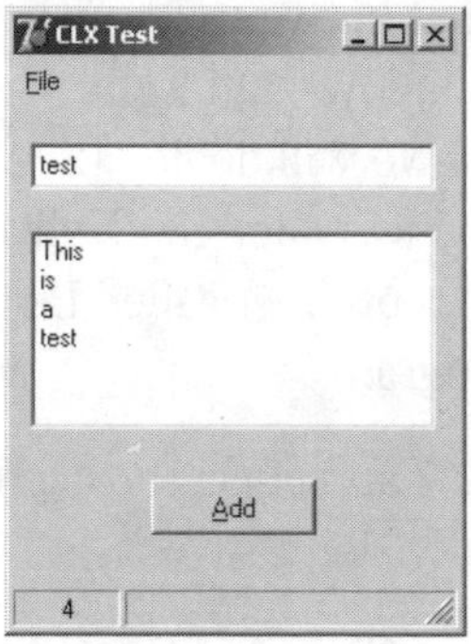

Figure 11-5

8. Copy (or save) the project to a Linux machine with Kylix 3 installed. Start Kylix and open the project. You will receive an error that Unit1.pas cannot be located in the path. Ignore the error and manually open Unit1.pas. If there is a path in the uses clause, eliminate the path so the line for Unit1 simply says Unit1.

9. Next, compile and run the program. The following should be displayed.

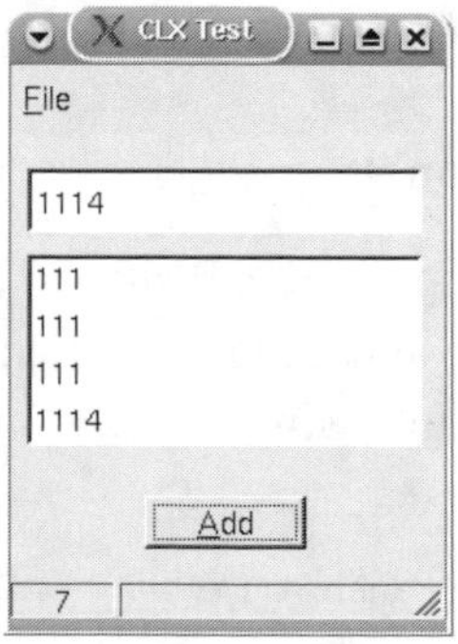

Figure 11-6

The program should run unchanged and look similar to the above output. Add text to the memo box and the program should function identically to the Windows version. Remember earlier we created a Windows DLL and Linux shared library for the device interface layer. To access the hardware layer we will add the shred objects to the project along with the definition files if required and write the logic to access the serial, Ethernet, and USB ports.

The wxWidgets Development Effort

Now, we will develop a simple application using wxWidgets and DialogBlocks. To begin we will design the user interface in DialogBlocks.

1. Start DialogBlocks and select **Sample Projects** from the main screen. A list of projects will be displayed. I chose the NoteBook dialog project shown in Figure 11-7.

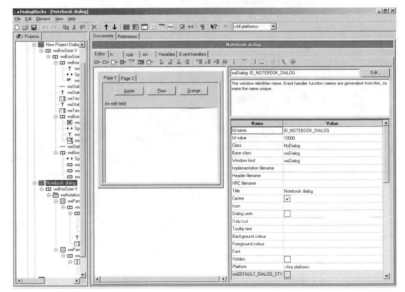

Figure 11-7

The far left window pane in Figure 11-7 shows the available components in our current project, the middle pane is our designer, and the right pane contains properties associated with the currently selected design element. The tabs across the top hold the editor, header, source code file, variable definitions, and event handlers. Anything defined within the DialogBlocks context will be in the source files. To add source and header files you need to generate the associated classes; otherwise you will not see any code created. The next step in the process is to create a C++BuilderX project and add the source and header files we just created as shown in the following figure.

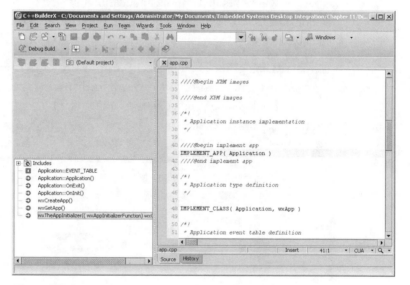

Figure 11-8

To compile and build the program with C++BuilderX, we need to also add the wxWidget libraries and add any remaining code and source files. When the project is complete, compile the project and link to the native wxWidget libraries for the chosen platform. wxWidgets takes a slightly different approach to development from Delphi/Kylix. I like to work with both and find Delphi and Kylix excellent products for developing solid applications quickly. I like to use wxWidgets and DialogBlocks when I have to support platforms that Delphi/Kylix don't support.

Distributing the End Results

Once the hardware prototypes are finished it's time to distribute the beta kits. There are many products that can be used to create install programs. If you want something that is quick and requires little effort, InstallShield is an excellent Windows product. If you want an installer that makes it easy to distribute and install Kylix programs, InstallMade is a must. InstallMade wraps the program and any required libraries into a single file for distribution and installation. The best part of InstallMade is that it will handle the distribution of OS libraries as well, which itself can be a task for Kylix.

The Sky Is the Limit

I hope this book has started your creative juices flowing. There are endless possibilities on what you can accomplish with the right knowledge. I hope this book combined with the companion files has provided you, the reader, with new ideas and fresh approaches.

Index

COMPONENT & INDIVIDUAL BOARD PRICING	KIT	ASMB
TTL / RS-232 INTERFACE BOARD	$19.99	$24.99

INCLUDES CIRCUIT BOARD, CAPACITORS, HEADERS, AND TRANSCEIVER

TIME / TEMPERATURE BOARD	$29.99	$34.99

INCLUDES CIRCUIT BOARD, RESISTORS, CAPACITORS, DS1620, DS2404, CR2032 BATTERY, BATTERY HOLDER, AND HEADERS

KEYBOARD / ALARM / I2C / LCD BOARD	$29.99	$34.99

INCLUDES CIRCUIT BOARD, BUZZER, PUSH BUTTONS, AND HEADERS

ALL PROCESSOR INTERFACE BOARDS INCLUDE THE FOLLOWING: CIRCUIT BOARD, PROCESSOR SOCKET, VOLTAGE REGULATOR, POWER CONNECTOR, AND HEADERS (PROCESSOR & POWER SUPPLY INCLUDED WITH COMPLETE KITS ONLY)

	KIT	ASMB
BASIC STAMP INTERFACE BOARD	$19.99	$24.99
dsPIC INTERFACE BOARD	$19.99	$24.99
PSoC INTERFACE BOARD	$19.99	$24.99
COMPLETE BASIC STAMP KIT	$199.99	$249.99
COMPLETE dsPIC OR PSoC KIT	$129.99	$179.99
POWER SUPPLY	$19.99	
BASIC STAMP 2p24	$79.00	
dsPIC 30F2010 (28-PIN DIP)	$10.99	
PSoC (28-PIN DIP)	$10.99	

SUBTOTAL _____

SHIPPING & HANDLING _____ **$10.00** _____

ILLINOIS RESIDENTS ADD 7% SALES TAX _____

TOTAL _____

NAME_____

ADDRESS_____

ADDRESS_____

CITY_____ STATE_____ ZIP_____

DAYTIME PHONE_____

EMAIL ADDRESS_____

ENCLOSE CHECK OR MONEY ORDER FOR FULL AMOUNT AND MAIL TO:

TIMELINES INDUSTRIES - EMBEDDED OFFER 1
5107 GREENWOOD PL.
MC HENRY, IL 60050-2376

YOU CAN ALSO ORDER ON THE WEB AT: **www.time-lines.com/embedded/offer/1**.

This offer may be changed or discontinued without notice. Prices subject to change without notice.

Development Tools for PICmicro MCUs

micro Engineering Labs, Inc.

Phone: (719) 520-5323
Fax: (719) 520-1867
Box 60039
Colorado Springs, CO 80960
All prices subject to change without notice.

Join the thousands of users who have discovered PICBASIC PRO™ Compiler. For more than a decade, we've been helping engineers, hobbyists, and students develop sophisticated, reliable code for PICmicro microcontrollers. PICBASIC PRO is much easier to use than Assembly or C, yet it generates code with efficiency and optimization that is comparable to either.

PICBASIC PRO Compiler is used by engineers in scores of major companies. It is the preferred tool when deadlines loom and code space is limited.

PICBASIC PRO™ Compiler $249.95

Full-featured Windows IDE or command-line compilation.

Direct access to internal registers and hardware modules.

True compiler with sophisticated code optimization.

Automatic bank and codepage switching.

Built-in commands for RS-232, LCD interface, I²C, analog conversion, USB, 1-Wire®, and more. No external libraries required.

Reliable, mature product proven by years of use.

MPLAB integration with source level debugging.

Single compiler supports all families of PICmicro - 12, 14, and 16-bit cores.

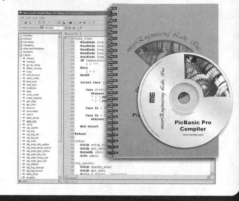

HIDmaker writes your USB code! No Need to be a USB expert!

HIDmaker $399 - Creates ready to compile PC & PIC programs that talk to each other over USB.

Choose your favorite languages!
PIC: PICBASIC PRO, CCS C, Hi-Tech C, Microchip C18, MPASM.
PC: Visual Basic, Delphi, C++ Builder.
Single chip solution: PIC with built-in USB.

HIDmaker Test Suite $149

USBWatch - Shows your device's USB traffic, even during 'enumeration', without expensive equipment.

AnyHID - Test any USB HID device. See what data it sends, even what the data is used for.

HIDCombo - HIDmaker plus Test Suite **$499**

LAB-X Experimenter Boards

Pre-Assembled Boards

Available for 8, 14, 18, 28, and 40-pin PIC MCUs

2-line, 20-char LCD Module (except LAB-X2)

9-pin Serial Port

Sample PICBASIC and PICBASIC PRO Programs

Includes Schematic Diagram and Documentation

LAB-X1 for 40-pin MCUs	$199.95
LAB-X2 for 28 or 40-pin MCUs	$69.95
LAB-X3 for 18-pin MCUs	$119.95
LAB-X4 for 8 or 14-pin MCUs	$124.95

EPIC™ Parallel Port Programmer starting at $59.95

Serial Programmer for PICmicro

$119.95

Includes:
Programmer
9-pin Serial Cable
AC Power Adapter
ZIF Adapter for 8 to 40-pin DIP
Software for Windows 98/Me/NT/2K/XP

Optional USB Adapter **$39.95**

PICProto Prototyping Boards

Double-Sided with Plate-Thru Holes
Circuitry for Power Supply and Clock
Large Prototype Area
Boards Available for Most PIC MCUs
Documentation and Schematic

Pricing from $8.95 to $19.95

Order online at: www.melabs.com

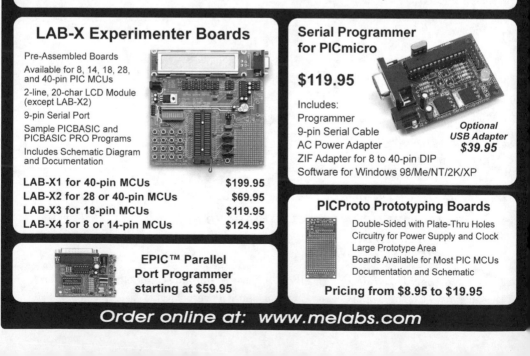

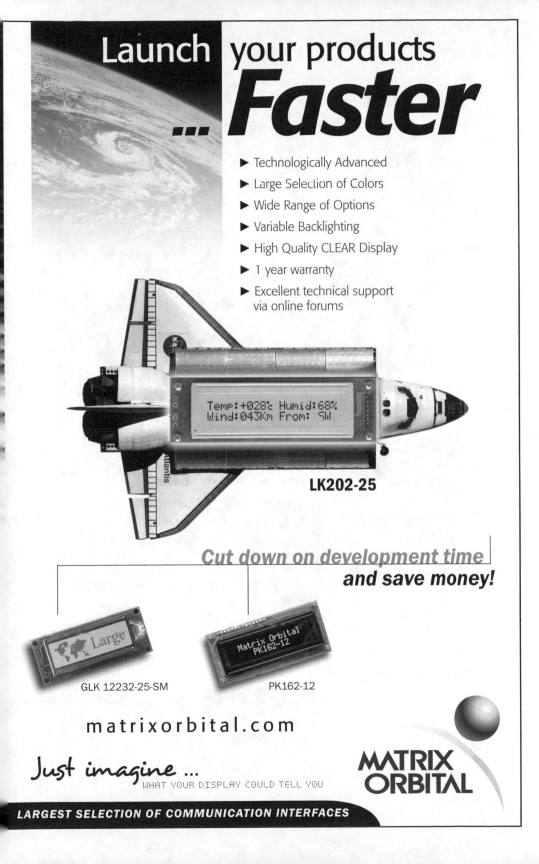

Learn to Program
Like a Pro!

BASIC Stamp® 2p24 Professional Starter Kit $209

BASIC Stamp
Syntax and Reference Manual

PARALLAX

www.parallax.com

The BS2p24 Professional Starter Kit includes the BS2p24 module, BS2p24/40 Demo Board, BASIC Stamp Manual v2.1, CD-ROM, serial cable, and a components pack. *Power supply not included.*

To order online visit www.parallax.com. To order by phone call our Sales Department toll-free at 888-512-1024 (Monday-Friday, 7am-5pm, PT).

BS2P24/40 Demo Board

www.**parallax**.com

© 2005 Parallax, Inc. All rights reserved. BASIC Stamp is a registered trademark of Parallax, Inc. Parallax and the Parallax logo are trademarks of Parallax, Inc. Pricing is subject to change without notice.